FRIENDLY POKER

FRIENDLY POKER

How to Host, Play and Love the
Classic American Poker Game

Mark A. Cochran

gatekeeper press

Published by Gatekeeper Press
3971 Hoover Rd. Suite 77
Columbus, OH 43123-2839

www.GatekeeperPress.com

ISBN: 9781619845626
eISBN: 9781619845633

Library of Congress Control Number: 2016958406

Printed in the United States of America

CONTENTS

CHAPTER 1

What Friendly Poker is All About

HEY, LOOK. IF your objective in a poker hand, in a night of poker, or in life in general, is to make as much money as you can possibly can, then this is not the book for you. It is not that there is anything evil or inherently wrong with those objectives. It is just that I don't believe that is what "real" poker is all about.

Poker is not really about maximizing how many dollars you take out of the game. We all have more than enough times when we have to try to optimize fiscal performance. The last thing we need is one more added to the list. If poker were really about money, then it would essentially be a job. And so it is for the professional poker players. Poor bastards. They have taken a beautiful thing and turned it into a grind.

And Poker is absolutely, positively not about gambling. Yes, there is money won or lost during a poker game. But the money really, truly is just the scorecard. Something of value must be at risk for the game to work, and so money is wagered. But that

1

money is not being gambled. Poker players come into a game knowing they will wager their money and invest their funds, in hundreds or thousands of decisions throughout a night. They fully expect their overall financial outcome to properly match the wisdom, skill, and expertise that they brought to all of those decisions. If they make poor decisions, they will come out behind. If they make good decisions, they will come out ahead. It is no more a gambling exercise than the efforts of a financial investment advisor. Shooting Craps is gambling. Poker is not gambling.

No, poker is a game. It is a contest. A fair match of skill versus skill. And any game or contest is a chance to prove ourselves, to show off. That's right. There it is. The object of poker, like all skill games, is simply to show off. To demonstrate to ourselves and to the world that we can prevail.

Guys in particular. . . .

[Let me stop right here for a second. It seems inevitable that I will offend some gender bias watchdogs by assuming that most readers of this book will be male. I should apologize in advance. In fact, I will. I am sorry. However, poker so uniquely springs from our need to outwit, outthink, outperform, outdo and outcompete with our peers that it is proper and fitting that we associate it with terms like "macho". What are all sports and all games, really, but a measuring contest? I believe that females are *not* congenitally *unable* to participate or perform as well as males in a poker game. But in my experience, it is much less common to find the hyper-competitive, win at all costs, kill-the-other-player-and-smile-while-doing-it, mentality among those with two "x" chromosomes. I am always, however, a firm believer that anyone with that mentality, male or female, will enjoy the heck out of poker.

In fact, one of the greatest and most famous poker players of all time was "Poker" Alice Ivers, a legendary figure in the Wild West. Although the most famous picture of her shows her as a grizzled, tough old bird smoking a cigar and staring in an intimidating fashion, she is said to have been beautiful and to have bought and worn to the poker table the finest and most elegant clothes obtainable from around the world. She is also known to have killed a man with her rifle, to have shot another man in the arm when the man was threatening her future husband with a knife, to have cussed with the experts of cussing and to have smoked and chomped on cigars while playing cards. She was religious to the extent of refusing to play poker on Sunday. But her motto was: "Praise the Lord and place your bets. I'll take your money with no regrets." Now, "Poker" Alice had the right mindset to bring to a poker game!]

Now where was I? Ah yes. Guys in particular seem to love to find ways to measure themselves against other guys. To test themselves and prove themselves worthy. To boldly go where no man has gone before. Was I to study anthropology or sociology, I might find that this need has always existed. But once we became civilized and stopped beating the crap out of each other to get a mastodon-burger, we needed other, more acceptable, forms of combat. Ways to give our internal cavemen an expressive outlet without having to clean blood off the living room carpet. So we came up with sports. And games. And corporate Machiavellianism. We crave opportunities to demonstrate our battle-worthiness and our continued desirability in the gene pool.

That's what games are for. And poker is the best game ever devised to simulate the Darwinist struggle for survival of the fittest. To allow us to say to ourselves—and to the whole damn world, for that matter—that "even if civilization were to fade away and I were left to depend on my wits for my very survival each day, I could still kick everyone else's ass. Not physically, mind you. Oh no. Leave that to the rugby players. But mentally, emotionally, intellectually, politically, psychologically . . . I am stronger, faster, better than you. "

The true object of poker is to show off. To demonstrate to the world that you can triumph in the arena. The object of running a regular poker game is threefold. First, to give the other gladiators fair and honest chances to show off for themselves over the long term. Second, to ensure that the contestants, *outside the artificial environment of the poker rules*, can remain friendly, cooperative, and mutually supportive. And lastly, to win the invisible and unannounced contest about who can host the best game. That is also a competition. And you want to win that one too.

When you get to show off and to win, of course, you want to do it in front of your buddies, your peers, your crew. It is infinitely more satisfying to pull off a clever victory in front of folks you know well and will see again, than it is to dazzle some perfect stranger in a casino somewhere. That is why you really want to have "poker buddies"—guys who understand the game and share a history of past conquests, bad beats, raucous laughter and appreciation for the irony and the fickle nature of justice that the game serves up in large doses over time. Developing a regular gang of "poker buddies" and creating the ideal environment for a terrific poker game takes effort and care and attention to detail. But it is well worth the trouble. A good "regular game" is a thing of beauty. And, as that great poker fan (who also dabbled as a poet), John Keats, wrote: "a thing of beauty is a joy forever."

In this book, I will try to relate everything I have learned about hosting a great regular poker game as well as some things I have learned about enjoying playing in a regular poker game. Now, you might be asking, what makes me such an expert? For that matter, who am I to be pontificating about what poker or games are "really" about? Perhaps I should use a softer word than "really". I suppose everyone has their own perspective on what is "real". Right?

Honestly, I have no official credentials—only experience and ideas. I am just a thinking guy with too much time on my hands and over 40 years' experience hosting regular poker games in several parts of the country. But, I like what the man behind the curtain in the "Wizard of Oz" said to the Scarecrow:

> "Why, anybody can have a brain. That's a very mediocre commodity. Every pusillanimous creature that crawls on the Earth or slinks through slimy seas has a brain. Back where I come from, we have universities, seats of great learning, where men go to become great thinkers. And when they come out, they think deep thoughts and with no more brains than you have. But they have one thing you haven't got: a diploma."

I don't have a diploma in poker either. But I do have deep thoughts. And I know that I can save you from having to do all that deep thinking yourself. Or, if you happen to be a deep thinker by nature, you can supplement you own deep thoughts with mine. I know you can use what has worked so well for me as suggestions for how you might improve or establish your own regular game.

The qualifications I can offer are these: I have established, hosted and enjoyed regular poker games with great "poker buddies" in locations across the country for over forty years. I still have guys in my regular games with whom I have played for over 40 years. I have played with more than a hundred regular players in nearly a thousand poker nights and I have never had anyone go home feeling swindled, cheated, abused, mistreated, or disappointed in their decision to play cards. Over the years and throughout all of these games, I have learned and can now relate the keys to making the experience so much fun—the little things and bigger things that separate the great games from the merely good games. I have always been on the lookout for new wrinkles or different approaches that add to the good times and can be incorporated into the games going forward. The list of recommendations has grown so lengthy over the years, that I thought I better write it all down, before I forgot something important.

> "There are few things that are so unpardonably neglected in our country as poker. The upper class knows very little about poker. Now and then you find ambassadors who have sort of a general knowledge of poker, but the ignorance of the people is fearful. Why, I have known clergymen, good men, kind-hearted, liberal, sincere, and all that, who did not know the meaning of a "flush."
> It is enough to make one ashamed of the species."
> —*Mark Twain*

Friendly Poker, or "Real" Poker

There are many different types of poker games. The range of variation is wide, deep and important to understand. Here are three fairly common examples of "poker" games:

- A $10 dollar limit, 7-card stud game at a casino in Atlantic City

- A single buy, "Hold 'Em" tournament for charity

- A monthly "dealer's choice" poker game among a group of friends/neighbors/ associates

Each of these examples are called "poker games". And each involves playing cards, wagering and a reasonably consistent definition of winning card combinations for each hand.

But the differences are more important than the similarities. The three games listed above feature completely different player objectives, different strategies and tactics, different rules and expectations, different participant characteristics, and different emotional outcomes.

The Atlantic City game is a single variety of poker hand, dealt by professionals, played by strangers, with the objective of making money for the casino owners. They player's objective is to try to come out ahead of break-even despite the house taking a slice out of every pot. There is extremely little socialization or banter among the players. New players come and go at random throughout the game as their fortunes dictate.

The "Hold 'Em" tournament is a single-winner elimination contest, again played among mostly strangers, and again featuring a single variety of hand played all night long. The objective is to raise money for the charity. The players' objective is to give money to charity and to try to be the one winner, the last man standing, at the end of the tournament. Everyone else goes home early. There is little socialization or banter among the players.

The "Dealer's Choice" game is a cooperative, regularly recurring, and very social evening of verbal, even boisterous, interaction among friends or at least folks who know each other well and wish to spend time with each other. Each player gets to deal a different game of his own choosing. The players' objective is to have a lot of fun, improve and show-off their skills (peer recognition), and enjoy the thrill of competing and outdoing each other. Everyone stays until the end. There are multiple winners.

No one but the casino owners get to host the first game above. Very few people will ever host a "Hold-'Em" Tournament. Anyone can, and many, many people do,' host a game like the third type.

7

Friendly Poker is the subject of this book because it is the "real" poker. Despite the internet poker sites, the televised poker championships and the growing number of casinos in the country, there will be far more people, having far more fun, playing Friendly Poker games. For purposes of our discussions here, Friendly Poker:

- Regularly recurs with many of the same players participating at most of the games
- Involves folks who know each other and wish to remain friendly
- Involves limited stakes that allow players to stay the entire evening
- Features a variety of different games, chosen and dealt in turn by each player

Why Friendly Poker is Worthy of Our Efforts

Before we devote such a high degree of time and effort to design, create and maintain a regular, friendly poker game, it might be useful to understand why the game is worthy of our attention in the first place. Why do we think the game has value? What exactly will we get out of our efforts to improve our skill levels at playing or at hosting a poker game? Isn't it "only" a game?

The short answers to these questions are:

- Games have always been part of socialization, but Poker has endured
- Poker is unique among games in its focus on human interaction
- Poker skills are life skills—easily translated back into the "real" world

Essentially, Poker is the greatest game ever invented to exercise our social, perceptive, persuasive, and interpersonal skills while giving safe outlet to the exhilarating exercise of cutthroat competition. The game has endured in popularity throughout generations of changes in society, proving its value and appeal. And most importantly, the lessons you learn from playing poker and *especially the lessons you learn from playing in, improving or hosting a regular poker game* are extremely valuable and transferable to any endeavor you pursue in all aspects of your real life—social, business, family, etc.

The Need for Games and the Endurance of Poker

Long, long ago, in a world that now seems as if it was from a galaxy far, far away, Americans routinely engaged in many social and friendly gaming activities. I know this is hard to imagine, but try to visualize what life was like before the creation of IPads, smart phones, Facebook, or even DVDs. Think way, way, way, way back.

All the way back to the 1970's when cable TV was a rarity, and TV had only a few networks and a couple of UHF stations. When no one had yet heard of 'digital' or 'electronic'. When phones actually rang and children had heard the sound of a bell, and no one had yet heard a "beep". I mean way, way back there. When movie theaters had only one screen, and thus only one choice of movie.

That seems like such a strange and different world. When someone left the house, you actually could not reach them to speak to them until they returned. It must have been horrible.

Now try to imagine or remember what in the world those people did to entertain themselves. And there was actually more leisure time then than there is now. All of our so-called gains in standard of living since the 1970's have come with increased working hours and increased workers per family. We had more leisure time then. (Hard to call it progress when you look at it that way, isn't it?)

People entertained themselves with TV, to be sure, but because houses typically had only one TV, it was a social event. People chose their channels and watched their shows together. And, when they were not watching TV, they often entertained themselves with another social activity called games. Wonderful games. Monopoly, Life, Risk, Scrabble, Stratego, Mystery Date, Clue, Masterpiece, Backgammon, Checkers, Parcheesi, Battleship, Blockhead, Operation, and on and on and on. The adults would play Mahjong, Chess, and others.

When they were outside, they made up and played more games. There were little league sports, yes, but really only a couple of sports, and mostly for the boys. Much more time was spent on pick-up neighborhood games of all kinds. And in family and neighborhood outdoor games like horseshoes, badminton, and croquet.

There were card games. Thousands of card games, fit for everyone. Bridge clubs, Gin Rummy games, Whist, Cribbage, Hearts, Canasta, and so on. And there was poker. Neighborhood poker games, where no one had ever seen or played "Texas Hold 'Em", but they played dozens of other poker games using their own 'house' rules and inventing things on the fly.

People have a basic, innate need to create social, interactive, challenging and fun contests. People enjoy the bonding, the rituals, the self-affirmation and the camaraderie that comes from friendly competition. People need to compete, but to do so in a civilized and controlled manner. And all of those great and no-so-great games supported and promoted that environment of friendly competition.

Poker, generally regarded as an American invention (but descended from the French game, "Poque"), has existed before the 1850's, and in some forms, significantly earlier. The definitive moment when "Poker" was invented is open to debate and interpretation. But the advent of steamboat transportation up and down the Mississippi and the huge cultural event that was the American Civil War were the catalysts for the rapid spread of the game throughout the country. The growth in Poker popularity was further assisted by the continuing transition from an agrarian culture to an urban one.

But Poker was initially limited in how fast it could spread into mainstream society by the fact that it was seen as immoral. It involved—gasp—gambling, and it was associated with cheating and violence and confidence swindles. These were significant limitations in a prohibitionist kind of culture and the shady moral standing of Poker should have all but prevented the game from becoming socially accepted. (For comparison's sake, think about craps, or dogfighting, or cock fights—they have never and likely will never make it into the mainstream) Yet Poker kept moving forward. Somehow, the game was able to satisfy more than those who were just looking to gamble. Its appeal reached beyond those who were only looking to swindle some rubes out of their money. Something in the game itself was so compelling that it did, indeed, cross into the mainstream and become one of the most popular and enduring games of all time.

Other than Poker, there are relatively few multi-player games from the early- or mid- 1800's that have continued to grow and gain in popularity into the 21st century. Radio and TV and the automobile culture provided other diversions that reduced interest in many old-time games. Electronic games and devices and reduced leisure time killed many others. But Poker endures. Understanding why the game has endured, what it provides to its players, and what drives its immense popularity is essential to determining exactly how your game should be structured.

> "Man is a gaming animal. He must always be trying to get
> the better in something or other."
>
> —*Charles Lamb*

Unique Attributes of Poker

"Playing the Man"

Poker is simply the best game ever devised to test and reward our ability to predict, understand, misdirect, persuade and influence the other players. Your focus during an evening of Poker is always on the other player, what he is thinking, what he is trying to accomplish, how you can influence his actions, how you can use his behavior for your own benefit and how you can outsmart him. The essence of the game is to outmaneuver the opponents and misdirect them through your actions, words, body language, facial expressions, and any other techniques you can think to employ. In many sports, there are opportunities to "play the man, not the ball". In poker, you must *at all times* play the man, not the cards. Poker is unique in its nearly 100 percent dedication to that purpose.

Understanding, Empathy, Discernment, Communication

Poker, more than any other game, rewards and requires the ability to understand human nature, to discern what the other players are thinking, to "get inside their heads. Poker demands not only that you see what cards are on the table, but that you see what the other players' *perceptions are* about the cards on the table. A good player will have to readjust his understanding of the cards and the probabilities many times per hand. But, more importantly, he will have to adjust his evaluation of his *opponents' perception* of those cards and probabilities many times per hand. And he will have to do it for five or six different opponents, all with different sets of perceptions.

And, as if that were not enough, the good player will have to decide what perception he wants the other players to have about his hand, and then creatively and subtly take actions or make statements that create that perception, and continue to adjust all of those actions and statements as he sees their reactions. At the same time, he has to spot his opponent's deliberately deceptive statements or actions about each of their hands. And carefully control his reaction to them.

All of that indirect communication, evaluation, and decision-making has to happen very quickly. It is actually not even possible to spot every clue and make a multitude of minute adjustments quickly enough to take full advantage of every opportunity. Good players will get faster and better at it. Poorer players will miss more of it and therefore not have as many tools at their disposal. But regular players will begin to do some of it reflexively, or subconsciously. Their brains will take in all the information, recognize and process the patterns and come up with conclusions that the players are hard pressed to explain later.

Because poker focuses so heavily on the other people at the table, and upon their perceptions and decision-making approaches, it is a much more dedicated exercise in socialization than almost any other game. To be sure, there are other games that emphasize team-building, cooperation, communication, and other aspects of social behavior. But Poker, particularly a regular friendly game, demands all of these behaviors and much more.

Poker requires the players to repeatedly look at the world through the eyes of each other player at the table, evaluate each players' attitudes and approaches and select an approach to best communicate a desired message in a way that person will be most likely to believe it. Then, Poker provides nearly instant feedback and relentlessly objective scoring for how accurately each player has been able to do that, so they can quickly become better and more precise at these assessments and communications. Poker requires empathy, understanding, goal-alignment, and great sensitivity to emotions, body-language, intimations, fears and anxieties of the other human beings at the table. The entire game revolves around this activity, hundreds of times an hour for every participant for several hours at a sitting.

Good or Bad?

Now, it is true that a good poker player, during the play of a hand, actually uses all of these skills and all of this understanding and empathy to harm the other player, rather than help. You might wonder how this can be a good thing. It seems a little like using "The Force" for Evil instead of for Good. Are good poker players only practicing the "Dark Side" of the Force?

Absolutely not. Keep in mind that the ruthless (or selfish) use of these skills and knowledge are applied with full permission and complicity of the eventual victims. Everyone at the table has given his consent to be tested and challenged in this way. And it is this contract with each other that allows poker games to remain friendly and productively social despite the ruthless behavior. By allowing each other to practice ruthless behavior, the players have created a system in which the <u>better</u> social skills can be accurately measured and tested.

Let me try an analogy here. Skip these two paragraphs if you do not like analogies. Two horse owners were complaining to each other about how slow their race horses were. They began to argue and eventually they made a significant wager about which of the two horses was actually slower. So they tried to race the horses against each other to settle the issue. But the race proved to be impossible. The jockey for each horse (an employee of the horse's owner), would simply slow his horse down purposely to be sure their horse did not finish first. Every race ended with each horse standing absolutely still, only a few yards down the race course from the starting gate. Finally, someone had the bright idea to have the jockeys switch horses. Now each jockey could only win the bet for their owner by racing the other owner's horse as fast as possible. They actually turned a key variable (which jockey rode which horse) backwards to achieve the desired effect of properly measuring the speed of the horses.

In a similar way, it turns out that one cannot measure a competition for how well each player has mastered the skill of discerning another player's thoughts, feelings, perceptions, and opinions simply counting how many selfless acts that player performs for his opponent. If there is any way to devise a game or a training exercise to develop and measure selfless, giving acts and abilities, I'd love to see it. One problem, of course, is that selfless giving would mean purposely losing the competition so the other guy could have the honor of winning. Everyone would be trying to give the game away and competition would be impossible. Just like the jockey's switching horses, though, if the players agree in advance to develop the empathy and understanding skills, but to <u>use them in reverse </u>to take from, rather than give to the other contestants, then they can measure their relative skill levels by the results achieved, and a real competition can be held that provides feedback and incentive for all players to become better at the desirable skills. It is always assumed and understood in a friendly game that the same skills that are used to make *taking* possible within the play of the game itself, can and will be used *"in reverse"* to make the players better at *giving and cooperation* and mutual support in the real world outside the play of the cards.

OK, the analogy is over, do we have everyone back? Good. Here is the main point: Poker requires and rewards empathy, understanding, communications, discernment, sensitivity to

15

others, and a whole host of other incredibly good and useful social skills. But, in the interest of creating a fun, competitive environment and a system of precise and immediate feedback, Poker measures those skill levels through the amount of <u>taking</u> each player can accomplish.

This is a fundamental principle of "friendly" poker. You treat friends selflessly in the real world. If you do not, they are not friends, merely people you use for your own ends. A regular game is based on the premise that you will want to continue to associate with your regular players over a long period of time, in further games and in "real life". Because you and your friends are good guys, it can be assumed that the skills you perfect and use to be successful at Poker will be used in a positive manner with your friends and colleagues outside of the game.

> "Whether he likes it or not, a man's character is stripped at the poker table; if the other players read him better than he does, he has only himself to blame. Unless he is both able and prepared to see himself as others do, flaws and all, he will be a loser in cards, as in life."
>
> —*Anthony Holden*

Self-Awareness

In addition to teaching and drilling players at perception, empathy, understanding and communication skills, Poker is also uniquely able to teach and drill players about knowing and controlling their own projected emotions, irritations, and complaints. A good "Poker face" is essentially a controlled, socially acceptable, non-communicative facial expression combined with neutral body language. There are many times when such a neutral expression and demeanor are essential and helpful in the real world.

There are also times when people in the real world show too little emotion or reaction. Do Poker Skills make the stereotypical, stoic, non-communicative male even more of a concern for his family and friends? Of course not. Poker teaches players to know and recognize when they have that non-communicative poker face on display and when they are actually communicating non-verbally and showing emotion. So, in theory, they help the overly stoic person recognize the difference between showing and hiding emotion which would be the first step in helping them choose the appropriate times for each.

Poker is unique in its ability to help you get to know yourself and the other players in some depth. Many poker fans have written about how the game helps them understand how other minds work. And everybody's mind works differently. One of the best ways to get to know how a person thinks, decides, communicates, and behaves is to play Poker with them. There is no other game that focuses as intently on human interaction and non-verbal communications.

Taking Poker Skills into the Real World

There have been many terrific books and articles written about how Poker teaches important people skills and enhances socialization and cooperation. One recent article that summarizes these ideas eloquently is "What Poker Can Teach Us", which appeared in the October 5, 2009 issue of the Chronicle of Higher Education and was written by James McManus (who also wrote the great books, Positively Fifth Street, and Cowboys Full). McManus teaches a course on the Literature of Poker at the School of the Art Institute of Chicago.

In the article, McManus writes about how Poker was a valuable learning tool for new Illinois Congressman Barack Obama:

> ... the bottom line politically was that poker helped Obama break the ice with people he needed to work with in the legislature. His favorite physical games were basketball and golf, but he seems to have understood that, as a networking tool, poker is a more natural pastime.
>
> Its tables have long served as less genteel clubs for students, teachers, soldiers, businessmen, and politicians of either sex and every rank and persuasion. Instead of walking down fairways 40 yards apart from each other, throwing elbows in the paint, or quietly hunting pheasant or muskie, poker buddies are elbow to elbow all night, competing and drinking and talking.

McManus' article goes on to describe how other presidents, captains of industry, generals and other leaders were poker fans who were able to learn skills and lessons at the poker table that helped them succeed in "real life". Bill Gates, for example, not only used lessons from poker in his approach to strategic planning with Microsoft, he used his poker winnings as seed money for the company's start-up costs. McManus quotes Gates as saying: "In poker, a player collects different pieces of information—who's betting boldly, what cards are showing, what this guy's pattern of betting and bluffing is—and then crunches all that data together to devise a plan for his own hand. I got pretty good at this kind of information processing."

A partial list of the skills that can be developed by playing poker and then used extremely productively in the real world would include the following:

- Understanding of probability theory and ability to quickly estimate and apply probabilities
- Understanding of "sunk costs", risk/reward, and other critical financial management concepts
- Game Theory and Strategy Definition
- Observational skills and eye for detail
- Ability to read non-verbal communications
- Ability to interpret verbal communications
- Recognition of deliberately and/or accidentally misleading communications
- Empathizing with others and identifying their motivating factors
- Persuasion, sales, marketing, and debating skills
- Self-awareness and self-control over your own projected feelings
- Faster and better decision-making
- Conflict resolution
- Consensus building
- Patience and equanimity in the face of short term misfortunes
- Graceful winning, and graceful losing
- Knowledge of how to bluff and courage to use bluffs.

And there are surely many more. Developing competence at all of these "real world" skills using only "real world" experiences takes a very long time. Poker can give you thousands of practice opportunities to learn and apply these skills in a single evening.

A good, regular Poker game is like having access to a human interaction simulator in which you can practice and drill hundreds and thousands of times as you hone your skills and talent. Poker is irreplaceable as a learning and development tool for anyone that will be going out into the world to interact with real, live human beings.

> "If you know poker, you know people; and if you know people, you got the whole dang world lined up in your sights."
> —*Brett Maverick*

Poker's Current Popularity Boom—A word about Texas Hold 'Em:

There has been a recent explosion in the popularity and mass awareness of Poker. I suppose this new surge of recognition is a good thing. Poker, as we know it, has been around for over 150 years and has enjoyed times of great popularity before. Both the Mississippi Riverboats and the Civil War played major parts in spreading the game throughout the new country. Poker's most recent popularity explosion is due to televised tournaments that use the "hole card camera". A second big factor is the spread of internet sites that allow people to play on-line. Unfortunately, both the televised tournaments and the on-line sites have emphasized one variety of poker above all others—Texas Hold 'Em.

A word about "Texas Hold 'Em": It sucks. OK, so that's two words. Here are some more: It is a spectacularly uninteresting and non-entertaining variety of poker to play or watch. And, despite the howls of so many "poker experts", it is not even particularly good at financially rewarding the better players at the expense of the poorer players, except over the very long term.

Then why is it suddenly so popular?

Because it received a lot of TV coverage from the World Championship of Poker. And even a poor poker game is a wonderful thing. Poker is such a great game, in general, that even the weaker varieties of it are attractive. When the tournament became televised and people saw how cool it looked to play poker (chips, betting, macho behavior, glamour) these new enthusiasts assumed that Hold 'Em was THE GAME. When I was much younger, many players would come to a poker game thinking "poker" was synonymous with "Five Card Draw". They had never been taught any other variety. Today's recently energized "Poker" lovers think the same way about "Hold 'Em".

We need to teach them better. And we should get to it before many of these potential 'real' poker lovers become bored and disillusioned by the monotony of the single and simple variety of poker they have seen on TV. A real poker game, a good poker game will include a wide variety of games almost all of which will provide more entertainment and a better reflection of relative skill levels among the players than will "Texas Hold 'Em."

"Hold 'Em" is very well suited (no pun intended) to the casino's desire to hold a poker elimination championship. It is quick and easy to deal, allows more simultaneous players than most poker varieties, and can force players to be eliminated faster than most games. This, in fact, is one of its big drawbacks—a better player can pretty easily be bankrupted while making all the right moves against an average player who catches a key lucky break or two from the deck.

"Hold 'Em" is antithetical to a regular, friendly poker game. Played with table limits, "Hold 'Em" will relieve players of all their money fairly rapidly, *whether they make any mistakes or not.* Thus, after you have gone through all the trouble to set up an evening for six buddies to play poker for several hours, and after everyone travels to your house and sits down and purchases their chips and is ready to play 'til dawn, you end up with two guys out of chips in 45 minutes, followed by a third guy out in 90. These three have nothing to do but watch (which is not really all that fun—how many viewers watch the poker shows on TV for hours at a time?) Or they can just go home early. Yee Haw.

"Hold 'Em" is designed to quickly move large amounts of money back and forth between players who have very little information. The opportunities to apply skill and calculation and intuition are there, but they are few and are limited in scope. It is a rarity for someone to leave a "Hold 'Em" game and honestly feel that they were outplayed. There are more 'bad beats' in "Hold 'Em" than in any other game I know. It is much more likely that a player losing a huge hand and getting wiped out will have had no reasonable way to see it coming and avoid his fate.

Here is the essence of how your typical "Hold 'Em" game might go:

You have studied up on which hands to play and which to pass on before the flop. You know the odds pretty well. And you even have a fairly good sense of how your opponent plays and some of his 'tells'. You get dealt the Ace Queen of spades and end up in a decent sized pot against two opponents. The flop gives you the King of spades, a red 10 and the 7 of spades. All kinds of options for you. Two shots at the nut flush and a straight draw, too. One opponent makes a large bet that you *correctly* read as an attempt to "buy the pot". You call. So does your other opponent.

Fourth Street. It's the Jack of spades. Hot damn, you have the top flush. You have a straight flush draw. And you have others in the pot to make it a big one. You are just hoping one of your opponents has two other spades to lose to your flush. You bet as much as you think they will call. One guy raises you. OK, maybe he's got trips. Maybe he has the two lower spades. Maybe he has a high straight. Maybe he is trying to buy the pot, himself. You study him and think through his 'tells'. You *correctly* decide he has a hand worth staying, either the trips or the two spades. You have him beat. Time to milk him.

You want to go all in, but you don't want him to fold, you want a big score. You want him to stay in with that weaker flush he could have—or with his trips, even though there is a small chance at a full house. You have *correctly* figured him for trips or a low flush. You know he is likely to stay. You raise big. The third guy folds. The other calls. You have more than half your remaining chips in the pot.

The River: The 7 of clubs. You are still very confident. But the 7 worries you a bit. A boat is possible. But the guy would have had to have had trip Kings, or trip 10's on the flop. Why would he only have called with three Kings after the flop? But if he only had trip 10's, would he have been gutsy enough to call the big bet on Fourth Street when your straight and flush possibilities were so evident? While you are thinking about it, he bets large enough to put you all in. You briefly consider the possibility of four sevens. But you *correctly* rule that out. He is not bluffing entirely, nor does he have the killer four of a kind. He could have a boat, but his betting pattern and 'tells' did not show you either trip Kings after the flop or trip 7's on fourth street. You figure him for a flush, but worry about the boat. But either way, there is no way you can fold your killer flush. Not with the pot being three times the size of the last bet. So you go all in. . . .

And he shows you a pair of 10's in the hole. A frickin' boat. You are busted. You start to ask why he had such confidence in the trip 10's after Fourth Street, but you notice that one of his hole 10's was a spade. He had trips AND a flush draw to the 10. Enough in his mind to justify the call. Maybe he was not smart to call with three 10s. Or maybe he was not smart to have slow-played his trips in the bet after the flop and let you catch your flush. Or maybe he is just so damn smart that he had you doped out exactly and made every move just right. You tell yourself it was a fun and interesting and skill-focused hand. But it was only five minutes of poker.

You look at your watch. It is 8:45pm, and you are out of the game. You wonder if your wife has started watching that chick flick that she rented yet or if there is still time to go home and watch it with her. Instead of playing poker. But, hey, you played "Hold 'Em" just like on TV. You had a real live showdown on a big, risk-it-all hand. So you have that going for you. Which is nice. And anyway, how bad can "The Sisterhood of the Traveling Pants" be?

Now, admittedly, a large part of the problem with Texas Hold 'Em is due to the "table stakes" betting limits usually applied to the game. If you played Five Card Draw with table stakes, you would suffer many of the same problems. Hold 'Em has so few points of information and so few opportunities for smart players to take advantage of good situations, though, that it almost has to be played with large stakes or it becomes very tedious. The excitement in a Hold 'Em game is exactly because anyone could get taken down for big bucks at any moment. If you play "Hold 'Em with a $.50 or $1 limit on betting, folks will tire of it very quickly. Actually, Five Card Draw is pretty much the same way. It is a bit tedious unless played with high limits, in which case it is more exciting but still rather arbitrary in how it redistributes the chips. "Hold 'Em" is a bit less tedious than "Five Card Draw" because "Hold 'Em" has four betting intervals, and most of the cards exposed, compared with "Five Card Draw's" two betting intervals and a card exchange with no cards exposed.

A good regular poker game will make players want to play for hours and will allow players to do so. A good regular poker game will feature individual games that incorporate a lot of strategy, observation, calculation and cleverness. When a player leaves a good regular poker game he wants to believe that many or most of the losses he suffered were controllable. That he made mistakes or got outplayed on some hands—not just outdrawn on the last card. After a good regular poker game, the losing players should have the sense that the winners (particular the winners who frequently win) have some skill and technique and savvy that the losers want to learn and master. Surely, there will still be luck in good poker games. But the best poker games are made up of individual hands that maximize the degree to which skill affects the outcome.

Think of it as a continuum. On one end of the continuum, you could have everyone put all their money in the middle of the table and just cut the cards. High card takes all the money and goes home. On the other end, you could play pure skill games like chess and the best chess player will leave with all the money. Your poker game should result in some element of luck and chance. But it should allow all players to play entertaining and interesting games over the course of several hours and to leave feeling like, to a big extent, the more skillful players do better, but everyone has a fighting chance. "Texas Hold 'Em" with table stakes is too far towards the "cut the cards for all the money" end of the spectrum. And if you limit the size of the betting enough to prevent large and arbitrary swings of fortune, and to ensure that skill gets rewarded over the long term, then "Texas Hold 'Em" fails in the "Entertaining and Interesting" categories. It has a very real skill component. But it takes hundreds and hundreds of pretty tedious hands at small betting limits to allow determined skill to prevail. There are many, many far better games which allow skill to prevail over a shorter series of hands and which therefore can support larger betting limits without the outcomes feeling arbitrary.

Some will always swear that "Texas Hold 'Em" is the best and most pure poker game ever devised. And there will be no dissuading them. 'Hold 'Em" is to "Poker" as "Bluegrass" is to "music". Sure, there are Bluegrass lovers who can rhapsodize about all the endless and subtle variations of Bluegrass and about the amazing depths to which one might be transformed while listening to or playing Bluegrass. But the vast majority of people, and the vast majority of music lovers are going to find deeper fulfillment in a far broader musical experience that might include a little Bluegrass but which includes much, much more.

> "So again, do not raise in No Limit Hold'em—especially tournaments—if there is a reasonable chance that a reraise will make you throw up".
>
> —David Sklansky

CHAPTER 2

Atmosphere and Flow of the Game

THERE IS AN emotional flow to an evening of poker. At various times, you and/or the other players will experience tension, suspense, aggravation, frustration, joy, delight, high comedy, low comedy, excitement, camaraderie, impatience, anticipation, and exhilaration among many, many other emotions. This emotional roller coaster and the challenge of maintaining your focus throughout the ride are key elements of why the game is so enjoyable. As the host, or as one of the players, you want to do everything you can to maximize the positive emotional impact and to mitigate the negatives.

I have played in games that were as quiet, solemn, and serious as a church service. I have played in games that were so noisy and boisterous that very few hands of poker were actually played with any level of skill or attention. The traditionalists will look down on anything but a quiet, serious, focused game with little banter and a lot of silence.

One of the best poker scenes ever to appear in the movies was the very early scene in Butch Cassidy and the Sundance Kid, where Sundance makes his first appearance. In that scene, and throughout the entire movie, Sundance says very little, and shows very little emotion. He is the epitome of reticence. Butch, on the other hand, is expressive, gabby, sociable, likable, and outgoing. When he comes into the poker room and sees Sundance and the other (also quiet and intense) player ready to have a shoot-out over the cards, Butch essentially good-humors the two of them into dropping the dispute. (It helps that Sundance has a hell of a reputation as a gunfighter, but note how Butch, talking and smiling a mile a minute gives Sundance a means to avoid shooting the guy and gives the other guy room to back down semi-graciously.)

Picture your regular poker game as a combination of Sundance Kid personality types and Butch Cassidy personality types trying to play poker together. There are some principles and guidelines that will help to create an atmosphere conducive to everyone enjoying the cards and the emotional roller coaster without feeling like shooting each other at some point in the night.

The Friendliness Dilemma

Are you playing with friends or adversaries? It is crucial to get this answer right. This book is not about playing with strangers. So you may think the best answer is to run the game as if you are playing with friends. At the big picture level, this is the best approach to a friendly, regular game of poker. In fact, the goal of this book is to convey how to create a friendly, mutually rewarding, regular poker game.

But that doesn't tell the whole story. Poker as an actual card game (as opposed to an evening of poker as a social exercise) only works as a competitive, win-lose, zero-sum, adversarial contest. It is not possible to play an individual hand of poker as a cooperative venture. The essence of the game demands that in each hand (and even across multiple hands) each player must do everything in his power to maximize his chance of winning the most chips from the other players.

So, as the host, you need to do what you can to ensure that the social/friendliness goal of your regular game does not interfere with the ruthless competition of the actual play of each hand. How? By properly setting expectations and speaking up when play runs counter to those expectations.

Let's say that towards the end of a hand, Albert is holding an unbeatable hand. Let's say he has a pair of Jacks showing and a Jack in the hole with all cards dealt in a 5-card stud hand. Bart, the only other guy left in the pot is showing a pair of 9s. Albert can't lose. He has a lock. The nuts. Albert opens the last round of betting with a check (betting nothing). Bart, with his loser 9s, raises $2. Albert calls and they show their cards, with Albert, of course, winning the hand. After the hand, you ask Albert what the hell he was thinking on that last round of bets. Why didn't he open with a cash bet instead of a check? Or, at the very least, why didn't he re-raise Bart's $2 once he had suckered him into the pot? Albert says "Well, Bart is pretty far behind on the night, and it wouldn't have been sporting to take another big bet from him when I knew he had no chance".

What should you do? You have to speak up. You have a problem. At least one of your regulars is trying to "be nice" instead of maximizing their results for the hand. This will screw up everything. For sure, Bart will return the favor some time to Albert and the two of them will reinforce their new set of expectations that being nice is important even in the play of an individual poker hand. Pretty soon, people will be letting folks win pots on their birthdays, or because they look sad. This will lead to even more conflicting sets of expectations. And you can be sure that, before long, when a competitive player makes a more ruthless bet, the "be nice" faction of players will act like he has broken the "niceness code."

Before you know it, someone will suggest that the money is not really important and why don't we just play for matchsticks. And soon thereafter, someone will suggest that you play hearts instead. And invite the wives. And they won't even play *that* game properly but will warn folks before they hit them with the queen of spades.

But if "being nice" *in the actual play of the cards and chips,* is one of the goals of the game, the only way you can do your best against that goal is to give everything away. And that prevents you or anyone else at the table from playing poker. The object of a poker hand is to win the chips. You simply must not corrupt that clear objective with confusing expectations or objectives relating to "being nice." It would be like trying to play Monopoly without charging anybody any rents. It would simply not be Monopoly.

It is critical to understand that you are doing two things simultaneously:

1. Providing a mutually supportive, friendship protected, camaraderie-inducing environment

2. Encouraging the controlled battles in that environment to be expertly and ruthlessly fought

Poker players and other sporting, competitive people enjoy the combat. You should provide an environment that allows the competitors to respect each other, know the expectations, support each other and win and lose with honor. But you cannot water down the actual combat itself.

Playing poker means ruthless, shark-like, adversarial play of the cards, the bets, the bluffs, and the deception. It doesn't mean you can't be a nice person while you do it and even laugh about it as you do it or commiserate with the victim after you do it. But you have to do it. Or you are not playing poker. It is inherent to the challenge and fun of the game. Within the rules of the game (cheating of any kind must not happen), you should encourage the most ruthless plays. The joy of a good night of poker is to experience giving and getting all of these ruthless slings and arrows within the reasonably safe confines of it all being just a game.

The game should provide a safe environment for friends to be ruthless and cunning and adversarial in an artificial game environment while protecting their long-term friendly and supportive relationships with each other in the real world. That is when the game is at its best. When the supportive and friendly behavior bleeds over from the real world into the game play itself, the essence of poker is lost. If you cannot *comfortably* and *simultaneously* exist in both the friendly real world and ruthless game world, then you will only be able to play poker with real adversaries or strangers. Because any game you play with your friends will become cooperative.

So, as a good host, you need to understand these concepts well and communicate them well to all of your guests. You should communicate and reinforce the "ruthless play / friendly reality" dichotomy in the invitations, greetings, table chatter, dispute resolutions, setting the date for the next game, and every other effort you make as the host. Use every opportunity to reiterate—we play the game ruthlessly, but outside the game actions, we support each other as friends and colleagues.

> "It's easy to be a tough competitor and still be the kind of person with whom people love to compete."
>
> —*Chuck Thompson*

The Players

To a large degree, the atmosphere of the game will be driven by the players who participate. If you sit down to play cards with five introverted, taciturn, scientific thinkers, you are not likely to have a rollicking, noisy, unpredictable, high spirited, evening of verbal humor, one-upmanship, crowing victors and vociferous losers. On the other hand, if you sit down to play cards with five extroverted, life-of-the-party types, you are not likely to find yourself several hours later in a serious, focused, competitive, and quick paced contest of steel and nerve, with few distractions.

If you like to think through the possibilities and make careful decisions, you may find yourself continuously feeling rushed when playing with five guys who decide everything within a nanosecond, right or wrong. Conversely, you may find yourself impatient beyond belief if you are the type who can make a good decision fairly quickly and you are playing with five "slow and thoughtful" types.

As the host of the game, you will be the one to choose players to invite, find a sufficient number of compatible players for each game, and determine which potential players might be better off in a different game than yours. It is all about the right combination of players.

I have never hosted a dinner party. I believe I am gender-disqualified from any such desire or impulse. My late wife, Laura, however, did host dinner parties (and probably would claim that I was the co-host, although I struggled mightily to retain only the title of "guest"). Laura told me one time that, from what she could observe, hosting a poker game had a lot in common with hosting a dinner party. She said:

> I see you keeping a list of potential invitees, choosing compatible participants from that list, putting out invitations, tracking responses and inviting alternates,

preparing the house for the game, welcoming the guests, ensuring their comfort throughout the evening and assessing afterwards the degree to which the night was satisfactory and lived up to your expectations and those of the guests. I see you appalled at the terrible breach of etiquette visited upon you by a participant who calls late to cancel, the scramble to adjust by finding replacements, and the relief you feel when the last guest arrives and you no longer have to worry about "no-shows". I see you in the days following the game, considering how the guests interacted with one another and adjusting your plans on whom should be invited in the future, and who should play with whom. It just looks a lot like a dinner party to me.

Well. I assured her it was nothing like a dinner party. I didn't cook. I tried to take all the guests money. I didn't have to dress up. And I didn't care who sat next to whom, or which fork was used. Furthermore, there was not one scintilla of polite chit-chat as every conversation was focused entirely on establishing and maintaining competitive positioning. And there were no thank-you notes, and no expectations of future reciprocity. So there. Laura just smiled and said, "OK." But I knew she was more right than wrong. And she knew I knew. I may also have internally adjusted my position a little on how cooperative I should be when she wanted to throw the next dinner party. I hope I did, anyway.

The point of that story is that, as the host of the game, you should pay attention to a lot of important pre-game decisions, including the critical choice of players to include in your list of regulars. A successful game requires players who enjoy playing against one another, trust one another's honesty, and enjoy one another's company, at least in a Poker setting. There are several factors to have in mind as you choose players for your regular game, as described below.

Number of Players

Six, five, seven, eight, four, ten, more than ten. In that order. But not nine. Never nine.

Let me explain. Some folks believe that you cannot play poker with more than seven players. This belief comes from the fact that many poker varieties are seven-card hands and you cannot deal seven-card hands to more than seven players without running out of cards. Well, actually you can. The casinos routinely deal Seven-Card Stud to eight players at a time. So you can do it. But you have to be clever about the rules. The casinos simply announce that if too many players stay in the game until the last card, such that there are not enough cards to deal each player a seventh card, then a single community card will be turned upwards and will be considered everyone's seventh card. Another rule I have heard to solve the problem states that if there are fewer cards in the deck than remaining players after the sixth card is dealt, the game converts to Six-Card Stud.

The point is that, with some creativity, almost any number of players can be successfully accommodated in a poker game. Some numbers are better than others, however. In my experience, the best number of players for a friendly Poker game is six. The next best number is five. Then seven, eight, four, ten or more than ten in declining order of preference.

If you have ten players or more, you simply have to have two or more tables going at the same time, with five or more players at each. It is certainly more challenging to find chips, cards, tables, beer, and other essentials for a bigger group. And there is more noise, more banter and distraction, and some squabbling over who plays at which table. But if you put out an invitation and you are lucky enough to have ten players who want to play, give it a try.

For a single poker table, you can easily handle up to eight

players by limiting the games you deal or by making minor changes to some of the favorite games. Play Six-Card Stud instead of seven (Six-Card Stud is actually a better game anyway, due to the lower luck factor when you eliminate the third down card in the end). Use community cards instead of individual cards for every round. It works. But eight-player tables in a friendly game feature a great deal of chit-chat. And you may be driven to distraction by all the delay involved in moving eight players through each betting decision. Eight players can also feel a bit cramped around a standard sized poker table.

Seven players is a better game than eight, simply because of the decrease in noise and distraction. Five players is a better game still—particularly if all are skilled players. The pacing improves, there is more focus on the cards, and it is much easier to keep the players from breaking into subgroup conversations. But, be careful if you have one weak player with four strong ones. In a five-person game, the weak player will have few places to hide and will take a worse beating than he will in the more randomized and less focused seven- or eight-player games. Also, beware of a game with only five committed participants. If any of the five have a last-minute emergency and have to cancel, you may have to cancel the entire game.

Six players is the ideal number. You can afford one last minute no-show. You can start on time if one player is late and you can play until the normal quitting time if one player has to leave early. You have enough players to get action on almost every deal, but not so many as to be unruly. You can play just about any poker variety ever invented. And there is a bit more personality at the table than there is with only five players.

Four players will only work if all four are very fast (to keep the game moving), and very good. A weak player will kill a four-person game by virtue of their slow, poor, or random play now representing 25 percent of the action. If you end up playing with four players, I strongly recommend playing double-handed, by dealing two hands to each player. High-low games work particularly well in a double-handed situation, as you are actually simulating eight-player action. There are a number of excellent games designed for double-handed, fewer player situations. These games are described in a later section of this book.

Nine is the worst possible number of players. It is really not enough to get two tables going. And it is too many for a single table.

So, when you are inviting players, try to ensure that you will have five (reliable) players at a minimum, and think about turning away players once you have eight, unless you want to try to run two tables.

Six, five, seven, eight, four, ten, more than ten. But never nine.

Wyatt Earp: [*to Doc Holliday discussing what to do with a card cheat in their three-handed game*]: "If we shoot him, we won't have anyone to play with."

Types of Players

It is helpful, although not always possible, to try to get a diverse group of players. You do not necessarily want to have a table of six aggressive players, or six extroverted talkers, or six silent types, or six "know-it-alls." Diversity is good. It makes the game much more interesting. If, for example, you have too many players from the same company and they start talking about some office issue, it can get annoying for the others who have no way to participate in the discussion.

There are certain player and personality types, however,

that are beneficial to your game, even if all your players share that type. Players who are competitive, for example are good to have. Players who will learn are important. Players who can stay focused on the task and are not easily distracted are desirable. And, of course, you want players that share the same objectives for the game that you have—players who want to have fun, show off, and compete intensely, but remain friendly outside the table.

One thing I have learned over the years is that it is hard to know, without actually asking, who would and who would not like to be invited to a game. And it is hard to tell who would and would not be a good poker player without actually playing with them. So establishing and maintaining your regular group of players is more about recognizing the good players once they have played a couple of times, and encouraging the players who will come regularly and play well, than it is about guessing up front who will make a good player and be worth inviting.

Player Skill Levels

Your game will be more rewarding and more fun if your players play well and continuously improve. So, in general, you want to find players with a high ceiling.

But most importantly, you want to avoid players who are significantly behind the group average skill level and who are slow learners. These players will lose a lot of money, which might be nice in terms of helping others feel like they are winning, but it will surely become awkward and disheartening. No one in a friendly poker game should enjoy taking money without much challenge from a poor player.

If you think you will have a player at the table who might be below the group average skill level, try to ensure that they are not isolated. Bring down the average a little bit by inviting another weaker player or two to that game. The advantage to this is twofold. The weaker players will not be so overmatched when up against each other. And the explanations and analyses (lessons) that are discussed by all the players after each hand are leveraged across a couple of players who need to improve and not visibly aimed at a single player.

Familiarity with Each Other

It is surprisingly unimportant that your regular friendly poker game players need to know each other well when they start playing in your game. Poker provides a natural language of phrases, actions, attitudes and behaviors that is actually much easier and far more enjoyable to practice than the so called 'art' of small talk. That is to say that a decent poker player can have an enjoyable and social evening with several people he has just met, even though that same person can hate the thought of meeting people at a party and making small talk.

It is somewhat important, though, that each player know at least one other player at the table pretty well. It is difficult to be comfortable playing and even more difficult to share the emotions of victories and defeats with an entire table of strangers. A player will have much more fun and be much more comfortable if he has at least one friendly face among his opponents.

Players who do not know each other will bond pretty quickly over a couple of evenings of playing poker. Two or three games is all it takes for most players to feel very comfortable throwing out the verbal abuse or sharing the humor that arises out of the evening's fortunes and misfortunes. So there is no reason to avoid inviting new folks to the game. If they can play cards, they will be insiders in no time.

Reliability

The most important "type" of player you want to find for your regular games is the reliable type. A player who answers the invitations promptly, can make the game most of the time, shows up on time, stays until the end, and always comes when he says he will—that player is an all-star. If you have been hosting a regular poker game already, you know how important it is to find players who are reliable.

Perhaps it is only my curmudgeonly inclinations, but it seems to me that society has been drifting rapidly away from the days when invitations were treated with respect and social commitments were important things that people would never break without extreme cause. Here are some examples of invitation responses that will be perfectly useless to you:

- "I'll try to make it."
- "I'll call you that day if I can get free to play"
- "I am hoping to be there"
- "I think I can make it by 10pm"

Do not accept these responses. If you accept responses like that from a few folks, you will get all set for your poker game and end up with only three players. Tell the invitee who responds in that (socially unacceptable) manner that you are sorry that he is not in a position to commit to playing and that you will offer the seat to others to ensure a full table. If he gets back to you and can properly commit before the table is full, you can choose at that point whether your game will be better with him in it or not.

If your players, on the whole, are prone to being unavailable three times out of four invitations, then you will require twenty five or thirty players on your invitation list to ensure that you can get six or seven players on any given night. If your players frequently cancel late or fail to show, then you will be unable to schedule a game with fewer than eight players so you can still have enough to play after a couple let you down. It is almost enough to make you sympathize with the airlines for deliberately overbooking all of their flights!

The best approach is to always keep looking for the reliability all-stars. Even if you have had no trouble scheduling games for the past year, you should keep looking for new players who might become one of your regulars. People move, or get married, or get a job that requires too much travel, or go to their beach house all summer, or become the coach for their kids' little league team, and just like that, all of a sudden, one of your regulars is out of action for a season, or a year, or for good. It takes some effort and some new blood to keep the number of reliable regulars high enough to keep your game running over the years. And there is nothing sadder than having to cancel a game for lack of enough players.

One of my favorite Poker cartoons was a single panel drawing showing a player arriving for a Poker game that was already underway. The clock on the wall showed the time was 9:30. The guy is explaining to his Poker buddies, "Sorry I was late, guys. It's my 25th anniversary and I just couldn't get away!"

Sign posted at the National Press Club:

"Your First Duty is to the Game—Then Come Mother, God and Country"

Casual or Formal?

One of the critical decisions you need to make as the host of a great regular poker game involves the degree of formality that you and your players will expect. How strictly will your game adhere to traditions or customs? How consistently will the rules be enforced? How 'serious' is your game going to be?

Some of this will depend upon the personalities of your regular players and ultimately, you will need to gain the consensus of the player themselves. But you should determine and take actions to establish the degree of formality that you believe works best for your group. And you do hold the final veto, since it is you who will issue future invitations and you can simply fail to invite players who don't abide by your determined degree of formality.

Here are some examples of behaviors that I have actually seen (some frequently, others rarely) at the poker table. For each of these examples, you might want to try to determine whether that specific behavior should be allowed/encouraged by your group or should be disallowed/discouraged. Once you work through these examples, you will have a pretty good basis for how formal (or 'tight') you want your game to be.

Loose (casual) game: Anyone can comment on the cards as they fall, and the dealer is not required to note anything.

Tight (formal) game: Only the dealer comments as cards are dealt and he should note pairs, new high cards, etc. as he goes.

Loose Game: A player, having folded his hand, leans over and looks at his neighbor's hole cards, offering advice and/or support.

Tight Game: A player is shot for trying to look at any cards that are not his own.

Loose Game: A player who has folded when he would have received the last card from the deck that hand begs the dealer to let him peek at the top card to see what he 'would have received'.

Tight Game: Players know better than to ask and dealers never let anyone peek at undealt cards.

Loose Game: A player trying to dissuade another player from making a big bet flashes the other player one of his down cards, saying "Don't get crazy, there, Johnny, everyone's got a pair by now!"

Tight Game: The player making this flashy move is ostracized for being too obnoxious

Loose Game: A player chatters about previous hands, or the Yankees' latest free agent slugger while a hand is in play.

Tight Game: All players remain silent except for declaring bets, declaring their hands at the showdown, or raising a salient question or concern about the current hand.

Loose Game: Many players complain about their hands as their cards arrive.

Tight Game: Complaining, like any other extraneous chatter, is heavily discouraged.

Loose Game: Two players who have folded take their two folded hands and look at them together remarking that between them they had nothing, or that it was no wonder they couldn't get anything, they had each other's cards.

Tight Game: No one looks at folded cards under any circumstances. No one comments on their folded cards.

Loose Game: Players betting out of turn, or making other mistakes, face no penalty

Tight Game: Players betting out of turn are penalized monetarily.

Loose Game: Players making an obvious error in declaring their hand, declaring high or low, or being unaware of the rules, or even folding by mistake are allowed to correct their mistake if possible

Tight Game: Actions are final. No take-backs.

Loose Game: A player exasperated by a particularly unfortunate deal involving his hole cards tosses them up on the table while folding so everyone can see just how unlucky he has been. "You always call two's wild and this time you say threes are wild, and LOOK at what you deal me! A pair of crummy twos!"

Tight Game: Any irregular exposure of cards that should be hidden is very strongly discouraged or disallowed.

Loose Game: A player, towards the end of the night and out of chips, grabs a few chips from his neighbor to cover the last bet and stay in a hand without making another chip buy.

Tight Game: Even if the neighbor doesn't cut off his fingers for dipping into his chips, the player who is out of chips must make a chip buy to keep playing. (Alternatively, a rule may be enforced that allows such players to be "all-in" when their chips run out).

Loose Game: If the dealer does not offer the player to his right a chance to cut the cards, nobody cares.

Tight Game: If the dealer does not offer the cut before dealing, it is a misdeal and must be re-dealt.

A "loose" or "casual" game might feature a lot of "table talk" among the players about developing hands, a lot of folding out of turn, players dealing without remembering to offer a cut of the cards, misdealt cards being rearranged without starting the deal over with a fresh deck, a good deal of complaining or gloating, folded players looking at active players' hole cards and offering their help, etc. A "strict" or "tight" game might disallow all of those behaviors and enforce a more rigorous adherence to a more detailed set of rules and practices.

There is no inherently right or wrong choice for the examples above or for the degree of formality you choose to have in your game. The deciding factor should be what makes the game most fun for you and your players.

I have found, however, that a more casual game is more fun, more friendly, and more in line with the principles of this book. Furthermore, the main rationale for many of the formal rules is to prevent cheating, which should not be a real threat to your friendly regular game. There must be some rules, however, and the permissibility of other casual practices should be plainly understood. The key is to ensure that everyone is on the same page and the expectations are clear.

> **From "A Big Hand for the Little Lady":**
>
> **Mary Meredith:** Gentlemen all. All such gallant gentlemen.
>
> **Henry Drummond:** Well, we're gallant on Sunday, this is Friday and we're playing poker. Now, you wanna play with us, you ante up $500!

House Rules

There have to be rules in any kind of game. The rules provide the framework of play, define the standards of expected behavior, put finite limits on the scope of combat and ensure that a clear line remains between game activities and "real life".

Since Poker is in the public domain, there is no 'official' set of poker rules published and overseen by the game manufacturer. Instead, you can find hundreds of versions of "poker rules" all of which differ in minor ways from one another. You may have heard the expression, "according to Hoyle". Hoyle published many books listing the rules of various gambling card games, including "Brag", one of Poker's many ancestors. But Hoyle was an expert, not an authority. So while many chose to accept his set of rules, many others did not.

The US Army, during World War II, commissioned a sleight-of-hand magician by the name of John Scarne to educate the troops on how to avoid cheaters, how to avoid the perils of gambling, and what rules they should use if they insisted on playing poker. (Scarne, by the way was the guy whose hands were shown doing all the fancy card manipulations done by Paul Newman's character in "The Sting"—a movie with another one of the greatest poker game scenes ever). Many US Servicemen learned to play according to Scarne's rules. But that does not make Scarne's rules the 'official' rules either.

If you learned to play poker from your Dad or your uncles, you likely learned their own set of "rules" and procedures. And they may have learned in the army, or from their family, or at their country club.

Previously published sets of poker rules have done an adequate job covering the basics of playing poker with strangers. But I have never seen a set of rules written to take full advantage of the richer and deeper experience of playing poker with friends and trustworthy colleagues.

To host a great friendly poker game, and to establish the best possible atmosphere and flow, you will need to adopt a set of rules. You and your players can evolve the rules over time as circumstances warrant, but you will need to start with a set of rules that everyone clearly understands. This particular set of rules that you adopt and gradually evolve becomes your very own set of "House Rules".

I have included, in this book, a set of rules that are perfectly compatible with other published poker rules, but which have a few nuances that make the friendly game more enjoyable. These nuances are not changes to commonly accepted poker rules (a flush still beats a straight!). Rather, they are additional rules and procedures to cover areas where the existing sets of rules are silent or ambiguous. I have also included the rationale or explanation for each of the rules so you and your players can more easily accept and adopt the rules or can more intelligently create your own variations.

Other Guidelines

In 1984, the movie *Ghostbusters* explained pretty clearly the difference between rules and guidelines:

Dana Barrett: [*possessed by Zuul*] Do you want this body?

Dr. Peter Venkman: Is this a trick question?

Dana Barrett: [*possessed by Zuul*] Take me now, subcreature.

Dr. Peter Venkman: I make it a rule never to get involved with possessed people.

[*Dana starts passionately making out with him*]

Dr. Peter Venkman: Actually, it's more of a guideline than a rule . . .

In addition to the House Rules dictating how the game will be played, your group will need other guidelines or rules that are more specific to your individual setting and players. Because they are, by nature, individual and specific to your game, you will have to devise them on your own. But here are a few examples from games in which I have played over the past forty years.

- Only one player may smoke at a time. (This was the compromise between the 'no smoking' faction and the smokers among the group. Mercifully, the games have all been smoking-free for 20 years now.)
- All drinks must be in the glasses provided and in the drink holders in the table
- BYOB. But all leftovers from previous games are up for grabs

- The host deals first, and also begins the last round of deals
- Each player returns his chair to the dining room on their way out
- Latecomers let themselves in the front door—no need to interrupt the game
- 727 (or substitute any other unpopular game here) can only be dealt one time in any round of deals
- Those having the furthest to drive cash out first
- Last guy to arrive pays a fine
- Everyone brings their own snacks or snacks to share. Non-oily snacks only (out of respect for the cards, table and chips)
- Absolutely no television on during the game
- Penalty of a red chip for asking the dealer to repeat the name or rules of the game because a player was not listening
- If more players are available than seats for an upcoming game, priority is given to the most regular player (or alternatively to the first person that reserved a seat)

These are just some of the types of guidelines or standards that might be adopted in your game. You will have others. It is not necessary to have all of these thought out in advance. In fact, it would look a little compulsive if you tried to do so. Just keep an eye out for where a standard is needed, and either pronounce it to resolve a dispute or just begin to expect and reinforce it as your games go on over time.

Size of Stakes

The amount of money at risk for you and your players will go a long way to determining the atmosphere of your game. If the amounts are too high, the players will be anxious or even fearful. That is no fun. And if the stakes are too low, the players can become bored or apathetic.

Poker demands that something meaningful be put at risk in each wagering decision. But it does not demand that losers must lose more than they can comfortably afford.

You need to determine the range of losses that, for your group of players, fall above the point where they don't care and below the point where they are significantly harmed. This amount changes over time and circumstances.

As a poor college student in the 70's, with very little disposable income, the loss of $2 or more in a few hours of poker would have been significant. And the risk of losing more than $2 was sufficient to keep many of our peers from learning or playing the game. So we set the buy-in, the antes, the betting levels, and the loss-limits (see poverty poker, below) to amounts that kept the big winners and losers within a few dollars of break-even.

As young professionals in our first career positions, the range had increased to winning or losing $10-$15 in a night. Later, when most players had houses, cars and kids, the range was up to $20—$30. And now, 35 years from those college games, the buy-in used by my regular group is $40 with big losers risking a beating of $60-$70 on an awful night. But, always adjusting to conditions, the great recession of 2008 had me strongly considering tweaking the buy-in and stakes to help the unemployed players stay under a $50 loss.

In order to set and keep the stakes at an appropriate level, you will need to pay attention to two principles which are stated here but explained in more depth (for those deep thinkers out there) in the footnote.*

---

* The trick in setting the stakes at the right level is to keep your eye on two related economic/financial concepts, 1) Marginal Utility of Money, and 2) The Risk Aversion Curve. You want the magnitude of the stakes or risk to fall somewhere in the sweet spot of the marginal utility of money curve where a dollar is actually worth a dollar. And you want the magnitude of the stakes or risk to fall somewhere in the sweet spot of the risk aversion curve where the value of taking a risk is close to the face value of the expected result and not diminished by the fear of uncertainty.

The marginal utility of money is a measure of the true worth of the next dollar of income you receive. And it typically decreases for people as the total amount of money they already have increases. Put in simpler terms, the richer a person is (or the further ahead he is during a night of poker), the less each additional dollar is worth to him. The less money they have (or the further behind they are) the more valuable each new dollar becomes to them. A player who is ahead $60 values the next $2 less than does a player who is behind by $30. The important corollary for our purposes is this: A player who is behind typically places more value on each pot and each dollar than a player who is ahead. So, to optimize the net emotional payoff across all of your players (i.e. to create the best average emotional experience) you want to set the stakes to minimize the pain of the losers, not to maximize the opportunity for winners to make a bigger score.

The Risk Aversion Curve shows the theoretical relationship between the amount of money at risk and the required payoff for taking that risk. As the amount of money risked gets larger and larger, the typical player's (or investor's) aversion to uncertainty will make him require higher and higher premiums over 'normal' expected values. If a person offered you the chance to lose only 49 cents if you called the flip of coin incorrectly but win 51 cents if you called it right, you would take that deal all day long. In the long run you know the math works out to produce a 2 percent edge for you (on average) for each flip of the coin. But, if the person offered you the chance to lose $490,000 for calling the coin flip wrong

The first principle is that the perceived value of the next dollar a player might win, earn, or lose changes based upon how much money he has readily available to him. Someone with little money, or someone who has lost money on the night, will value the next $1 he might obtain more highly than someone with a lot of money or someone who has won money over the course of the evening. The implication is that the net emotional impact on your players can be more positively impacted by helping the losers avoid more losses than by helping the winners win more money. Focus on mitigating the loser's pain. The winners will take care of themselves.

---

but win $510,000 for calling correctly, would you really take that deal? Most of us would be financially wiped out and bankrupt by a single bad call. The amount of the wager overwhelms the expected mathematical value of the deal. Almost none of us would have the courage (or the indifference to risk) to take the deal. We'd rather keep the $490,000 we might be able to scrape together than risk losing everything for a chance to get another $510,000.

Actually, understanding the concepts of risk aversion, discerning an opponent's level of risk aversion, and using bullying skills to trigger fearful reactions are an important part of table-limit, winner-take-all poker tournaments such as the World Series of Poker. The players may all be able to withstand losing their entire buy-ins without being financially ruined. But as their stacks dwindle and they fall behind those with more chips, their fears of each hand being the one that busts them out of the tournament weigh into every decision they make. The short-stack (few chips remaining) players' marginal utility of money is higher than the chip leaders, and their risk of being busted out on a given hand is much higher. So their risk aversion instincts consciously and subconsciously factor greatly into their play.

But this book is not about those kinds of poker games. For a regular, friendly game, you do not want your players to bust out, go broke and go home. You want them to buy in again and keep playing until it is quitting time.

The second principle is that risk aversion diminishes the quality of play. Players who fear that a loss is too big for them to comfortably handle will play more poorly and enjoy the game less than those who do not suffer such fear. If the stakes of your poker game are too high, you will have some or all of your players making too many of their decisions while being overly affected by their risk aversion.

Braver players, and those who get ahead during the game will be able to "bully" the risk-averse players, or players nearing their loss limits, simply by betting large amounts. Not only does this make the game much less fun and literally too scary for many of the players, but it also decreases the poker skill involved and replaces it with 'bullying' skills. You want to keep the fear (the risk aversion) to a reasonable limit to prevent the game from becoming too 'intense'. Some fear or anxiety can be fun. There ought to be occasional big hands or big bets that put a player's bravery to the test. But not so often, or so hard a test, as to ruin the player's enjoyment of the evening.

> **From "The Odd Couple":**
>
> **Oscar Madison**: I'm $800 behind in alimony. Let's raise the stakes.

Controlling the Stakes and the Risk Level

There are four key variables that you need to control in order to have set the stake and risk level properly for your friendly, regular Poker game:

- The amount of the initial buy-in (what it takes to get started)

52

- The amount of the maximum bets per betting turn (how much can be wagered on a single decision)

- The amount of foreseeable total losses that might be incurred by a player having a really bad night (typically 3-4 times the buy-in amount or 50+ times the maximum bet)

- Any special "poverty poker" or "loss-mitigation" rules that you might install in your game.

Let's look at these one at a time.

Initial Buy-In Amount

The **initial buy-in** amount is the price the player pays for his first purchase of chips. In some Poker games, a player can buy as much or as little as he chooses in the first or any subsequent buy. There are a couple of good reasons, however, why it is helpful to make this a standard amount in your game and consistent across all players. First, a consistent initial buy makes the overall banking, accounting and tracking easier. Secondly, it makes it possible for the host to have pre-counted out sets of chips to have ready for the players as they arrive. Third, it demonstrates that each player, at least initially, intends to put an equal amount of money at risk in the contest. And fourth, it allows a standard expectation of sorts to be set regarding how much capital is typically required to get most players through the first hour or so and to the point where they have won some and lost some pots. Too small an initial buy-in will lead to unnecessary mid-game subsequent buy-ins by players and slow down the game. (By unnecessary, I mean that you do not want to have players making mid-game buy-ins after only a few hands, simply because they haven't had a chance to play enough hands to get their first win. Obviously a subsequent buy will eventually be necessary when there is too little winning over time to make up for the steady stream of non-winning hands).

The initial buy-in, especially if it is a standard amount, is important to the atmosphere of the game because it serves as a general indication for how much is "at play" during the game. It is the amount that players tell themselves and their wives that they are placing in harm's way. ("It is a just a friendly game, the buy-in is only $20 so we are not playing for blood and no one goes broke.") Of course, every player knows that they may end up making more buy-ins during an evening. So, the initial buy-in amount is kind of a reassuring oversimplification. But it is a simplification (or rationalization) that is psychologically important to ensuring the players' comfort level. And we know how important rationalizations can be from *The Big Chill*:

Michael: I don't know anyone who could get through the day without two or three juicy rationalizations. They're more important than sex.

Sam Weber: Ah, come on. Nothing's more important than sex.

Michael: Oh yeah? Ever gone a week without a rationalization?

The Maximum Bet per Turn

The second variable in setting the stakes appropriately is the **maximum bet** per betting turn. This defined amount controls the speed with which the players' chips can be consumed over the course of the evening. Since you want your players (and you, too) to enjoy a long night of cards, it is essential that this variable is not set so high that someone can be wiped out in only a few bets. It is the size of the maximum bet, more than any other factor that separates poker tournaments from friendly games.

Having watched far too many poker tournaments on TV, players may come to your neighborhood poker game for the first time and expect that you will be playing "table-limit," or, worse still, "no-limit" poker. They may feel that anything less than "table stakes" is insufficiently manly or that it will somehow lessen the interest and excitement level of the game. You will need to explain to them that table stakes games or no-limit games are for contests where the object is to eliminate the other players from the game and to then leave with all the money. Table stakes are for contests where the best approach is to lurk and wait patiently for the few killer opportunities to take down an opponent.

You are not hosting this type of game. You are playing a friendly poker game. A regular poker game. The object across all the hands you play is still to win as much money as you can. But your game requires that this can only be done by subtle skill differences applied over several hours and sharper play over hundreds and hundreds of smaller decisions over the course of the evening. It is, really, a completely different game from the no-limit tournaments. And it is a lot more fun.

In your regular, friendly poker game, there is an implicit (or explicit) agreement by the players that they will play for the entire evening. It is a cooperative venture among the players to enjoy an evening of cards. Forcing a player to leave the game early is not part of the purpose or intent of this evening. It would be like getting a foursome together to play golf, but forcing a player to quit the game as soon as he shoots over par on a hole. Sure, you *could* see who can go the longest at par or better and who will be the last man standing. And that would be a game of some type. But that is not golf. And it is not what 18 holes of golf are supposed to feel like or look like for a foursome out to compete over an entire day on the golf course.

In "no-limit" poker, there is no limit to how much can be bet on any decision. In "table-limit" poker, the limit you may bet on any decision is equal to all the chips you currently have on the table. For both of these types of games, there is usually a rule that allows a player with insufficient chips to go "all-in" and play the hand out for whatever money he does have left. The problem is, of course, that as soon as a player loses a single big pot, he is broke or well on his way to broke and leaving the game.

In "limit' Poker, which you will be playing with your regular gang, there is a fixed (and much lower) maximum limit for the amount that can be bet or raised on a single turn. No matter how good your cards are or how well you have set the trap for your opponent, you can still only bet the maximum limit. It will take many, many such bets over the course of an evening to cause opponents to buy more chips or to eventually reach the point at which you have become the night's big winner.

Set your maximum bet per turn to be high enough to make a player think before throwing it in the pot. But keep it low enough that a player can make 20 or so of these maximum bets before exhausting his initial buy-in of chips. Keep in mind that a single round of betting in a poker hand might not get raised above the minimum or may even be a "free card" round if everyone "checks". But a round of betting can also start at the maximum bet limit and be raised two or three times before all three raises are exhausted. So, those 20 maximum bets that are contained in the initial buy-in might cover substantially more or substantially fewer than 20 actual betting rounds.

Different Maximums for Different Deals

Your regular Poker game will be "dealer's choice", meaning every deal might feature a different game. One player, for example, may deal straight Five-Card Stud, and another player may choose to deal Seven-Card High-low. Still others will choose wild-card games, or community card games, or any number of others. Your evening of friendly poker may end up featuring as many as 15 or 20 different poker varieties.

Each of these poker varieties will come with their own unique betting characteristics. Some games might have only one or two betting intervals. Others may have as many as seven. Some games will have multiple winners splitting the pot, others will have a single winner. Each different game played might benefit from a maximum betting limit tailored specifically to the characteristics of that variety of poker hand. However, substantial confusion would result from different betting limits for every different game.

The compromise answer that works very well is to have a "standard-limit" that applies in most cases, and then a second, "max-limit" that applies to all remaining situations. In my regular game, for example, the standard-limit on bets and raises is $2. This applies throughout all high-low or split pot games. The max-limit, on the other hand, of $10 bets and raises, applies to single-winner games and is also the maximum penalty required in any "match the pot" variety of poker. This solution works especially well for our players because about 70 percent of our games are split-pot games. (So, most of the time, we are playing at $2 limits and only occasionally do we have a game where someone can and does bet $10). If more of our dealers favored single-winner games, I think we would have to lower the "max-limit" to $5 or so to prevent the entire evening from basically becoming $10 limit poker.

I strongly recommend that you keep the max-limit fairly low. It should be no greater than one eighth of the initial buy-in (or a couple of times larger than the standard-limit) unless you are sure it will be used very infrequently. Furthermore, you may find that your group of players does not even need to have a max-limit. The standard limit may be quite sufficient to cover all situations that arise in the set of games that your dealers play. We introduced the max-limit in our game only after a few players who watched the tournaments on TV expressed concern that the pot sizes made it impossible in our game to use the standard limit to force anyone to fold. We did not want to increase the standard limit, because it decreased the participation and action in the high-low hands. So the max-limit was born for single-winner games. If you use it, just make it two or three times the standard limit and see how that goes for a few games. Then, adjust as needed.

> "Learning to play two pairs is worth about as much as a college education, and about as costly."
>
> —*Mark Twain*

Amount of Foreseeable Total Losses

Probably the most important variable you need to keep under control in your friendly poker game is the amount of foreseeable total losses that might be suffered by a player having a horrible night. If a single evening of cards contained enough hands to ensure that luck balanced out equally across all the players, then players would all come close to breaking even for the night. If luck and opportunity were perfectly balanced, only the skill differential would cause wins and losses. Of course, a skill differential could be significant enough to cause a big loss even under those conditions, but it would be less likely and more correctable over the course of several games as the poorer player learned to play better.

We all know, however, that neither the quality of the cards nor the timing of good hands will be completely balanced over a single evening. Someone will get the worst cards of the night (typically the cards that finish second most frequently). And someone will have the worst timing (i.e. getting great hands when everyone else has nothing, or getting a strong hand exactly when someone else gets a killer hand)

Players who have both of these misfortunes happen to them in a single evening will lose the most money. This can be mitigated by how skillful they are relative to the other players. But players of average or below-average skill compared to the others at the table will suffer their worst losses on nights when their cards and timing are both cold.

While this bad luck and bad timing might be evenly distributed among the players over the course of a year or so of poker, that fact will be little consolation to the player the morning after a bad beating, when he is explaining to his wife why there was an extra ATM withdrawal and where that money went. You have to help your players manage their worst outcomes. You have to keep the worst outcome affordable for yourself and your players. And you have to be able to tell potential and invited players what the 'worst case' can be.

Dr. Egon Spengler: It would be bad.

Dr. Peter Venkman: I'm fuzzy on the whole good/bad thing. What do you mean, "Bad"?

Dr. Egon Spengler: Try to imagine all life as you know it stopping instantaneously and every molecule in your body exploding at the speed of light.

Dr. Ray Stantz: Total protonic reversal.

Dr. Peter Venkman: Right. That's bad. Okay. All right. Important safety tip. Thanks, Egon.

Your players will only be comfortable, much like Venkman in *Ghostbusters*, if they have at least some concept, coming in, of how much they might lose on a bad night.

In general, (and there will always be players out there pushing the envelope), a once-a-year, really bad night for a below average player might see them able to lose as much as 60-75 times the maximum bet. If the maximum bet in your game is $2, a player might, on a really bad night, lose $120 or more. But it would have to be a really bad night. Now, of course, your mileage will vary. Your players might be much worse than just below average. Or you might have players that very frequently throw the maximum bet or raise out there on every turn. So it could get worse. But, in my experience, the losers lose between 1 and 25 times the maximum bet. The really big loser for the night might lose 30-50 times the maximum bet, and the epic loser might, once or twice a year, lose 60-75 times the maximum bet.

Controlling Against Epic Losses

What can you do to prevent the really big losses that may cause a player to want to quit the regular game? There are a few important things you can do to keep things more under control. Each item on the list below will help decrease the size of the biggest loser's losses for a night of poker. Keep your eye on outcomes for each of your poker nights, and tweak some of these items to help keep it friendly:

- Lower the size of the maximum bet per turn. If there is a max-limit in addition to a standard limit, keep an eye on where the losers are taking their beatings. If it is in a few giant hands, lower the max-limit or eliminate it altogether. If the beatings are just a steady drain through every kind of hand, lower the standard-limit.

- Try to discourage (or avoid entirely) the "match-the-pot" variety of games that can disproportionately affect the entire night's outcome on just a few bad hands. Never play a match-the-pot game without a max-limit that kicks in once the pot gets bigger than five times the standard-limit bet. (And don't give in to any player who howls about how that is taking the fun out of it. There is excitement in cutting the cards for all the money at the end of the night, too. But it is arbitrary gambling thrills, not poker fun. Tell those players they can go outside after the game and flip a coin for their cars' pink slips if that is what they are looking for. You are running a poker game.)

- Encourage the players, particularly those who are behind for the night and looking weak on a particular hand to remember to "soak up raises" by raising the minimum amount instead of just calling when they are whipsawed between two other betters who will be raising the maximum. It is surprising how many players forget this loss-mitigation tactic. The three-raise limit rule is there to keep the weaker hands from being whipsawed in the first place.

- Make sure that fewer high-value chips, and more low-value chips are distributed in the opening buy and subsequent buy-ins. You will be surprised how much of a difference this will make in the frequency of lower-sized bets in the early rounds of all of the games.

- Be gracious, not insulting, to players who are behind and who choose to sit out the last 45 minutes of the game rather than make yet another buy-in that will put them at risk of losing more than their comfort level can cover. Go ahead and insult any of the winning players who do this.

- Discourage unnecessary betting rounds in longer games that have more than a few betting intervals already. The longer games tend to create the situation where the pot odds are compelling, and players, even with weaker hands, stay in longer, make more bets, and lose more money.

- Allow/encourage the natural tendency in a friendly poker game for the table to sympathize with and root for the player who is behind in any hand where he is up against a player who is ahead. This is effective not only for the psychological support and comfort it provides the player who is behind, but also because advice flows his way that will help him see possibilities he might have otherwise missed. "Watch out Chris, Tim's low cards look like they could be a straight and the slimy dog has certainly been betting them that way."

Most of these techniques will have the effect of decreasing the speed of money flowing into the game, which, in turn, lowers the magnitude of the biggest win or the biggest loss. The magnitude of the biggest potential nightly wins or losses is a key factor for you to control to keep the game friendly, regular, and in line with your expectations.

Of course, you could simply rely on the players themselves to use their own judgment. When they have lost too much for their comfort level, they can simply quit playing. Isn't that the simplest and most common practice? Perhaps. And, surely, no one should be forced to stay and play beyond his financial capabilities. But using the players' own financial limitations as the only control against overly high losses leads to some unfortunate consequences.

First, players may need to quit in the middle of an evening, leaving the table short-handed for the rest of the night. That, alone, is a very significant drawback that should be avoided if at all possible. Secondly, a player forced to quit by financial considerations is embarrassed twice—once by losing and a second time by not being financially able to keep going. Embarrassing your friends, colleagues and neighbors is not really the goal of establishing a friendly poker game. And finally, you have robbed that player of the possibilities of a comeback. Had the stakes been better controlled, his losses would have been lessened and he would have had the resources to play longer and perhaps see his fortunes change. Friendly poker is a game of highs and lows. If the peaks and valleys are too steep, you risk depriving everyone of the full journey.

So use the tools outlined above to mitigate the risk that one or more of your players are forced out of your game by their financial limitations. It is supposed to be an evening of fun and camaraderie, not an evening of worrying about finances.

> "The saddest words I ever spoke
> Were "Deal around me boys, I'm broke."
>
> —*unknown*

Poverty Poker and Loss Limits

The most powerful variable you can control to keep the stakes at the appropriate levels for your group of players is the application of "loss limits" or "poverty poker." These are rules or systems that directly prevent a player from losing more than a previously agreed upon amount *but that allow the player to continue to play for the entire the evening.* The downside of these systems is that they are essentially funded out of the winnings of those who finish the night ahead. But the upside is that these systems are incredibly effective in keeping your game friendly and fun. And since the goals of your game are to provide an atmosphere for showing off, friendly and fair competition, and camaraderie, you do not want to ignore such an important factor in keeping it all friendly and fun.

Allow me to reiterate here for emphasis:

Loss Limit rules are the most powerful tool you have to ensure that your poker game will succeed as a regular, friendly poker game, and that your players will remain friends after the game is over.

Now, obviously, if you are only looking for angles to play, for ways you can come out ahead in all of your interactions with your neighbors and associates, then you may not become a fan of loss limit Poker. But if you are looking for Poker to be an amazing game you can play and enjoy with your *friends* or with other people who you would like to treat with respect and care, then the Loss Limit rules are the key ingredient that allows you to do so.

The Loss Limit rules are what allows you to play the cutthroat, ruthless game of Poker as it should and must be played, while simultaneously protecting your friends (and yourself) from any financially significant harm. The limits also protect the big winner from being perceived as having a purely financial motivation for playing. The big winner ends up cheerfully accepting fewer real dollars than he has technically won during the game. If his goal was purely financial, he would find a game that was not loss-limited. His goal must, therefore be beyond financial—it must be the same thrill of the competition, and the same camaraderie and fun that everyone else is seeking.

The loss limits simply establish boundaries within which the ruthlessness can be practiced in a socially permissible and non-lethally harmful way. The limits do not make losing a big hand painless. They do, however, limit the pain to the pre-established pain thresholds of the participants.

You may be thinking that you have played in many great poker games and that you are not at all familiar with any Loss Limit systems. You may think it is a totally strange concept altogether. But consider the variety of Loss Limit systems listed below. At least the first few should be familiar to you:

1. Playing for peanuts. Or matchsticks. Or other non-monetary quasi-assets. This is the most commonly tried approach to limiting the financial risk and motivation. Unfortunately, while most of us have tried this approach at some time in our lives, we quickly discover that the total lack of real risk renders the game boring and, essentially, unplayable.*

---

* It is possible to be intensely competitive over points in a game of Hearts or Bridge, or to be competitive in a game of Risk or Monopoly. So why is it impossible to play Poker with the same intensity if the game is only being played for "peanuts" or "matchsticks" or "points"? I believe that the answer lies in the thousands of decisions made during the course of an evening of poker. For poker to work, each of these thousands of decisions must have a tangible, real-world risk/reward associated with it. A player knows that the chips he uses to ante, call, bet, or raise have direct real world value. In Risk, the individual armies are each important to winning the game, but they have no true value in the real world. In Monopoly, a house or hotel or title deed has importance in the game, but no value outside the game. But in poker, for every chip a player chooses to bet, he has spent real money in the real world. And when he folds instead of calling a big bet, he has saved those chips and thus saved real money.

2. Playing for Pennies. The next most common approach
   to loss limits is to play for very small stakes, such that

---

Furthermore, the playing pieces in other games are typically used to build or progress on intermediate goals related to the player's overall strategy for emerging as the winner. A Risk army is used to build up a force that can help the player retain control of a country, which eventually helps him retain control of continents, which leads to control of the world. In Monopoly, the houses or the properties help a player create more income opportunities, which eventually help him gain more income for yet more houses and properties, which help him bankrupt another player, which yields more property and then more revenue until he has all the money. But in Poker, each hand is essentially independent of the other hands. A player might set traps or learn lessons during one hand that he can use later on another hand, but each hand is essentially an independent event with a winner or loser that is not necessarily the biggest winner or loser over the course of the evening. If there were no real-world value to the chips captured in a single pot out of the 60–150 pots in an evening, there would be insufficient incentive for a player to care too much about any individual hand. Unlike Risk or Monopoly, successful early plays will rarely have great importance to later hands.

Finally, poker is a game where a player's victory is weighed against break-even. Unlike Risk, or Hearts, or Monopoly, there can be multiple winners in a poker game. A lot of the game's intrigue and interest comes from the fact that even if you are not going to finish as the top winner or even the second highest winner, you have a monetary incentive and a pride incentive to come out "ahead." That conveys an importance to every hand during the night. But it is an importance that relates solely to whether the hand helped the player gain against break-even or not. If the chips have no real-world value, if you are playing for matchsticks, there is much less pride from coming in third or fourth. Break-even would just be an arbitrary score somewhere between the big winner and the big loser. But with the chips being tied to real money, break-even is the difference between wasting or losing money and earning or winning money. That is a bigger emotional payoff.

no one can be truly financially impacted by their total winnings or losses. Unfortunately, as many of us have discovered, this ends up feeling exactly like playing for matchsticks or peanuts. It also renders the game boring and unplayable.

3. Playing for money, but allowing those who have lost all of their chips to reach out to a friendly winner and take some of his chips so they can keep playing. You will see this style of loss limits applied often in family games. Good old Uncle Bob never minded you taking some of his chips if yours ran out. Although this approach works better than playing for matchsticks, it is really sort of like riding a bike with training wheels instead of a Harley. After the first or second "borrowing" of chips, the players realize that the game has lost any semblance of real poker with real scorekeeping and real risk/reward decisions. So the skilled players stop competing, and the game goes on for a while as teaching exercise for the kids before all the grown-ups find something more entertaining to do.

4. Playing for real stakes, but allowing a player who has lost all of his initial buy-in to get a second rack of chips for free. If he loses those, he is out. If he can pay the free chips back at the end of the night, he can also begin to win back real money. Now we are getting somewhere. The players know they can only lose their initial buy-in amount. And they have a safety net that keeps them in the game if they run into bad fortune right out of the gate. And they have incentive to play smartly with their free chips because they are out of the game if they lose them. The drawbacks to this approach are that you can still have one or more

players forced out of the game early in the evening, leaving the rest of you short-handed. Also, as in any loss limiting system, the winners are providing the funding for the free chips through deflation of their winnings at the end of the night. Some systems deflate all chips equally, others deflate only the net winnings, redeeming all initial buy-ins at full-value and then allocating the remaining deflated chips among the net winners.

5. Playing for real stakes, but allowing players who have lost their initial buy-in to get as many subsequent chip buy-ins as they need, all at no additional cost. The idea (and the main advantage of this approach) is to prevent anyone from ever being forced out of the game early. The disadvantage is that players who get more than a couple of buy-ins behind begin to realize that they have no hope of paying off the free chips and regaining any of their initial buy-in money back. So, especially as the game approaches the quitting time, the players playing on "free chips" have very little incentive to ever fold. A second disadvantage of this approach is that the deflation of the winners' net winnings can be more severe. This approach actually works pretty well, however, particularly if the initial buy-in is set high enough. (You want few, if any, players to lose the initial buy-in so quickly that they need three or more "free" buy-ins to complete the evening).

6. The same as #5 above but with a couple of tweaks to prevent bad play from those too far into the free chips to have a reasonable hope of recovering. The main tweak is that if any player playing on "free chips" wants to call or make a large, max-limit bet, he has to actually pay for the chips needed to do it. As long as

his bets, raises, or calls remain within the standard-limits, he can use the free chips. This mitigates wild, loose, desperate play at the end of the night by those playing on free chips. But it is complicated to administer, as it requires tracking of which chips were free and need to be paid back before collecting any money, and which chips were legitimately paid for.

7. The West Chester Progressive System for Player Protection. This system is detailed in a later section of this book. Essentially, it requires a fairly high standard buy-in at the start of the game and gives players who lose this entire buy-in additional buy-ins for only 25 percent of the face value of the chips. Every chip, even the second, third or fourth buy-in from a losing player will have some real value in this system, so there is sufficient incentive for smart play even as the clock winds down and break-even is no longer possible. Also, the winnings are deflated less because the initial buy-in is larger (and at face value) and because the subsequent buy-ins require at least some new cash to go into the bank. The one drawback to this approach is that on a really historically awful night, a player will lose more real money than in the systems described above.

Any of the last four systems described above will work well for most groups of players. I would recommend the West Chester system. But, mostly, I would very strongly recommend that you implement some system of loss limits in your friendly, regular poker game. Once again, **Loss Limit rules are the most powerful tool you have to ensure that your poker game will succeed as a regular, friendly one, and that your players will remain friends after the game is over.**

> "No wife can endure a gambling husband,
> unless he is a steady winner."
>
> —*Thomas Robert Dewar*

Table Talk

Distinct from idle chit-chat, which will be covered later, "table talk" is commentary by players regarding the cards in play. Examples would be:

- "Hey Barney's just got another Queen! Didn't he bet big after getting that first one? I bet he has trips!"

- "I'd raise, if I were you. Joe's only got a pair. I am sure of it.

- "Well he can't have three Jacks, because Bill has one showing and Dave had one showing when he folded!"

- "Bet whatever you like, fellas, I am gonna fold anyway."

Because of the creativity and imagination of human beings, there is an infinite variety of types of comments that can be made and topics upon which a player may opine. The intent of the player making the comments may be purely sociable, or it may be whining or sympathy-seeking, or it may be cleverly calculated to influence the other players.

In traditional, strict poker games, table talk is highly discouraged. In games with strangers, in casinos, for example, the players normally won't respond well to it, either. It is not considered "taking the game seriously."

I think this view honors tradition, and is appropriate for some games, but I think it is shortsighted for a regular friendly poker game. The game of poker is all about deception, misdirection, influencing others' actions, and seeing through others' attempts to deceive, misdirect and influence you. Oh, and showing off—never forget showing off. Taking away table talk greatly reduces the scope of the contest.

If the players play in silence, they have only their actions with which to exercise their wits and cunning. If players are allowed to say whatever they want in pursuit of their objectives, the game becomes much more complex, more interesting, and more challenging. You wouldn't tell an artist that he must restrict himself to working with blue watercolors. Why force poker players to only work in actions? Give them the full palette of actions, words, pauses, facial expressions, lies, truths, humor, and anything else they can imagine. It just seems arbitrary to restrict verbal communication, and it makes the game a lot less fun.

I suspect that the tradition to frown upon "table talk" comes from the same thinking that frowns upon the check-and-raise (betting zero with the high hand in hopes that someone else will be emboldened to bet into you, and then raising them when they do). But, just as the check-and-raise must be permitted and is a logical and valid technique to maximize the value of a hand, deceptive table talk should be allowed as well. Poker is a game of intentional deception. It is counter-productive to allow some types of deception, and to arbitrarily prohibit others.

Yet, that is the goal of those who would prohibit the check-and-raise. Their argument is something like this: Because check-and-raise appears to be ruthless, it is not nice and must be forbidden in a "nice" poker game. Similarly, since verbal lying is telling a lie, it is not nice and must be forbidden. Of course, that slippery slope leads to outlawing bluffing of any kind. But bluffing is the basis for the game in the first place. The actual play of the poker game, *including verbal communications,* must allow for ruthlessness and cunning. That is the point. Let all of the other actions not relating to the play of the game itself be restricted to the conventions of niceness and mutual respect and good sportsmanship.

Having said all this, however, there are certain types of "table talk" that should be forbidden. Players should not be permitted to disclose actual information that is not supposed to be known by the other players and that might hurt another player's chances. The most obvious example of this would be a player showing his folded hole cards or telling people what they were while the hand is still in progress.

> **From "Rounders":**
>
> **Worm:** [*Interrupting the other two players' conversation in Russian*] Hey! If you want to see this seventh card you're gonna stop speakin' fuckin' Sputnick. I'm sure you guys were talking about pierogis and snow but let's cut that out.

Is there a line that can be crossed if table talk is allowed?

In our game, almost any forms of deception that do not involve actual cheating are permitted. There can be some pretty subtle non-verbal kinds of table-talk deception. A guy who is waiting for his turn to bet, for example, might visibly count out the maximum bet in chips to pretend that he will raise or bet the maximum when his turn comes. Or, in an attempt to represent weakness, he may start to gather or pick up his up cards as if he is getting ready to fold, only to raise when his turn comes around.

Another player might use a bit of almost 'sleight of hand' to convince an opponent that he has a chip in his fist when it comes time to declare high or low. His hope is to scare the other player into going the other way. Then he opens his fist at the actual declare, and he has no chip after all. I've actually seen a player show his opponent the chip in his hand, then close his fist. When the opponent has his fist ready and it is time to open the hands and see, the chip is no longer there. The clever player has dropped it silently in his lap while the opponent was not looking. Technically this is not cheating, because at the time of the declare, the player only declares one way and does so without knowing what the opponents are doing. But the artifice of showing the chip ahead of time and then hiding it while everyone else gets ready for the declare is pretty sneaky.

I have also seen a player 'accidently' drop the chip he takes under the table and wince when it noisily hits the floor, revealing to everyone else that the chip is not in his closed fist. But when the fists were opened, lo and behold, he had a chip inside and was going high. He had taken two chips under the table so he could drop one for misdirection.

I've seen a player look his opponent in the eye and tell him, "You know I don't have three fours because you can see Joe has a four and, if you remember, Rick folded the four of hearts earlier." But at the showdown, there were the three fours, including the four of hearts in the players winning hand.

So, is there a line you can cross? Well. Bluffing is misrepresenting. Checking a strong hand is misrepresenting. Misrepresenting is dishonest lying. Dishonest lying is therefore permitted (and encouraged) in the play of a poker hand. So, I say there is no line. If it isn't cheating, it is permitted.

There is a very old Henry Fonda movie called *A Big Hand for the Little Lady* that makes this point very clearly. For those of you who will ever want to see it yourselves, I will tell you to skip the rest of this paragraph so as not to spoil the ending. A couple with a young child is passing through town just as the five richest poker players are sitting down for their big game. The husband (Fonda) is a reformed gambler, but he succumbs to temptation and joins the game. Pretty soon he has lost the entire family savings. In his last hand, he does not have the money to stay in and he dies of a heart attack while arguing about it with his wife. Faced with a dead husband and no savings, the wife is advised by a kind stranger to continue the hand to the end because it is such a good hand and it is her only hope of recovering her money. She knows nothing about poker, so she has other folks help her too. They all think her hand is a winner. To continue the hand, she has to go borrow money from the town banker who never loans money without collateral. In front of the other players, the banker looks at her cards and immediately loans her $5,000 no questions asked. She raises the other players the $5,000. They are sure from the banker and the other townsfolks' reactions that she must have killer cards. So they fold. But she's got nothing. It was all a bluff. A fake heart attack, a banker who was in on the scam, all that tearful acting by the little lady, everyone being willing to help when they saw her cards . . . all of it. Actually, it was a pretty unexpected ending if you haven't read this spoiler. But the movie makes the point as well as it can be made. As long as no one is actually cheating, any other method, verbal or otherwise, should be fair game to trick the other players. Why not? That's the heart of the game, isn't it?

Idle Chit-Chat

Unlike "table talk" which is an integral and desirable part of every fun, friendly poker game, "idle chit-chat" should be strongly discouraged. The more players you have at the table, the bigger a problem you will have with this issue. Idle chit-chat is casual conversation involving two or more players that has nothing to do with the hand being dealt and that distracts the chatty players and others from concentrating on the game.

Allowing too much chit-chat will absolutely kill the pacing of the game and severely annoy those players who are eager to have everyone quit yakking and get their heads into the current hand. Then, when you have finally regained the attention of the Chatty Cathy's, they will cause more frustration , irritation, and delay by needing to have the dealer repeat everything he has already announced about the game he is dealing and what the rules are. If the chatting continues into the hand, itself, there will be delays in the gabby ones' betting or calling bets. Followed once again by someone having to bring them up to speed on the previous players' actions that happened while the social butterflies were tittering over their conversation.

And idle chit-chat is terribly contagious. Once it gets started, it spreads easily, infecting one player after another and flaring up multiple times per night in those that suffer from the affliction.

The reason that idle chatting and its related delays are so annoying in a poker game is that, at any given time, many players at the table are hard at work trying to maintain their patience, equanimity, good humor, and calm. There are players who have just suffered a loss on the last hand, or who are still seething about a bad loss a couple of hands earlier. There are players who are behind on the night, and trying to play disciplined poker to maximize their chances of recovery. These guys may have folded early the past couple of hands and are now waiting impatiently for their next winning opportunity. Poker is game with emotional highs and lows, and maintaining a smooth and even demeanor can be a significant challenge.

A player who is battling his own frustrations or impatience is said to be "on tilt." A player struggling to avoid being "on tilt" really does not want to see the carefree winners of the last hand or those that are ahead for the night happily engaged in gossip from the neighborhood or in prolonged shop talk. And no one wants to see the night's losers engaged in sidebar conversations when they damn well ought to be paying more attention to the game so they can get a little better at it.

Wait a minute, you might be thinking, what happened to

friendliness, social interaction, and camaraderie? We haven't forgotten about those objectives. But it is important to recognize that the socialization and camaraderie and bonding come from the fact that poker is a group activity. It is done in a group, with all the players involved at the same time. The problem with sidebar chit-chat is that it divides the group. Some will be involved in the conversation, the rest will be waiting for those few to come back to the group activity.

It is fine if the entire group is having a single conversation about the last hand, or listening to a joke, or having some other verbal interaction in which all players are involved. That is not an irritant because everyone is included. But even with these whole group conversations, you need to be careful that the focus does not drift away from the game for very long. People came to play, and the next hand, with all of its own intrigue and discussion-worthiness, awaits.

So if a couple of players repeatedly launch into extended conversations with each other, you should feel free to encourage the rest of the group to rein them back in with gentle hints, direct requests, and verbal abuse as needed. And, if the entire table is distracted by a conversation that involves everyone, look carefully for the first sign of impatience from any of the players and act quickly at that point to get back to the game.

There is one approach that might help you control the chit-chat but still allow some outlet for your chatty types to satisfy their need for gab. Take a "halftime" break midway through the game. Maybe order a pizza and take a 20-minute break when it arrives. Just be careful that the 20 minutes does not morph into 45 minutes or an hour. The relatively few total minutes in your life that you get to spend playing poker with your crew are priceless. Idle chat sessions are a dime a dozen.

From the author's life:

My Wife: So, how was Brian? Is he doing all right?

Me: Yeah, I guess so. He ended up ahead by $20 or so.

My Wife: I mean, how is he doing in general? I haven't seen him since St. Patrick's Day.

Me: I don't know. He didn't say. I think maybe he mentioned one of his kids getting married. Or arrested. I don't remember.

My Wife: You don't remember? How can you not remember something like that? Didn't you just spend six hours sitting at a table with him?

Me: We were playing poker.

My Wife: Well, did you congratulate Lou on his new job?

Me: It didn't come up.

[Pause]

My Wife: I hear you guys down there laughing and shouting for hours and hours and you can't remember anything meaningful you talked about? You don't ask each other basic questions? What do you spend all that time shouting and laughing about?

Me: It's a poker game, honey. That's what it is.

Pacing

The atmosphere of your game will be dramatically affected by how smoothly and quickly it is paced. The natural tendency is for people to take their time, and for play to move at a leisurely rate. The player who is "under the gun" (the one whose turn to act is next) may not feel that he is delaying the game by taking his time. But the other players at the table will perceive anything but immediate action to be too slow.

There are time delays for decision-making or preparations multiple times per hand. It will take time for:

- The cards to be shuffled and cut
- The dealer to decide what game he will deal
- The dealer to announce the game and outline any specific rules
- The dealer to ante or forget to ante and to be reminded and then ante
- The dealer to distribute the cards (each card)
- The players to figure out who has the first bet (each interval)
- Each better to decide an amount, gather their chips and execute their bets or raises (each action)
- The showdown to occur
- The pot to be collected (or split and collected)
- The post mortem discussion
- Any buying of chips from the bank

In order to keep the pace from dragging and keep the players focused and intrigued, you will need to make efforts to speed up the game at some or all of these potential delay spots. You don't want to be a nag or to rush the play to the irritation of the other players. But you will need to use techniques to keep the game moving. I have never seen a home game move too quickly for the players' enjoyment. Occasionally, the casino-dealt poker games can move a bit fast for the comfort of some. But home games have an almost universal tendency to slow down to a pace that is perceived by the players as too ponderous. While no individual wants his decisions to be rushed, most, if not all, players want the game to move along briskly.

There are several helpful techniques that can be applied to keep the game moving at an enjoyable pace that is neither too fast nor too slow:

- Be sure there are two decks of cards being used and be sure that the one not being dealt is being shuffled and prepared so it is ready for the next game.

- Dispense with the ritual of the "cutting of the cards," or if that is too sacrilegious for your group, at least decline to cut the deck when it is your turn to do so.

- Use gentle verbal persuasion to help the dealer understand that by the time the deal comes to him, he should have already contemplated the options and chosen a game. No need to be obnoxious or rude, but the Al Czervik (Rodney Dangerfield) line from *Caddyshack* will do nicely: "Let's go. While we're young!"

- Have the dealer ante for the table. (see the house rules section)

- Keep the rules for each variety of games consistent where possible

- Have additional "buy-in" racks of chips pre-counted and ready

- Teach the players the most efficient way to split the pot for high-low or other two-winner games. And enforce the practice. There are few things more annoying than watching one or two players fail at multiple attempts to split the pot evenly and have to start counting again! Yet it happens quite often unless players are taught the proper procedure. The procedure goes like this:

▷ One player does the splitting.

▷ Using two hands, scoop up one same-colored chip at a time simultaneously in both hands until both hands are full.

▷ **Always start with the highest value chips and work down to the least value.**

▷ If there is an odd number of the color chip being scooped, just scoop the last of those color chips in one hand, while taking two of the next lowest value chips in the other.

▷ When you have your hands full of chips, place the handfuls in two separate piles in front of each of the winners, but not into their chip piles. That way, everyone can do a quick visual inspection to ensure the two piles look equal before they are comingled with the winners' other chips.

▷ With the remaining chips in the pot, fill both hands again, using the same method as above.

▷ If, at the end of splitting the pot, there is a single (lowest value) chip left over, it goes to the high hand by convention. (It has to go somewhere, so this is the rule.)

• Encourage the other players to pay attention to pacing and encourage quicker action. If a player's delay is caused by carelessness or inattentiveness, it is appropriate to chide him a bit. Salieri's line in *Amadeus* is a good one if anyone else has seen that movie. "Tempo . . . Tempo, Your Majesty . . . "

- Ensure a variety of games and try to get the quicker paced games interspersed with the longer, slower ones. Too many long, slow, tricky games in a row will get the players in the habit of slow action. Mix in a Five-Card Stud hand or even a whole round of Stud hands to pick up the speed a bit.

- Choose pace-compatible players. You need to be aware if one of your occasional players is a major culprit at slowing the game to the detriment of everyone else's enjoyment. Ideally, if you have a 'beginners' group, you can invite the slower player to play in that game. But, one way or another, you will need to exclude a chronically slower player from killing the pace of your regular group.

- Encourage folks to take their bathroom breaks, grab their snacks or get more beer during the completion of hands where they have folded. Try not to let the next game wait for player who gets up just before the deal and wanders away from the table. Just ask that player "should we deal you out for this hand?"

- Keep outside distractions to a minimum. Refuse to let cell phones and smart phones intrude on the game. Try to avoid playing where kids, spouses, pets, or neighbors will interrupt you every ten minutes.

Notice that one item that does not appear on the list above is to somehow try to hurry a player taking time to make a decision. A large bet or a difficult call or fold decision should be accorded the time it requires to get it right. **In general, you do not want to hurry an individual player who is thinking through his options during a hand.** On the other hand, if you have a player who routinely takes much longer than everyone else to make decisions, then you may owe it to him and to the rest of the group to exclude him from the invitation list for future games.

Players like to see as many hands per hour as possible. Each new hand is a chance for glory. And the best way to get over the fact that you did not win the previous hand is to focus your attention on the next hand to come. Conversely, players seeing too few hands per hour will, out of impatience or boredom, begin to play hands they should be folding and the quality of play for the whole evening will decrease.

Pay attention to how efficiently, smoothly, and comfortably quickly your poker game moves. Always be on the lookout for ways to increase the pace without being obnoxious. It is almost impossible for your home poker game to move too fast for the enjoyment of the players. So enlist your group's assistance in keeping everyone focused and keeping the action moving.

My Little Chickadee:

Cuthbert J. Twillie: During one of my treks through Afghanistan, we lost our corkscrew. Compelled to live on food and water—

Gambler: [*interrupting out of frustration*] Will you play cards!

Cuthbert J. Twillie:—for several days.

Variety and Mix of Games

Although I presume there can be regular, friendly poker games that play the same game all night long, I have never personally seen or played in one. One of the strengths of friendly poker vis-à-vis casino poker or Hold –'Em tournaments is that the variety of different games being dealt makes for a much more challenging and interesting evening. The variety of games keeps the players fresher for each new deal and challenges the players to learn more skills and techniques to cover the different games.

The convention of having each dealer name the game to be played, define any special rules, and then deal the cards throughout the hand is important. It essentially places each player, in turn, in a leadership role. The fact that the leadership role rotates makes the friendly poker game a truly cooperative, group exercise. When the house deals every hand, there is an inevitable sense of playing against the house, instead of competing with the other players.

Dealer's choice poker also ensures that every player will like at least some of the games being dealt during the night. Every player has his favorite game. And, even though he may not have gone out and found six other players wishing to play that particular favorite, here they are. For at least his share of the deals, that is the game that they all will play.

To emphasize the advantages of Dealer's Choice, you can take some important steps to encourage the variety and optimize the mix of the games being dealt. If, for example, there is a new game that you believe your players will greatly enjoy, make sure you use your deal to choose that game a few times in a row. Eventually, if you are correct in your assessment, others will choose to deal that game on their deal, and you can move onto something else.

If there has been a preponderance of complex games, use your deal to play a simpler game as a change of pace. If possible, use the "two times" rule to deal it twice. Or if the last several deals have been split pot games, make sure you deal a single-winner game. Players can fall into the habit of playing the same two or three games without thinking too much about their choices. Use your deal to ensure that a change-of-pace happens at least some of the time.

In addition to pure variety, you want to use your deals (and encourage other players to use their deals) to choose games that fit the objective of rewarding skill over luck. It is fine to play a few games that are heavy on the luck factor. But do what you can to ensure that those games don't become predominant. It is the skill play that you want to encourage over the course of the evening.

Through your choice of games to deal and through persuasion and encouragement, when it is someone else's turn to deal, try to ensure that the mix of games is balanced in terms of:

- Duration—even split of time spent playing the long games vs. short ones

- Complexity—even split of time playing the difficult rules vs. simple games

- Single Winner vs. Split pot—both should get a fair share of the total playing time

- More time on 'skill' games vs. those decided with a higher 'luck factor'

- Not too high a proportion of "big pot" games. Maybe 25 percent or less

Teaching Games to New Players

As noted above, one common characteristic of a friendly Poker game is the wide variety of games that players will bring to the table. In spite of having fairly regular attendees at your games, there is a good likelihood that, on any given night, there will be at least one new game being taught to the group or one or more 'old' games being taught to new players. It is also likely that players may need a refresher course on games that they have played before, but forgotten in the time since they played it last.

It is important that the explanation or teaching of these games is done well and efficiently. Contrary to what some people believe, not everyone who is an expert in a subject is able to teach effectively. Pay attention to your players as they all pitch in to try to explain a game to a new player. Some will make factual errors. Others will be factually correct, but explain things in a very confusing manner. Still others will get some of it across well but leave out some key element.

Identify the best teacher in the group and ask him to explain the game to the newcomers. This will save a lot of time and confusion and will make the newcomer feel well treated (considering part of good teaching is respect for the learner and sensitivity to what he is understanding and what he is missing). This seems like a pretty obvious point, but it has more importance than you might think. A new player is in a bit of an awkward spot, requiring explanations to begin with. If three or four players jump in with a jumble of partial explanations, the new player is going to simply pretend to understand the game rather than ask questions of the multiple explainers.

Then, the new player is at a severe disadvantage trying to play the game which makes him feel uncomfortable and isolated. This situation also creates a high potential for a misplayed and then disputed hand. The end result is that your new player may end up feeling unwelcome, or somehow taken advantage of. His recollection of the evening later might be "they played a lot of confusing and weird games for which even they did not even seem to understand the rules. It did not seem much like Poker to me." It would be far better for his recollection to be: "they played some pretty cool varieties of Poker which made the game more interesting. I can't wait to get another shot at those games now that I have played them a few times myself." If you take care to ensure clear and accurate teaching of the games, you are much more likely to get the second, more favorable impression from your new player.

It really helps, when teaching anything, to present the information in a logical order that allows the learner to relate each new piece of information to the ones presented earlier. Here is a recommended sequence of information to provide when teaching a new game:

- What will win (i.e. high poker hand, split pot high-low, closest to 7 or 27, high hand splits with low spade, etc.)

- The format, if it is a common one (i.e. "It is a Seven-Card Stud game," or "It is like Hold-'Em, except...")

- Any odd dealing peculiarities such as choice cards, twist cards at the end, community cards, etc.

- Any wild cards

- Any qualifiers (minimum hands needed to win)

- Values of the hands that will win in an average deal (i.e. "This game is rarely won with less than a boat, but occasionally a flush or a boat bluff will sneak in there")

- Any other oddities that the experienced players know to expect (i.e. "Because everyone's low hole card is wild, and some players will pair it up, almost every winning hand will contain at least two wild cards)

Notice that the last two points are particularly helpful to reassure the player that you are not deliberately trying to take advantage of his inexperience. This is important to keeping the game friendly and fair and to keeping the new player feeling respected and included.

One last point on teaching: make sure to solicit questions from the new player during and after the hand. You want him to learn quickly, and asking questions with real examples in front of him is the best way to accomplish that goal.

> "The poker player learns that sometimes both science and common sense are wrong; that the bumblebee can fly; that, perhaps, one should never trust an expert; that there are more things in heaven and earth than are dreamt of by those with an academic bent."
>
> —*David Mamet*

CHAPTER 3

Key Environmental Factors That Impact Player Enjoyment

THERE ARE A number of very important environmental elements to a great poker game. These factors enable the participants to truly enjoy themselves, provide everyone with opportunity to win, and bring out the incredible intrigue, fun, and suspense of the actual card game itself. When a guy gets up after playing several hours of poker, he can feel exhilarated, satisfied, eager to come back, vindicated, and fulfilled. Or he can feel like it was a painful, boring, tedious, annoying evening that he would never wish to repeat.

Most people assume that the degree to which a player comes out monetarily ahead or behind will completely determine whether he feels great about the evening or lousy. This is just wrong. A player's fiscal result partly determines whether they felt the night was *productive*, but not whether they had any fun.

There is a scene in the Woody Allen movie "Love and Death" where Boris wants to make love with his wife, Sonja. Sonja tells Boris, "Sex without love is an empty experience." Boris replies: "yeah, but . . . as empty experiences go . . . it is one of the best."

Well, winning money without being challenged, having fun, showing off, or feeling like you swindled it fair and square can be an empty experience too. Of course if you are talking about significant amounts of money, it can be a good empty experience. But it is empty nonetheless.

I have had a few nights where the cards I got were so ridiculously good that I was by far the big winner without being truly challenged or having to be smart or creative. I was bored. And I have had nights where I came out significantly ahead, but the pacing of the game was ssslllllooooooowwww or the lighting gave me a headache, or someone was smoking in my face, or there were too many commercials blaring from the radio, or the dog was running in and out and barking, and so on. I never wanted to go back. And I have had losing nights where the music, food, company, pacing, competition, and environment were so much fun that I had a great time despite losing money.

If you are going to host or play in a regular poker game, you can significantly improve the game by paying attention to some easily controllable and very important environmental factors. The more regular the game, the more important it is to optimize these factors. A "regular game" is defined here as a consistent group of players playing with a set of understood house rules and having a game multiple times per year. If you have just been named the best man for a wedding and you are trying to set up a poker game at the bachelor party with folks who will never play together again, you won't need any of the tips provided on the following pages. Just get lots of booze, a stripper or two, and everything will go fine. The suggestions in this book apply to those who really want to play poker, not those who deal a few pretend hands of poker at a drinking party.

The key word is "regular." If you know you will be doing this again and again with the same people, then getting the details right will have a significantly positive impact on everyone's enjoyment over a long period of time. And you know that you will have committed poker players, not folks looking for a party. Plus, you will be on your way to winning that award for Best Poker Game Host.

Here is a list of the some of the factors that will have a huge impact on the success of your regular game:

Equipment:
- Poker Chips
- Playing Cards
- Other Equipment
- Table
- Chairs

The Room:
- Lighting
- Music
- Ambient noise
- Distractions from outsiders
- Temperature in the room and air quality

Food, Drinks and Amenities:
- Amount of alcohol expected/encouraged
- Spill Prevention and Cleanup

- Amount of smoking expected/encouraged
- Food—types and amounts
- Ice, napkins, drink glasses, other such supplies

Leadership, Money and Banking

Player Responsibilities

Scheduling and Invitations
- Frequency of the game
- Weeknights or weekends
- Start and end times
- Optimum numbers of players to invite
- Type and tracking of invitations
- Style of the invitations

It really is important to get each of these many factors optimized to the degree possible. Any poor performance on any of these items can have a significant effect on the players' enjoyment and satisfaction over a 5+ hour game and over many games per year. So take advantage of the information below. Take the time to do it right. You and your poker buddies will be glad that you did.

Equipment

The quality and style of the cards, chips, markers and any other equipment you use in your game does matter. If you have ever played backgammon, you may remember more about the nice set you used than you remember about the game itself. Maybe there were ivory stones or dice, or maybe the board was marble, or the dice cups were high quality leather. But the way the equipment felt in your hands or looked to your eyes had a direct bearing on your enjoyment of the game. Same thing with chess sets, golf clubs, hand tools, kitchen gadgets, bed linens, etc. People like nice "stuff". Quality matters and 'look and feel' is important. So make sure you have the good poker "stuff". It will make people want to come play.

> "Besides lovemaking and singing in the shower, there aren't many human activities where there is a greater difference between a person's self-delusional ability and actual ability than in poker."
>
> —*Steve Badget*

Poker Chips

Never, ever, use cash if you can possibly use chips. Cash is ugly, smelly, doesn't stack well, makes your fingers taste funny, and makes the game look crass and low class. Get some poker chips. And get some nice ones, not the plastic ones from the drug store. Remember that the poker chips—the piles of chips in the middle of the table, the stacks of chips in front of the winners, the few chips in your opponents hand as he considers calling your bet on your unbeatable hand—are the objects of attention in the game. The objects of desire.

Poker chips in your game are what Alfred Hitchcock used to call the "MacGuffin" in the movies: the object around which the action revolved or in pursuit of which the characters exerted their efforts. (Think of the falcon statue in *The Maltese Falcon*, the "*Casablanca*" letters of transit, the ark from *Raiders of the Lost Ark*, the Ring in *Lord of the Rings*, the shark in *Jaws*, the hooker's reward money in *Unforgiven*, the briefcase full of money in *No Country for Old Men*, Private Ryan in *Saving Private Ryan*, the big contract in *Jerry Maguire*—I think you should understand what I mean by now.)

You want the actual chips to be worthy of all that attention and desire. You want to play with the best chips you can get.

So which chips are the best? Well to some degree (maybe to a great degree), it is a matter of personal taste. In general, you are looking for some important characteristics.

Weight: Heavier poker chips feel more substantial in your hand as you toss in that last raise. A minimum of eight grams per chip is needed to have the proper heft. Nine to 11 grams per chip is even better. (Keep in mind, though, that when you have 500 of them in a set, they get pretty heavy to carry around.)

Material: Old fashioned, interlocking plastic chips are *not* what you want. Although the interlocking edges make stacking easy and tight, the grooved edges are a dead giveaway that you bought cheap chips. These chips do not have sufficient weight to get that serious feel when calling the big bluff. Even a stack of them will not make a satisfying *thunk* when you place it in the middle of the table at a crucial and dramatic moment.

But the worst thing about the cheap plastic chips is their sound. They make a high pitched chirp or screech when bouncing off each other or falling onto any hard surface. It is a harsh and cheap sound. And sound is important. You use your five senses to gauge the quality and desirability of objects. You want to use poker chips that look good, sound good, and feel good—and don't smell or taste funny. Inexpensive plastic chips sound awful. And feel cheap. The sound you want is a substantial and solid *click* when two chips are struck together. Many players will absent-mindedly shuffle, stack and restack, or play with their chips as the game goes on. The sound of chips colliding is a big part of the atmosphere of any poker game. Make sure you get chips that make a pleasing sound. I was once playing with a group that used the cheaper plastic chips, and the unpleasant noise drove us to institute a ban on unnecessary fiddling with the chips.

But don't immediately rule out all plastic. Many decent and reasonably priced chip sets today are made out of high grade plastic that is weighted with a built-in lead or other heavy insert. The better plastic is soft on the hands, pleasingly smooth to the touch, and can be colored with shades and patterns that are not available in pure clay chips. A high-quality, weighted insert, plastic chip in a decent color scheme can be very nice indeed. Many players, even in higher class settings, will prefer them over clay.

Clay chips are also popular, but you should know that clay chips are often composites of various materials which may or may not include clay. Pure clay chips get their weight from the heavy clay itself. Composite chips, made from a variety of materials, can be weighted by an insert to offset the lighter weight materials. The other materials are mixed with the clay (or even used instead of clay) to add strength, durability, or texture, or to reduce cost.

Some clay chips have a significant metallic content. This can have the unpleasant side effect of imparting a metallic taste to the players' hands, which is never fun. In general, however, good quality clay or clay composite chips from reputable suppliers are easy to find and will perfect to use in your game.

You can find poker chips in many other materials including ivory, metal, wood, bone, Bakelite, rubber, enameled metals, paper, or cardboard. Some of these, of course, are no longer mass-produced. Unless you are wealthy enough to spend several thousand dollars on a set of antique ivory chips and then proceed to use them casually in a regular game (which would be a misuse of an antique treasure, wearing down the engravings and rubbing off the color dyes), you will be most satisfied with clay or high quality weighted plastic.

Texture: Most clay chips will have a fine grid on their surface texture, but the edges will be smooth. The quality plastic weighted chips can be smooth or textured. The texture of the surface of the chip is a matter of personal preference. The casino chips that I have seen in many casinos and card rooms have all had some degree of textured surface. In my experience, however, people prefer the feel of smooth chips. This may only be because the smoothies are different than casino chips and are, therefore, less familiar. Again, it is really a matter of individual preference. The smoothies can be more difficult to find.

Another important component to how the chips feel is whether they have a "square edge" or a "round edge." Casino chips are almost universally square-edged, meaning that the chip can be made to stand on edge and that there are sharp "corners" between the two main surfaces of the chip and the edge of the chip. A round edge or rounded edge chip has a smooth curved edge with no discernable corners. Some people prefer the square-edge chips, due to the smooth surface created by the side of a stack of chips. Others simply like the precise look of the corners. But consider the advantages of the rounded edge before you purchase your set. A rounder edge is smooth to the touch, feels more natural, and maybe most importantly, makes the chips easier to push together into piles. The square edge chips will simply collide edge-to-edge and push each other around when you try to scoop together a big pot and drag it into your pile. The rounder edged chips will slip on top of or beneath each other allowing a deeper pile to be more easily created and hauled in. My preference is for the rounded edges, but others love the square. It's up to you.

Age: Nothing adds the feel of authenticity or quality to your regular poker game like a nice set of antique or vintage poker chips. These can be a bit tricky to find, but I urge the serious poker hosts to make the effort. eBay or other antique vendors will yield fine sets of chips if you look for them. In eBay, just search for "(antique, vintage) poker chips" and you will see several sets listed. I was lucky enough to have my grandfather give me a beautiful set of 600 heavy clay smoothies in perfect condition that were produced in the 1920s. But I have also put together a several antique sets of embossed or inlaid chips for my own use and for presenting as gifts. There is an extra thrill involved in playing with the same poker chips that may have been used at the turn of the century on a Mississippi riverboat or in a speakeasy during prohibition. I have poker chips made and used before the Civil War, and I have full sets of chips from the late 1800s.

If you are not an eBay or antique market fan, you can still make an effort to find the old poker chips stashed away in the attic of a family member. Just ask around. Your uncle, or your grandfather, or your Great Aunt Myrtle might have played poker during the '30s or the '40s and have a classic set gathering dust somewhere.

If you are interested in the antique chips that were made and sold over the past 150 years, there is a great book that can be used as a reference source or a collector's guide. It is Dale Seymour's *Antique Gambling Chips*, and it is well worth finding and owning if you become a poker chip connoisseur. It contains photographs and descriptions of poker chips and a history of their manufacture. Pre-Civil War chips were often beautiful ivory and bone sets. By the turn of the century, clay smoothies were produced and sold via catalogues. To deter counterfeiters who would "ring in" to a game with identical plain clay chips, manufactures began in the early 1900s to produce fancier clay chips embossed, engraved, or inlaid with hundreds of different designs. The carousels, cases, and holders were often works of art all by themselves. During the War Years came the development of Bakelite plastic, followed by more modern plastics, which by the 1960s had become the standard material for most home games. But clay chips were still preferred in "better" poker games or clubs, and today are most players' idea of "top of the line."

The Container: Beautiful chips, well chosen and appropriate to your setting, will add to the players' enjoyment of the game. But the effect can be spoiled somewhat if you store them in an old shoebox. The case for the chips should match the prestige and class of the chips themselves. If you find nice antique chips, they may or may not come with an antique holder. Some of the nicer antique carousels or chip cases can draw oohs and aahs even when they are empty. If you buy some new clay or quality weighted plastic chips, a nice holder, antique or otherwise, will properly show off your good taste and will make your players feel like big shots when they purchase or sell back chips to the bank.

The trick with an older container is to find one that holds a sufficient number of chips. Many old cases or carousels only hold 200 chips, which is too few for a regular poker game. One approach is to just get two matching or different cases. It can be quite a show if you pull out a nice 75-year-old carousel with 200 chips and then pull out another 50-year-old mahogany box case holding 300 more. So, if you can, find a nice antique or vintage case or cases to hold and display your fine chips.

If you don't have the time or the inclination (and it takes both!) to find antiques, then just be choosy when buying your new chips. You can buy chips in sets with a little briefcase or with a wooden box or carousel. Or you can buy the chips in cardboard boxes and buy the holders separately. Shop around and get something you will be proud of and that you will want to hand down to your poker-playing sons (and discerning daughters!) There are plenty of beautiful and high-quality poker chip cases and poker chip sets out there.

You will appreciate the sturdy briefcase style holder for your chips if your chips and the game will rotate from house to house, or if you will be taking the chips back and forth a lot from the beach house, college, ski-lodge, or such. Chip sets are heavy, and the chips can beat the hell out of all but the sturdiest holders during transit. In general, you want to choose a case or cases that look good on display, but you might need to think about how much you travel as you decide.

Colors: The colors of poker chips are extremely important to the actual playing of the game and to the visual appeal of the room. Different chip colors will represent different values. Stacks, piles, and pots will contain chips of all values, so you want colors that will look good together. There are also "standards" for the assignment of colors to values. If you go with non-standard colors, you will regret it, as you will confuse players who play in other games and you will surely suffer their constant mistakes and/or griping. So you want your poker chips to conform to the color standards.

Although some games or houses vary, the most commonly accepted value/color standards are:

Value	Chip Color	Example
Lowest	White	.25
Next Lowest	Red	.50
Higher	Blue	1.00
Still Higher	Yellow	2.00
Even Higher	Green, Black, Purple, etc.	4.00, 8.00, 16.00

Fortunately for aesthetic considerations, white and the three primary colors (red, blue, yellow) look fine when piled together in any combinations; however, if you get pure clay chips and you get odd shades of the basic colors (like mustard yellow, or pinkish red, or olive green), then you may end up with a really ugly look when the chips are all piled together.

Also keep in mind that the piles or stacks of chips will be sitting on your table top, in your players' trays, or in their chip case. If you have a green felt table top, the chip colors have to look good on that background. Some table tops are red felt or red leather. The red chips can easily clash or disappear from view depending on the shades of red involved. Brown chips can look awful on a clashing brown table or chip case. Of course, brown can be a pretty ugly color all by itself and is probably a poor choice for a poker chip anyway.

Your best bet is white, red, blue, yellow, and green with the shades of those colors being non-garish and clear to go well with your table surface.

Designs: You can have multi-colored, almost checkerboard-looking chips, or you can have solid-colored chips. You can have embossed or engraved initials or pictures. You can have stamped on letters, numbers, or pictures. You can have colorful paper inserts into the chip. You can have numbers on the chips to try to keep their values straight. There is essentially no limit to the combinations and permutations. Here are some important design hints:

- *Multi-colored chips.* Most players like the checkerboard look, especially when looking at the edges of a neat stack of chips. Most casinos use multi-colored designs. My advice is to keep it simple. If you go multi-color, use white as the highlighting color for the red, blue, yellow, and green chips. Or, you can leave them a solid color. While the individual chips can be pleasing to look at, even with intricate designs and mixed colors, you don't want a chaos of colors when you pile up a bunch of chips in a sweet pot. Red chips with yellow highlights sharing a pot with blue chips with olive highlights and yellow chips with orange highlights would probably look just awful. Then again, your vision may be to emulate a Vegas environment instead of an old-fashioned refined and moneyed poker club from the turn of the last century. Suit yourself.

- *Numbers.* If you have numbers or values stamped onto the chips, you may make it easier for your players to remember the value of each color. You will not be able to use those chips, however, in different games where the stakes might be higher or lower. Chips marked with 5, 10, 25, and 100 might make sense for a game with nickel bets and quarter limits. But the chips will be distracting and confusing if you graduate to playing quarter minimums and two-dollar maximum bets. Skip the numbers so your chips don't become obsolete with inflation or limited to one group of players.

- *Initials and other designs.* Some players like the idea of a last name initial or a simple symbol on the chips. One of the nicest antique sets I have has an inlaid "C" on each chip. But be sure that the process used to add the initial to your new chips creates a high-quality image. In almost every new initialed set of chips I have seen, the proud owner's initial has been stamped onto the surface of the middle of the chip, usually in gold metallic ink or paint. The initial looks like an afterthought, with none of the care and quality of the rest of the chip. It looks like a decal that has been slapped onto a classy finished product. In the antique chips I mentioned, the initial was inlaid into the chip along with other chip highlights in the initial manufacturing process. The color of the initial perfectly matches the main color of the chip and is set into a white background in the center of the chip. The initial itself is made of the same material as the rest of the chip. The result is that the initial is an integral part of the chip itself, not an "add-on." Whether you are getting initials or designs or symbols on your chips, pay attention to the details of how that initial or design or symbol will be put there. Don't ruin a nice looking set of chips with a shoddy hot-stamped initial. It may end up looking like an automobile dealer decal stuck to the back of a new Ferrari.

> "The one who bets the most wins. Cards just break ties."
>
> —*Sam Fahra*

Quantities: The total quantity of chips you will need and the quantities of each color will vary according to several factors, including:

- Whether players can sell chips to each other or must go through the bank
- Values of the chips vis-à-vis the maximum betting limits

- Number of different colors in the set
- Desire to encourage or discourage looser play
- Maximum number of players expected at any given time

There is no scientific formula to combine all these factors into the "ideal" number of chips for a good poker game. But I have come to a couple of interesting conclusions through my experiences.

First, a player with fewer than 40 or 50 chips in front of him, regardless of their relative value, tends to play tighter than his normal style (that is to say he is more reluctant to call or make bets). Maybe it is human nature to hoard dwindling supplies even if the items remaining and being hoarded have high value. (By the way, this observation is useful as a "tell." A player showing no reluctance to throw in some of his last 10 chips is more likely to have a strong hand than the player casually tossing in a few chips while he has hundreds in front of him.)

Secondly, with fewer than 30 chips in front of each player, an inordinate amount of time will be taken "making change." That is, players will be trading high-value chips with neighbors for lower value chips to provide the right chips to call or make small bets. For some reason, not many players think to "make change" with the pot.

Lastly, if everyone has hundreds of chips in front of them, there is too much time wasted in chip counting exercises at the beginning and end of the game and at any subsequent buy-ins.

One clear requirement is the need for enough chips to allow all players their initial buy-in (and for a few players to make subsequent buy-ins throughout the night). The value of all the chips available has to be high enough to cover the amount all players will invest in the game through buy-ins.

The fourth and fifth chip colors are very helpful to ensuring that there are neither too many total chips on the table nor too few to go around. The fourth and fifth colors also give the bank a lot more control and flexibility to ensure that everyone's total assets—small to large—can be represented by a reasonable number of chips. Consider a $.25, $.50, $1 game. White chips are a quarter, reds are 50 cents, and blues are a buck. Pretty simple. But having yellow chips and green chips to represent $2 and $4 will significantly improve the bank's flexibility and reach. With yellow and green chips available, a $40 stack of chips can be represented by as few as 10 chips (all green) or as many as 160 (all white). So a player that gets far ahead for the night does not require three or four times the number of total chips that made up the initial buy-in. Instead, his winnings can be represented by reasonably few chips, of higher value colors. And the hundreds of lower-value chips he would have otherwise needed can be available for others to use for their subsequent buy-ins.

It is important to have the fourth and especially the fifth color represent a value in excess of the maximum standard bet in your game. You simply do not need to have too many denominations of chips between the minimum and the maximum bet. And you always want the values to increase by doubling. If you have ever tried to set chips equal to a nickel, a dime, and a quarter, you know what happens. You spend half the evening making change so people can call a two-dime raise or make a 15-cent bet. Doubling the value works best for simplicity and speed. If your minimum bet is a buck, then make white chips worth a buck, reds worth $2, and blues worth $4. Yellows should be $8 and greens $16. If your minimum bet is 25 cents, then whites should be a quarter, reds fifty, and blues a buck. Yellows $2 and greens $4.

If you only have four colors and you absolutely need to stretch their total value to cover all your players, you can make the highest value chip worth five or even 10 times the second-highest chip. But only do this with the highest-value chip and make the first three levels a doubling progression.

I have generally found that 300 chips are too few for a regular game of five or more players. Between 400 and 500 chips work significantly better. But before going out to buy a set of 400 chips, be careful of the distribution. Older poker chip sets have an unfortunate tendency to include too many of the lowest value (white) chips. When you bought 100 assorted poker chips at Sears, for example, they sent you 50 whites, 25 reds, and 25 blues. This is not an ideal distribution, which I will soon explain.

You can make 400 chips work well for your game if there are only 50 of the lowest value (white) chips and if you have at least 50 of a fourth color and 25 of a fifth color: 50 White, 125 Red, 125 Blue, 75 Yellow, and 25 Green, for example. I have played for over 30 years with my grandfather's set of 600 chips. It has 150 white, 150 Red, 150 Blue, and 150 Yellow. I never used even half of the white chips. I would have been fine with only 500 chips, doing without 75 of the white ones and 25 of the yellow ones.

You can make do with fewer than 400 chips, but the drawback is that you may have to force some winners to sell chips back to the bank so the bank can issue chips for another player to make a second or third buy-in. Of course, you could let a player sell excess chips to another player who needs chips, but this is not optimal for many reasons, as described below. It is better to have the bank handle all buying and selling of chips.

Some winners will want to keep all their chips until the end of the game and will not like being forced to sell back chips to the bank or to other players. They might consider it bad luck to pocket winnings early. Furthermore, many players hate to see winners cash in chips early, because it makes it less apparent where all the money is. They don't want to see any winnings "tucked away" or "rat-holed" off the table. And finally, early cash-in by winners can add significant complexity to settling accounts at the end of the night if any "poverty poker" system is being used. So your best move is to ensure that you have enough chips and enough colors of chips in your set to avoid these pitfalls.

Get a set of chips as follows:

Luxury—600 Chips	Preferred—500	Acceptable—400
75 white	75 White	50 White
150 Red	150 Red	125 Red
150 Blue	150 Blue	125 Blue
150 Yellow	100 Yellow	75 Yellow
75 Green	25 Green	25 Green

White Chips: The reasons that the lowest value (white) chips are not needed in great quantity are that 1) relatively few bets or raises are made of the minimum value, and 2) it is easy for someone to "make change" with the pot if they don't have the one white chip needed. Conversely, if there are too many white chips in the game, players will throw four of them into a pot instead of playing a precious blue chip. This just causes more time and trouble when splitting pots in high-low games and when trying to verify if a player really put in the correct bet. It also causes more difficulty in transactions with the bank.

Generally speaking, you need fewer than half the numbers of white chips in the game than you need red or blue. The game goes more quickly and smoothly when the distribution of white, red, and blue chips matches more closely the frequency of minimum, medium, and higher bets.

Playing Cards

Higher-quality cards will produce more satisfaction over the long term. They feel better in your hand, resist creases and marks, and are easier to shuffle. They also look better than the cheaper ones. You and your guests will spend the whole night looking at cards, holding cards, dealing cards, looking for cards, praying for cards, shuffling cards and, discarding cards. Make the experience as rich as possible.

You need two decks with contrasting back colors so that one can be in use while the other is being "prepared" (gathered, shuffled, cut, etc.) for the next hand. Although the backs should be clearly contrasting, (i.e. blue and red), the two decks should be a matched set with matching designs. Otherwise, it looks about as stylish as wearing mismatched socks.

Paper or Plastic: The debate rages. High-quality paper cards (always plastic-coated) are a joy when they are fresh from the box. And they will last a few evenings before they start to feel "used." High-quality plastic cards look and feel great for a much longer time. They can be wiped or even washed if something is spilled. And they will cost less over the long term while retaining their like-new look and feel. Some players feel that the plastic cards never quite match the look and feel of brand new paper cards. But most players agree that after 50 deals or so, the paper cards are beginning to fall behind their plastic competition on the look-and-feel scale.

Plastic cards can be a bit "slippery" when shuffling, especially when they are first opened. But nothing matches their silky smooth riffle shuffle. It makes every shuffler look like a pro.

Casinos and card rooms dealing poker (as opposed to Black Jack and other games) routinely use plastic cards. And if they do not have a fancy machine-shuffler, the dealer will often shuffle the deck like a five-year-old. He will keep them all face down on the table and swirl them around and around just like we did when we were too young to shuffle and bridge the deck.

I recommend the plastic. You will have to buy new paper cards every other game or so to even come close to the feel of good plastic cards. Paper also gives you a much higher risk of a dog-ear or a crimp or some other blemish that will first give the observant (or malicious) player an advantage and then cause you to throw out the deck and maybe be stuck playing the rest of the night with only one deck (slow) or with mismatched decks (tacky).

Size Matters: We always knew this. There are poker cards and there are bridge cards. Poker cards are wider (helping you see them better across a big poker table). You do not need to hold 13 of them in your hand at one time (which is why bridge cards are narrower). Get poker cards so you have the right tools for the job. Most players may not notice, but the real poker fans will.

There are Jumbo Index and Standard Index. You can't find any with no index any more. That went out of style around 1880. This is a matter of taste, I suppose, but for the two decks you use in any one evening of poker, make sure they have the same size index. Dealing Standard Index cards for one hand and then Jumbo Index cards for the next is like alternating bites of a burrito and a chocolate soufflé. Either is nice. But it won't do to keep switching back and forth.

I think the Jumbo Index are more dramatic as they fall face-up in front of the players. I also think that players' age and eyesight falters over the years and over the course of long night, making the bigger face and numbers helpful. Anyone needing an extra second to squint and read the cards on the table (or in extreme cases, in his own hand) will slow the pace of the game and become irritating, so I go with the Jumbo Index.

Back Designs: Yes, even this has an impact. Choose something you think is classy and something you will want to look at for hours and hours and game after game. And make sure that the two decks you will use in the evening have matching patterns and contrasting colors on their backs. They should be a set. Traditionally, there will be a blue deck and a red deck, but again, this is open to your own sense of style and preference.

If you intend to use paper cards, choose decks you can order in bulk. Buy at least two identical sets if you will use plastic cards. When a paper or even a plastic card is damaged or marked beyond use, you will need to throw out the entire deck. (Some plastic decks will send you a replacement card for a small fee). If you don't have an identical deck to swap in for the ruined deck, you will have to play with only one deck for the rest of the night (too slow) or you will also have to remove the contrasting but matching deck from play and find two new decks. You could, I suppose, swap in a different deck, but then your two decks will not match. Can't have that. In the long term, it is handy to swap in an identical deck for any ruined deck, while allowing the ruined deck's contrasting mate to be used until it reaches the end of its useful life. No one wants to trash two full decks of cards because a single card is damaged.

Any style of design will work, but the busier ones hide stray marks or imperfections better. Bicycle decks are classic, but I got sick of their overly ornate backs and the fat little winged cherubs on the bikes many years ago. I go with plastic decks that closely emulate the small, diagonal check design of Bee Playing Cards. Simple and timeless and geometric, not Gothic or Romantic or Rubenesque. Covers up dings. A man's deck of cards.

Humorous decks are good for a laugh, but maybe not up to the rigorous standards described above. Break them out for a deal or two and then switch back to the "regular" cards. My favorite deck of cards (and one of my favorite all-time Christmas presents) was given to me by my brother, after a big family poker game in which he fared poorly. They were a set of two decks in classic dark red and midnight blue, with refined and understated gold borders. Each card also bore a one sentence inscription written in gold lettering in a formal font: *"Make all checks payable to Mark A. Cochran"*

> "Marriage is like a deck of cards. . . . In the beginning, all you need are two hearts and a diamond. But years later, you'll be wishing for a club and a spade."
>
> —*Unknown*

Other Equipment

A stylish holder or box for the playing cards is a very nice touch that can add to your décor. Antique ones can be found that lend a degree of tradition to the game, or you might just look for attractive ones in game shops. Make sure they hold two decks and are wide enough to fit poker cards, not just bridge cards.

You may wish to have markers or indicators (not the chips themselves) to be used for specific purposes throughout the night. For example, if you use a poverty poker system, you will want markers for players making their second or third buy-in of the night. It is sometimes handy to have a dealer button, which indicates who will deal the next hand. If, despite the drawbacks of the game, your players like to deal Texas Hold 'Em and if they want to use rotating deals and small and large blinds, you may want a Small Blind and Large Blind marker.

You can find a variety of markers from the on-line poker chip stores. Or you can find and use other unique items for the same purpose. A pocket watch, a silver medal, wooden nickels, a few poker chips from a different set, a pen knife, whatever. Use your imagination, but keep it in synch with the rest of the atmosphere you are creating.

You need somewhere to hold the money until it is time to cash out. A pile of bills and change lying around is tacky (not to mention prone to lost coins or bills). Find a nice looking box or container that complements the rest of your equipment and use that for the bank. Keep the extra markers in there with the money. It doesn't hurt to keep several quarters in there aside from the buy-ins so that the cash-ins don't have to be rounded to the nearest dollar.

The Table

The table is an extremely important part of the atmosphere and the aesthetics of your game. If your poker game were like a baseball game, then your table is the playing field. When you walk into Camden Yards or Wrigley Field or Fenway Park, it is the field of play that really grabs your attention. A perfectly prepared playing surface, ready and waiting for dramatic contests to be fought and heroes created. The scene of past triumphs and past heartbreaks. The arena. If you are lucky enough to have the perfect poker table, then savor it. If not, try to come as close as you can to perfection with the table you choose to use—and look forward to acquiring the perfect poker table at some point in the future.

Here is what to look for:

Size: Your table needs to be large enough to fit the players around it comfortably, but not so big as to make people have to stand to reach the chips in the middle when they have won the hand. A round or octagonal table, 48-54 inches across, will fit six players comfortably. If you intend to have seven or eight players regularly, they will fit at a 48-inch octagonal table, but you will be better off with the 54-inch width. Of course, the width of the chairs makes a big difference, too. Chairs with arms, or wider chairs in general, will be more crowded and you may not all be able to get eight chairs pulled up close to even a 54-inch table.

Shape: I hate playing poker at a rectangular dining or conference table. Some players don't seem to notice. But I find that you have to be very careful not to expose your hole cards to or see the hole cards of the folks on your left and right. Even worse, you cannot see everyone's face well enough to keep an eye out for tells. Nor can you see their expression when they make a funny comment or caustic complaint. Because you can't see them, it follows that they can't see you and that you have to work harder to get your intended messages across to everybody. Poker is a game that heavily relies on body language, facial expressions, reactions, and non-verbal cues. This is true for the actual betting and bluffing itself, and for the associated banter, jokes, and trash talk that make the game so much fun. It is just much harder to nonverbally connect with others at a rectangular table. Sometimes it is impossible. If your neighbor along the long side of rectangular table is sitting back in his chair as the guy across the table throws in a big bet, it is just not possible to watch both of them at the same time. One of them is directly in front of you and the other is almost behind you. You simply lose the ability to keep an eye on your neighbor's reaction to the big bet. A tactical point of interest that is lost to you forever. Just because the table is wrong.

Round tables are best, because any number of players can be evenly spaced around them with no one having to sit on a corner. Hexagon (six-sided, for those of you who cut geometry to play poker) or octagon (eight-sided) shapes work well also. Square tables are difficult unless there are only four players.

Construction: The table has to be sturdy. Guys will be leaning their elbows on it and banging their feet and knees against the legs. Drinks and stacks of chips will also be sitting on the table, so if the table is not sturdy, it will wobble, drinks will spill, and stacks will be scattered. The ubiquitous square-card tables with folding metal legs with little latches/braces at the corners will simply not do. Even with a different table-top laid over the card table, the whole thing will teeter back and forth. Find a solid table or play somewhere else.

The table legs on some tables can be a big obstacle. If the legs are at the corners of the table surface, they will block where chairs and knees can fit under the table. If the legs are attached farther toward the center of the table, or if the table has a single center pedestal, then there is more flexibility for chair position, but potentially less stability for the table. As long as the legs are recessed back from the table edge by eight inches or so, they should be relatively out of the way of players' knees.

Playing Surface: One can debate whether the ideal surface is felt, leather, vinyl, or something else entirely. To some extent, it is simply a matter of individual taste. But there are some important considerations that apply and that you should know before choosing a playing surface.

The surface should not be hard or rigid. If you play on wooden, glass, or marble surface, you will encounter a few problems.

- The chips will make a lot more noise when being tossed into the pot. This louder noise can become quite annoying over the course of an evening.

- The chips will also bounce a lot more and will be much more likely to roll out of the pot and into someone else's stack or even off the table altogether. This is a hassle if it happens multiple time per hand

113

over the 50 -100 hands you play in an evening. You don't want to spend 20 percent of your time fetching errant chips or retrieving another player's chip from your pile.

- The cards will glide or slide across the table much more quickly, causing more exposed cards and misdeals as they fly off the table's edge.

- The cards will be much harder to pick up off the table. The hard surface makes it difficult to pry up the edges of the cards, which means that the cards have to be slid all the way to the table's edge to get a grip on them.

- The chips are harder to pick up, and they will collide with each other edge-to-edge rather than sliding over and under each other when pushed into the pot or raked in by the winners.

- Any raised imperfection on the surface of the table will scratch the cards, potentially marking the backs and rendering them unusable.

The surface should be easy to clean or dry. Spills happen. Even with some of the drink holders and techniques described below, there will be spills. If you have particularly careless players, or if the table is small enough that any spill will likely spoil the area where cards and chips have to be played, then you want a surface that can be quickly and completely dried with a paper towel. If you have more careful players, better drink holders, and a large surface such that a spill might only impact the edge of the tabletop, then you can get away with felt.

The surface should be uniform and neutral in color and should not have designs, markings, or printed layouts for cards or listings of ranks of hands. The table surface is the background. The focus is on the cards and the chips. You do not want designs or lettering or even the single uniform color of the table to distract from or conflict with the chips and the cards. If you buy a table with lettering on it (made to look like Vegas blackjack tables, for example), you will find it ugly to use for anything but its specifically designed use. Think about it—those tables do not even look classy in the casinos! Stick with understated, uniform colors.

Do not use a tablecloth unless it can be tightly attached to prevent sliding of any kind. If the tablecloth has any "play" in it whatsoever, the cards and chips will snag on the cloth when they are passed around. You will end up removing the cloth and playing on the hard surface despite the concerns listed above. You can, however, buy a round vinyl cover that is designed with a drawstring around its entire edge so it can be pulled very tightly over a round kitchen or dining room table. Perhaps such a cover could be also be made from pool table cloth with a rubberized backing underneath and a drawstring that would pull the edges up tight underneath the table's edges.

The surface should be slightly padded. I made the mistake of having my antique poker table re-covered with a beautiful billiard cloth without asking for a thin layer of padding underneath. The surface is beautiful, but the cloth, luxurious as it is, does not have the thickness required to completely mitigate some of the disadvantages of a hard surface.

Poker Table Tops: Most of us are not blessed with houses large enough to allow the poker table to remain permanently in place. We have to make do with a folding table or a removable table-top or a converting table or some other compromise. Here are some tips regarding these options:

There are many types of **folding tables** where the legs fold under the table top for storage. When choosing one of these, take extra care to ensure that the design and construction are such that the table feels sturdy and solid when standing. Consider the points mentioned earlier about size and shape.

A **folding poker table-top** might be a good choice if you have a sturdy and properly shaped table for it to be placed upon. Generally speaking, a 42-inch to 50-inch round kitchen or dining room table can make a good base for a poker table top. If your kitchen table is square, remember to measure diagonally so the corners do not stick out from your round or octagonal poker table top.

If you use a poker table top, take care to ensure that it stays snug on the table you choose for underneath. If it slips around, get some rubber carpet mats or other device to put between the table and the poker top so it does not slide. And remember to center it properly on the underlying table.

If the table top is going to fit over a regular table, keep an eye on the regular table's legs. If they are all the way out at the corners of the table, you want the poker table top to extend beyond the edges of the regular table's surface by at least six or eight inches so your players aren't bumping their knees or dodging the legs. But, if the regular table's legs are recessed already from the table's edge, then you don't want the poker top to extend beyond the surface too much. Players will lean their elbows on the edges of the poker table top, and a player could actually upend the entire poker top if he leans on it hard enough.

There are many types of folding poker table-tops available online and in retail poker supply houses. In general, you want round or octagonal, as sometimes you will have more than six players and a hexagonal table is uncomfortable for more than six. Also, there are many options for chip racks and drink holders. Both of these can be very handy and helpful, but the drink holders (and sometimes the chip racks too) tend to be too shallow to be of much use. Try to get drink holders deep enough to actually prevent easy spills. Alternatively, get a table with no drink holders but with a padded rail, under which you can slide add-on drink holders like the ones they use in the casinos. It is unlikely that you will use the lettering or the markings that appear on some tables unless you are planning to play the specific game for which the lettering is designed, so get a tabletop with no lettering. Spend enough money to get a table with sufficient thickness to prevent warping or bending when players lean on the edges.

Table Covers can be purchased or maybe even constructed at home to stretch over a round kitchen or dining room table. If you have a sturdy table of the right size and shape, such a cover might be worth a try. You want to get a cover that has a drawstring underneath that will tightly secure it to the table, and you want to ensure that the material is thick enough or is padded so that it provides the right feel. Also, you want to ensure that the backside of the cover is rubberized or is slick vinyl or will some other way properly 'stick' to your table so it doesn't slide around at all. If you get a vinyl cover, you might be able to both pad it and adhere it better to the table with some thin rubber anti-slide carpet mats.

Convertible tables can be purchased that have a dining or smooth wooden surface on one side of the table-top and a fancy poker surface on the other. In theory, you simply flip the table-top to change your dining room table into a nice poker table. This can be a very nice option, for they are typically sturdy, use a central pedestal instead of knee-banging legs, conserve room, and usually come with matching chairs. The drawback is that they can be very expensive. Also, it may be hard to convince the person in your life who controls the selection of dining room furniture to limit his/her options to those that convert into poker tables. Perhaps you have a game room or an office where the smooth side will come in handy without having to be used for formal dinner parties. If you can afford them, and if they fit your house décor, these tables are hard to beat.

> "When a man with money meets a man with experience, the man with experience leaves with money and the man with money leaves with experience."
>
> —*Anonymous*

Table Features—Pockets, trays, drink holders, etc.: Poker tables and tops can come with various features that range from very useful to worse than useless. Some of the common features are covered below:

Drink Holders—Many tables have built-in drink holders. Poker and drinking, of course, are intertwined. Almost no player will go through a night of poker without drinking. Partially, this is due to the advantages of alcohol in relaxing folks in a social situation and in asserting one's manhood and autonomy. And partially, this is due to the simple needs for liquid over a five- or six-hour stretch. Whether they consume water, beer, liquor, sodas, or something else, most, if not all, of your players will have drinks sitting somewhere throughout the game. Drinking goes great with poker, but liquids can be hell on playing cards. So, as the host, you want to be do what you can to keep the players and the drinks connected, while keeping the cards and the drinks separated. In short, you need a plan.

While many poker tables will have some kind of drink holder built into the design, many of these holders will be all but useless at preventing spills. They are more like coasters than drink holders, and they are not very good at being coasters, either, because they often have a hard plastic surface that gathers and does not control or disburse condensation.

There is no real point in having a quarter- or half-inch plastic indentation supposedly designed for your drink. Other than potentially designating whose drink belongs to whom, they serve no purpose, and the uneven surface makes it more likely, not less likely, that a drink is spilled. Look for deeper holders or cork lined coasters or skip this feature all together. If you get a table with shallow plastic holders, get some cork and cut some circles to put into the bottom of the plastic holders.

If you forgo drink holders in your table, you can use higher quality coasters on the main surface, or you can have folks keep their drinks off the table, such as on side tables if this is possible. I have also seen players use foam-rubber can koozies, because, despite their awful aesthetics, they are very useful at making spills more difficult (broader base for the drink) and at preventing and controlling condensation. Perhaps you can find some classy looking koozies (good luck) and enforce their use.

Some nicer poker tables and tops have a **padded rail** around the edge of the table (as featured in most casino card tables). If your table has this feature, then you can get very effective drink holders that are several inches tall and that have a thin plastic tab on the bottom that will slip securely under the edge of the padded rail where it meets the playing surface. Again, you may want to insert some cork into the bottom of these holders, but this is an effective way to avoid spills.

There is one other very convenient and nearly foolproof drink holder approach that I want to mention here because it works so well. I have an antique poker table that had 2-1/2" diameter holes which originally held steel ashtrays around the edges of the table. Because the table edge (and ashtray depth) is two inches deep at the site of these holes, and because there were two holes per player position, my original thought was to use half the ashtrays as drink holders. It turns out, however, that beer cans and almost all drinking glasses are more than 2-1/2" in diameter. Furthermore, standing a tall narrow glass inside a shallow ashtray created a high potential for spills. I saw the perfect solution while looking for skinny glasses that would at least fit the holes. Old-time Coca-Cola or 7-Up glasses that were used in soda-shops were narrow at the bottom and then flared out at the top. Turns out that, not only do they fit neatly in the holes, but, once I removed the ashtray altogether, the glasses sit down low enough in the holes that they are virtually un-spillable. Even better, they are large enough to hold a 12-oz. beer. Any condensation that forms on the glass mostly falls harmlessly to the floor. So, if you should have a table where a hole can easily be made all the way through the table top, you can find glasses to fit inside the hole and be held snugly in place.

Padded Rail—In addition to providing a place to secure a casino-type drink holder, the padded rail around the edge of some poker tables has a few other advantages. It is comfortable for the players as a forearm or elbow rest, and it keeps cards or chips from sliding off the edge of the table. The rail provides a natural wall against which each player can stack his remaining chips without fear of the stacks falling over.

Chip Wells or Trays—Poker table-tops and tables often come with built-in recessed trays, pockets, or "wells" to hold each players' chips. Sometimes these trays have a flat bottom and sometimes (more often now in newer tables) these trays have curved columns for holding stacks of chips in a horizontal position. These trays are generally very useful. Players like the curved stack holders, particularly those players who like to keep careful count of their remaining chips at all times.

On the other hand, only a fixed number of chips can fit in the curved stack holders. Players lucky enough to have gathered more chips than will fit need to trade chips in for higher denominations or they will have extra stacks piled on top of the table. Furthermore, the curved holders provide a less-than-ideal place to throw car keys, a wrist-watch, a cell phone, or anything else a player may want to keep handy in front of him.

The flat chip trays are a bit more flexible in that they can hold more chips, players can stack chips vertically in the tray and steady them against the wall of the tray, and pocket paraphernalia can be tossed into the tray without problem. Generally speaking, the flat-bottomed tray will be larger and hold more chips and other things than the molded curved stack trays.

One other consideration is the manner in which the trays are built into the table. Modern poker tables with molded plastic curved stack trays usually have the plastic tray set flush into the table top, which results in the tops of the stacked chips sitting higher than the table surface. This design can get in the way of a typical player who will pick up his hole cards (or his dealt hand) by sliding the cards to the edge of the table where they can be picked up more easily. A properly padded table can help reduce this issue, but most players will very often drag their cards off the edge of the table when picking them up. You don't see this much on TV because the casino tables have the padded rails around the playing surface, so everyone has to pick their cards up from the table surface without using the table edge. Typically the curved bottom molded plastic trays are directly in front of the player and directly in the way when he wants to use the table edge to help him pick up his cards.

The flat-bottom trays are usually set at the very edge of the table. Players will drag their cards to the edge of the playing surface (which is the front edge of their recessed tray) and use the depth of the flat bottom tray to get their thumbs under the cards and pick them up. Even a tray full of chips will not exceed the height of the playing surface or get in the way of this action.

The last option is no trays at all. With a larger or non-crowded playing surface, this works fine (although it works best in combination with a padded rail to prevent chips from falling off the edge). Players simply pile or stack their chips a bit to the left or right of directly in front of them. If the table is big enough, there is plenty of room so everyone can clearly see their remaining chips.

Summary of Table Recommendations

1. A sturdy, round, 54-inch poker table (folding or not) with a padded felt or vinyl surface and recessed flat-bottomed trays around the edges with useful drink holders, or at least proper drink coasters.

2. A 48-inch round, sturdy table covered by a folding 50- to 54-inch round poker table-top with a padded, unlettered, vinyl surface and a padded rim, but no chip trays or built-in drink holders, combined with eight casino style drink holders with a tab that secures them underneath the padded table rim.

From the Cincinnati Kid:

Cincinnati Kid: Listen, Christian, after the game, I'll be The Man. I'll be the best there is. People will sit down at the table with me, just so they can say they played with The Man. And that's what I'm gonna be, Christian.

The Chairs

The chairs you use for your poker game can add or detract significantly from the overall experience. But it takes some thought to get the right ones. The very expensive table and chair sets you see in catalogues or game room supply showrooms are not really optimized to a regular poker game of six or seven players. The chairs are always too large for that big a crowd. Ideally, your chairs should be:

- Sturdy—No one likes to sit in a wobbly or shaky chair. Especially not for five or six hours at a time.

- Appropriately sized—You need to fit seven or even eight chairs around your table comfortably. The bigger the chair, the tighter the squeeze. Actually, the wider the front of the chair, the bigger diameter table you will need.* Eight players fit comfortably around a 54-inch diameter if the chairs are only 17 or 18 inches wide in the front. If you figure on never playing with more than six or seven players, then the chairs can be a bit wider.

- Appropriately shaped—If the chairs are high-backed, people will have trouble getting out of their

---

* I once did a lot of math to figure out how big a round dining room table should be to comfortably seat eight people. I was very surprised that the experts in the furniture showrooms had no math to support their generalizations. I figured it would be a matter of how many inches of table edge would be needed per person multiplied by the number of people. (And then divided by pi to turn the circumference measure into a diameter). Wrong. It turns out that the key variable was the width of the front edge of the chairs that would be used. When pushed together, the chairs formed an octagon with their front edges touching each other at the corners. You can't squeeze them in any tighter than touching. And you can't back them up any farther than a few inches inside the diameter of the table, or the person would be too far from his dinner plate. Chairs vary widely in the width of the front edge. But once we knew what chairs we were going to use, it was a simple matter of geometry to figure out the minimum diameter for the table.

seats, since the backs of their neighbor's chairs will pin them and their chair in.

- Supportive—Folks are going to be sitting there a long time. Adequate back support and thigh support is important.

- Padded—If you have players older than 30, they will appreciate a little seat padding. If you use simple wooden chairs, you can get some cheap chair cushions at WalMart to put on them.

- Armless—If you are going to have a full table, arms on the chairs will make it much harder to get in and out and will be more crowded in general. If you are going to have five or six players at a big table, arms would fit as long as the chair is not too wide.

- Swivel-equipped—It is ideal for easy access and comfort.

- On wheels—For ease of access and egress and for pulling up to the table to rake in that big pot.

- Matching—It always looks best to have a matched set. Or at worst, a few from two sets.

- Stackable, foldable, or easily stored—Remember that the chairs have to be somewhere when they are not being used for poker.

Really, kitchen or dining room chairs work pretty well. They are designed for use with a table and you are more likely to have matching sets. Also, it is easy to add a cushion to them if need be. Desk chairs can be really nice too, and are probably ideal, especially with their height, seat-back angle, and back support adjustments. Keep an eye out for offices going out of business, or pick up inexpensive ones from Staples. Just remember to keep the size workable, and keep in mind that they don't stack and store easily.

The Room

Although you may have only one or, at most, a couple of choices for which room you will use for your game, there are quite a few factors about your room that can be controlled. People do not typically sit in one room, without a break, for six or eight or ten hours at a time. You want to take steps to optimize the environment so that you and your players will enjoy the setting as much as possible. Some of these suggestions can be implemented before the first game you play there. Others should be items you watch over time, making improvements toward the ideal, as you assess how the games are going.

Lighting—One of the most important elements of the proper poker environment is the lighting. It is one of those things that most people do not notice right away, but it can cause players to get headaches, or to get overly tired too early in the evening, or just to be irritable without knowing why. There was a great short story called *Ex Parte* by Ring Lardner, in which a couple goes over to another couple's immaculately decorated home for an evening of dinner and cards. The visiting husband, who is the story's narrator, is amazed that the other three think the house is so wonderful. When they sit down to try to play bridge, he reports that after a full 30 minutes of dragging floor lamps and end tables around, they are able to tell the black cards from the red cards, but still can't tell a club from a spade. Now he is likely exaggerating, as he does throughout the story, but his internal grumbling about the lighting conditions makes it clear that he noticed and was annoyed by trying to play cards in a sub-par environment.

Keep in mind that your players are going to be sitting in one place for many hours. If there is a light shining in someone's face, it will eventually wear them down. Think about how shopping malls and restaurants make every effort to eliminate harsh lighting and all unpleasant sights or sounds and to create the most relaxing and inviting atmosphere possible. That is what you are shooting for.

There needs to be a good light that shines directly on the table surface from above. A hanging lamp, whether it is poker-themed or not, will take care of this nicely. Get one that will do as a start, and then keep your eyes out for one that perfectly fits the décor or the style of your table, chairs, and chips. But do not compromise function for style. The table needs to be well lit. It is the center of attention. The light that hits the table can't come from over the shoulders of the players on one side of the table. If it does, it will be in the eyes of the players on the other side of the table.

There needs to be some ambient light from table lamps or floor lamps or other sources to illuminate the players' hole cards or other cards that are held in their hands and not laid on the table. Because the player will hold his cards right in front of his face, this light does not have to be bright or direct. If it is too much of either, it will be an irritation for the players across the table. Just be sure there is diffused light coming from a few sources around the periphery of the room.

Pay attention to how well the lighting is working throughout one of your games. It is easy enough to get a lower or higher watt bulb, or to leave a lamp turned off, or another one turned on. You can even get warmer incandescent or cooler fluorescent bulbs to fine tune the lighting further. Once you think you have the optimum mix of wattage and sources of light, then just duplicate that every time you play.

Music—Music is essential to a poker game. In addition to setting the right mood, it provides something for the players to do while they wait for the next hand or another player's decision. Played well, poker requires a lot of patience. In almost any regular poker game, a new player can come out ahead for the night just by having a little more patience and playing a little more conservatively than everyone else. This is because most players like playing even a poor hand better than they like sitting and waiting for a good hand. For reasons described elsewhere in this book, you want to encourage the best play possible. And you want to encourage everyone to have the best time possible. Background music will make everyone less impatient. Players will play better and enjoy the evening more because of it.

I would not presume to tell you what kind of music will work best with your group. It is largely a matter of the individual tastes of the collection of players you have. I am sure that there are poker games out there somewhere where the perfect music for the evening is opera. But that is not game I could tolerate well. I offer the following tips and approaches that have worked well for the many groups with whom I have played:

No commercials—If you are forced to use the radio, then you will be bombarded with commercials. Perhaps you can use a radio with a remote control to switch stations or mute the commercials. But commercials are a big problem. Companies spend millions of dollars to find, attract, and retain those rare, few human beings on the planet who have ridiculously great talents in devising clever schemes to barge into your thoughts, interrupt your concentration, and hijack your attention. These incredibly talented individuals create breathtakingly ingenious schemes to destroy peace and quiet, to end all contemplation and reflection, and to eliminate any chance of coherent thought. For this, they are handsomely rewarded with all the riches our free enterprise system can bestow upon them.

They may use ingratiating and infuriatingly persistent

127

jingles, humorous but, upon ceaseless repetition, annoying visual or verbal sketches, treacly and sappy slice-of-life heart-tuggers, or just the tried-and-true yelling and screaming and crashing of cymbals approach. But whatever their approach, these evil advertising geniuses have tremendous success in quickly dragging our minds and our subconscious far away from what we were enjoying, and focusing our attention fully or partially on whatever it is they are peddling at the time. They are an anathema to any relaxing or intriguing activity. They prevent anyone from going placidly amidst the noise and the haste. They ARE the noise and the haste. And their vile output, their evil spawn, their cursed commercials, will greatly diminish if not completely extinguish anyone's enjoyment of a poker game.

OK, I may be overstating it a bit. But keep in mind that the very intent of radio commercials is to grab your attention away from whatever else you were enjoying and compel you to focus on the advertiser's message. This is the very definition of an uninvited distraction from the game.

Despite the benefits of having music playing during a poker game, it is far preferable to play in silence than it is to play while besieged by commercials, so FM radio is a very poor and problematic choice for a source of good poker music. Fortunately, there are many other sources of commercial-free music among which you can choose. CDs, iPods, commercial-free Internet and Satellite radio are much better choices.

Variety—You are likely to have a variety of musical tastes represented by your roster of regular players. Thus, it would be unpleasant for at least some of the players to have all of the music come from a single artist or even a narrow genre over your five- or six-hour evening of cards. Have a little sensitivity and find out what your players like. And try to have a mix of music that covers most tastes while not being truly objectionable to any player. Remember the owner of the rural night club where the Blues Brothers had their first gig? Asked what kind of music they usually had there, the owner replied, "oh we have both kinds of music here—Country *and* Western." That really wouldn't be a sufficiently wide spectrum to keep a diverse group poker players happy for several hours.

Pleasing everyone can be a bit tricky. When I was younger, 30 years ago, the big problem was that half the table wanted Country music, the other half wanted Rock. Another group I played with years later had those two factions and a third group that wanted what was then called Rap music. At some point, I settled the disputes by letting anyone who complained about the music be the one who chose the next tape. (*Yeah, cassette tapes. I mentioned that it was a while ago.*) There were no such things yet as CDs or iPods so we had to change tapes every 45 minutes or so all evening.

When VCRs came out a few years later, the tapes could hold eight hours of video on the "Extended Play" setting. I got the bright idea of using an extended play VCR tape to record eight hours of "poker" music that would be reasonably acceptable across the board. It took me a couple of days, but I created the biggest mix tape that anyone had ever seen. I used only hit songs and I alternated between rock (but no heavy metal), country (but no extreme twang), and folk/pop (Paul Simon, Jimmy Buffett, James Taylor). It didn't have any Rap music, but it had a smattering of great Motown stuff. In short, I chose songs that everyone could at least tolerate and had some things (probably at least two songs out of three) that each player would actually like.

I didn't tell any of the players about the VCR tape, I just had it on in the background as they began showing up at the door. I waited for someone to notice that it was a mix tape. An hour went by. And another hour. I was on to something. Finally, in hour three, one of the country music haters (who had by then heard at least 15 country songs on the tape) asked me whether we could switch to rock music for a while. I said, "Sure, when this tape is over, just choose whatever you want for the next one." Satisfied, he turned back to the poker game. Because the next song was rock, and the one after that was Jim Croce (*let's call it Pop*), and the one after that was The Temptations, he never noticed after his initial request that he was getting tired of all that Country. And he never noticed that the tape never ended. I was definitely on to something.

Over the next few games, I had one or two players ask if they could choose the next tape. But it wasn't until many games later that a player finally realized that the tape never ended. They were all pretty surprised that they had listened to so much music outside the genre of their choice without noticing it as a problem. It turns out that if you don't play the same group more than one song at a time and if you avoid some of the more "extreme" examples of the different genres, and if there are no commercials, and if all the music is reasonably well known (hits), and if you have a genre or two that is pretty universal (soft rock or pop/folk), everyone is pretty happy and the music debates go away.

> "[Poker is] as elaborate a waste of human intelligence as you could find outside an advertising agency."
>
> —*Raymond Chandler*

Ambient Noise—You are trying to eliminate all bothersome or annoying distractions in your poker room. Ideally, there will only be high-quality background music, the beautiful sound of the chips clicking together as they are tossed into the pot, the occasional happy sound of beer cans being opened, and the priceless verbal banter, laughter, howling, and other interplay between your players.

As you prepare the room, take the time to listen for distracting noise intrusions. Is there a fan squeaking somewhere? Does the dishwasher make an annoying noise that is audible even in your poker room? Is the dog barking in the house or outside the window? Do the fluorescent light bulbs hum in a way that might irritate folks? Does your mini-fridge cut on and off and make a lot of noise while it is running? Is there too much traffic noise coming through an open window? Do the chairs screech across the floor surface?

Oil it, shut it, turn it off, muffle it, muzzle it, fix it, tighten it, move it, pad it, schedule it, end it. Do whatever it takes to make the irritants disappear. You will be surprised how big a difference this can make over multiple hours sitting in a room, trying to concentrate.

I once had the experience of trying to play cards in a home where the host owned a couple of those large, squawking pet birds. Not parakeets, mind you, but those big ones that shriek in the jungle as loud as the monkeys. Without warning, and at arbitrary intervals every few minutes or so, for several hours, there was a horribly loud and unbearable scream from the next room as one of these fugitive Perdue oven-stuffers let out a yell that stood up the hair on the back of my neck. It was a nerve shattering experience. And one I never care to repeat.

Distractions from Outsiders—It is important to limit the traffic through your little poker paradise. Every interruption breaks the rhythm and interferes with the atmosphere you are trying so hard to create and maintain. This goes for dogs running in and out, teenagers coming to ask for car keys and get directions, wives or roommates coming and going, delivery men ringing the door bell, people getting called to the telephone, neighbors borrowing a cup of sugar, (*does that even happen anymore?*), family members running in to search for something, small children wandering in to talk to Daddy, and any other break in the focus of the game. Eliminate these interruptions to the extent humanly possible.

Watch out for distractions from "insiders," too. You and your players might feel it is no bother to check the ballgame score, move the laundry to the dryer, jump up multiple times for the microwave popcorn, run the kids across the street to the movies, check for messages or e-mail on their smartphones, show you something real quick on YouTube, or say "hello" to your family. But each distraction is an irritant and a mood-breaker. And they add up very quickly. Try to plan around any such need you think you may have and to discourage your players from this kind of behavior as well. You don't have to be the ugly enforcer, but you and your game will benefit greatly from some attention to the task of reducing the interruptions.

Temperature and Air Quality—It seems pretty obvious that you don't want your players sweating all over the chips or shivering so much from cold that they can't pick up the cards. But there are a few subtle points to consider in this category.

First, you should be aware that many modern, energy-efficient heating and cooling systems do not cope particularly well with six or seven people in a small or even medium-sized room over a period of several hours. Secondly, some types of hanging lamps or other lights that you need to illuminate a poker table may emit more heat than usual for that room or that space, particularly if they are left on for several hours at a time. The result of these two issues is that the room temperature can become uncomfortably warm during a poker game, even if there is no such problem at any other time. This is particularly likely if you have seven or eight players at the table.

With a little bit of advance planning, however, you can mitigate these issues. Ensure that the air registers and air returns throughout the house are set to positions that keep cooler air flowing to your poker room in the summer, and prevent warmer air from going there in the winter. You can ensure that there are fans ready to circulate the air throughout the house or apartment or even to draw air in from a nearby window in the wintertime to keep the room cooler. You might also use CFL light bulbs which stay significantly cooler.

In general, increased air circulation around your poker table will help both the temperature and the air quality, particularly if you allow smoking at the table.

Proximity to Facilities—If you have a choice of rooms for your game, consider the locations of the bathrooms when deciding where to play. (Also, in all your preparations for the big game, don't forget to check the condition of the bathroom and the availability of supplies there!)

If you are going to keep beer in the refrigerator—instead of in a portable cooler, for example—you will want the table to be pretty close to the kitchen. If you have a mini-fridge dedicated to the poker room, that is even better. (Refrigerators do make noise and emit heat, though, and more so when being opened frequently, so keep that in mind when trying to manage the temperature and the ambient noise levels for the game.)

Food, Drinks, and Amenities

I suppose this could have been a section that only contained a single word: "beer." But, at the risk of stating the obvious, and in the interest of completeness, there are a few more things to consider.

Alcohol—It is hard for me to imagine a poker game with no alcohol. I suppose I must have played in some such games in my youth. My early youth. Poker is a social game. Alcohol is a social lubricant. Part of the macho culture that fits with the image of poker is the image of drinking. And swearing. And any other bad boy behaviors that we don't often get away with when the womenfolk are around.

It should be prearranged with your players whether they bring their own bottles (which is by far the most prevalent and easiest system) or if it will somehow be provided for them. But one way or another, it will be there. Beer has always been and continues to be the most popular drink at the poker games I have hosted. But I had one player once who would drink peppermint schnapps all night, if you can imagine that. Another player brought blenders and milk and made mudslides on some nights and white Russians on others. So, to each his own.

You should be ready to do what can be done to prevent someone who has been drinking all night from hopping in his car at 1 a.m. for a 45-minute drive home. If your players like drinking to that extent, you might need to brew coffee during the last hour of the game. In our game, as we have all grown older, we have become much more moderate in our consumption. But your group may vary and you should keep an eye out for late night drinkers.

Does alcohol help the play of the game? It depends on the players. A drink to "take the edge off" might help an agitated player play calmer and avoid going on tilt. But give an average player three or four drinks in an hour and I will show you a below average player until he slows down on the drinking.

Spills—All players will have something to drink during a five-hour poker game. It is useful to have ice, water, and soda on hand to supplement whatever alcoholic beverages the players have brought. The biggest impact of all that drinking is the high potential and inevitability of spills.

A spilled drink is a major interruption to the poker game and a real threat to the condition of the cards and the table, among other things. So you want to plan ahead on how to minimize spills and be prepared for them when they happen. As described earlier, there are several different types of poker table designs and features (involving well-designed cup holders) that can significantly reduce the number of spilled drinks. The shape of the glasses or containers that your players use will also affect the propensity for spills. And the guidelines you establish and enforce for keeping drinks in appropriate containers and in appropriate places (i.e. off the table, on the coaster, in the holders) will reduce the number of spills. Condensation from containers is also an issue and should be controlled with coasters or with special cupholders.

But despite all of your planning and monitoring (and you don't want to be Felix Unger, either, and just harangue your players about coasters all night), there will be spills. Just have a dishtowel or two handy and try to minimize the damage. If you are playing on a felt surface, you want to blot that quickly and try to avoid the damp spot with the cards for the rest of the night. It is extremely helpful in this situation to be using plastic playing cards. If you are using paper cards and they get wet, you need to retire the wet deck and break out a new one.

If water or diet soda splash on the poker chips, just wipe them dry. The lack of sugar will make this pretty easy. If beer or a sugared drink hits the chips, you need to wipe them more thoroughly and be sure you get every one of them or the chips will stick together and become discolored.

Always remember to heap the proper amount of verbal abuse on the miscreant who has spilled the drink and interrupted the game. That is one of the upsides of spilled drinks at a poker game.

Smoking—If your game features cigarettes or cigars, you can be assured of losing potential players who do not smoke. Most non-smokers simply cannot tolerate being around cigarettes and will not play again (and maybe leave the current game) if anyone is smoking. If you smoke, however, and you can find enough players who are smokers, then have at it.

Smoking creates a need for ashtrays and for keeping the cigarettes away from the cards, the table and the poker chips, all of which can be permanently damaged by cigarette burns. So be forewarned on that score. As a collector of antique poker chips, I have seen many an old set ruined by numerous burn marks from cigars and cigarettes.

I have had smokers play in our regular game, even though smoking was not permitted in the house. They would just leave the table for 10 minutes at a time once or twice an hour to go have a cigarette. It kept the poker game and the house free of smoke, but it played havoc with the pacing of the game as you never knew for sure when they were about to leave and when they would come back.

There are people who, by tradition, believe that cigars must be involved if there is to be a poker game. Unless everyone likes cigar smoke and the game is outside on the porch or patio or deck, I do not see how this works. I have played in a game, though, where a 20-minute recess was called in the middle for cigars and brandies. That was rather nice, even though all the players smelled like cigars for the rest of the night. If you had a cigar, though, you didn't notice so much.

For you southern boys, I should mention that chewing tobacco should be prohibited from the game, too, unless every player is going to be spittin' along with you. I did play poker one time with a guy who brought his Skoal and his spit cup to every game. I eventually got used to it (although I am pretty sure he cost us a couple of potential regular players who could not take having to witness his whole routine). My poor wife, however, almost cut short my days of hosting poker games forever when she found old Billy Bob's spitting cup sitting up on the dining room hutch the next day. Half full. I can't say as I blamed her too much for putting her foot down over that one. (Actually, now that I think about it, she reacted more negatively to that than to the marijuana stash another player left behind on a different night!)

Thirty years later, as my stepdaughter attended a southern university, she, too, became familiar with southern boys who carried around their spit cups. One of them was borrowing something from the top shelf of her closet and managed to spill his nearly full cup of spit and tobacco juice all over her nice clothes which were hanging neatly on the rod. I suspect it was the trauma of that moment, as much as anything else, that caused her to transfer back up north at the end of the semester. The point I guess I am making here is that although you and/or some of your players might love the practice of chewing and spitting, or smoking or toking, you can be quite confident that other players will be revolted by such habits. So, in the interest of keeping it fun and enjoyable for everyone, unless all will be partaking, you should probably just rule out the nastier habits during your poker games.

From "Butch Cassidy and the Sundance Kid":

Card player #1: Well, looks like you just about cleaned everybody out, fella. You haven't lost a hand since you got to deal. What's the secret of your success?

Sundance Kid: [*pause*] Prayer.

Food—Six or more hours is a long time to do any activity without having food of some kind. So you can count on people eating during the poker game. While the types of food to have on hand will be literally a matter of individual tastes, there are a few important guidelines that always apply.

The most important guideline on poker game food is that it cannot be oily, greasy, juicy, prone to dripping, sloppy, or in any other way messy. The table, the chips, and the cards will suffer greatly from messy foods, no matter how careful the players think they will be. This is a guideline that you will need to enforce, but you will get help from most of the other players. No one wants to play with greasy cards.

You should also discourage particularly aromatic foods, as at least some of your players will dislike the smell.

And you should try to avoid high-maintenance food—snacks that require of lot of effort and dishes and trouble. Stick to non-messy, easy to consume, preparation-free snacks. Again, your players' tastes will vary, but here is a list of snacks that work particular well, versus those that do not:

Snacks that Work Best

- M&M Peanuts ("melt in your mouth, not in your hands")
- Skittles
- Pretzel Rods (Not as loudly crunchy as other pretzels, and the cigar-like shape is nice)
- Dry Roasted or Raw Almonds (for the health-conscious)
- Twizzlers
- Dry cold cut sandwiches (prepared away from the table and served on paper plates)
- Granola Bars (non-sticky ones)
- Cookies (non-greasy ones)

Snacks that DO NOT Work Well

- Potato Chips (much too greasy)

- Cheetos (you end up with red cards, black cards, and orange cards)

- Italian subs, Sloppy Joes (or any other oily, aromatic, and messy sandwich)

- Donuts (sticky)

- Popcorn (greasy)

- Bananas (aromatic)

- Chocolate bars (melt on hands and get everywhere)

- Hot hors d'oeuvres (someone has to prepare them and keep them hot, and who wants to do that? Too greasy anyway.)

I recognize that these lists are pretty much a matter of common sense. But I have been surprised to see players show up with some of this stuff without thinking about the practicality.

Which brings me to another point—who is bringing the food? It is pretty easy and effective to have players bring a bag or package of snacks for all to share. That will likely evolve over time as the practice, even if nothing is explicitly stated. But if you enjoy setting out a spread for everyone, I am quite sure they will be appreciative. If you put too much effort into the food, however, you will risk duplicating the poker scenes in the classic Neil Simon play and movie *The Odd Couple*:

Felix Ungar: [*serving refreshments at the poker game*] Cold glass of beer for Roy...

Roy: Thank you.

Felix Ungar: Where's your coaster?

Roy: My what?

Felix Ungar: Your coaster. The little round thing that goes under the glass.

Roy: I think I bet it.

Oscar Madison: [*tosses the coaster back to Roy*] Here, here, here. I knew I was winning too much! Here.

Felix Ungar: Always try to use your coasters, huh, fellas? A scotch and a little bit of water...

Speed: Scotch and a little bit of water and I have my coaster.

Felix Ungar: I don't want to be a pest, but you know what glasses can do.

Oscar Madison: [*under his breath*] They leave little rings on the table.

Felix Ungar: They leave little rings on the table!

Oscar Madison: [*under his breath*] And we don't want little rings on the table.

Eventually, of course, that kind of behavior gets Felix thrown out of the game and the apartment.

Oscar Madison: Listen, he was driving us all crazy with his napkins and his ashtrays and his bacon, lettuce, and tomato sandwiches. All of you said so.

Roy: We didn't say kick him out, Oscar.

Oscar Madison: Well, who do you think I did it for? I did it for us!

Roy: Us?

Oscar Madison: Yes, that's right. Do you know what he was planning for next Friday night's poker game as a change of pace? Do you have any idea?

Vinnie: What?

Oscar Madison: A luau! A Hawaiian luau! Roast pork, fried rice, spareribs—they don't play poker like that in Honolulu!

So, whoever brings the food, remember it is a poker game with some snacks around. Not a luau with some cards.

Amenities—You will need to provide a few other necessary items to go with the food and drink. These accoutrements can be easily forgotten, so you may want to keep them all in one place to pull out for your games. Here is a partial list of what you may need to have ready for each game:

- Ice bucket
- Beer towel (to dry off bottles and cans that have been in a cooler of ice)
- Cooler and ice (unless you have a refrigerator. In that case, you just need the ice)
- Bottle opener
- Napkins and/or paper towels
- Paper plates if needed
- Small dishes to pass snacks around the table (find ones with a cool "look")
- Coasters (Felix lives!)
- Multiple trash cans (lined with bags) and recycle bins (for bottles and cans)

- Ashtrays and matches (if all are going to be smoking)
- Drinking glasses that work with your drink holders
- Dish towels (for quick cleanup of spills)

With each of these items, and any item you add to this list for your own environment, you can use standard Walmart issue products, or you can take the opportunity to find classy, unique, and stylish examples that really add something to your game. I recommend that you start with things that work, but that, over time, you keep your eye out for the unique and stylish. For example, I had perfectly acceptable bottle openers that I would put out for the first 20 years I hosted games. But then I came across a vintage, silver-handled bottle opener with a molded design that featured old-time poker players, cards, and chips. Eventually, over a long period of time, you can get to the point where every item related to the game is a high-quality, stylish, and unique expression of the atmosphere you are trying to create.

Leadership, Money, and Banking

It can be helpful to have a de facto "leader" of the game. By default, this role usually falls to the host. After all, the host does the inviting and the game takes place on his turf. But in games that rotate among several locations, or in situations where more than one person does the inviting, it can be a bit more difficult to identify the leader. It is not absolutely necessary to have a single declared leader. A poker game is a cooperative venture (*despite the actual play being ruthless!*). However, there must be a clear-cut means for deciding dates, times, and places for future games; deciding who is invited; resolving who gets the seats if there are too many players; and other similar issues.

Even if the regular game moves from location to location,

it is important that there is consistency in the game rules. You do not want to be in a situation where someone asks "In Jack's house, Aces can only go high, right?" The rules and procedures should stay as constant as possible regardless of the venue.

In each night of poker, there should be one person designated as the banker. This can be the host/leader or another player, but it should be only one person for the entire evening. There are several processes that the banker should perform and for which he has accountability. These might include:

- Counting out chips for each player's initial buy-ins. It is best if the initial buy-ins (and a few subsequent buy-ins) can be counted out before the players arrive. It takes some time to get the chips counted properly and in the right distribution of colors, so, ideally, you want to avoid having potential *playing* time taken up by this administrative function.

- Ensuring that the correct amount of money is received from each player in exchange for the initial buy-in. Encouraging players to use smaller bills for their buy-ins so the eventual cashing out can be easily accommodated. Totaling the money from the initial buy-ins to double check that all have paid.

- Having counted chips ready from the bank for subsequent buy-ins needed by players. Collecting the money from the player and issuing the counted chips. Issuing any markers required to keep track of subsequent buy-ins.

- Checking all stacks of chips being cashed out at the end of the night. Following the procedure for any Poverty Poker or Loss Limit cash outs and reclaiming those markers as needed. Cashing out all the chips for all the players.

- Ensuring that the cash out was satisfactory to all players. Leading any conversations regarding potential discrepancies and their resolutions.

> "The game exemplifies the worst aspects of capitalism that have made our country so great."
>
> —*Walter Matthau*

Player Responsibilities

Each player at the table has certain clear responsibilities and duties to the game. If you are a player in a regular poker game, you should be certain that you are fulfilling these responsibilities. If you are the host or the leader of a poker game, you should not only fulfill your responsibilities as a player, but also teach and encourage the other players to hold up their end.

The Ten Commandments for Poker Players

I.   Thou shalt respond promptly to invitations and fulfilleth all thy commitments. Never shalt thou fail to appear as promised.

II.   Thou shalt show up on time and stayeth until the end. Thou shalt have eaten dinner, visited the money changers, and performed all other preparations ahead of time.

III.   Thou shalt bring thine own libations, but bringeth food for many

IV.   Thou shalt bring bills smaller than Twenties

V.   Debateth in good faith, but thereafter supporteth the decisions of the group

VI.   Sloweth not the pace of the game at any point, but instead, hasten to take all necessary actions with alacrity

VII.   Stay thou at the table, rising only after thou foldeth thy cards in a hand that continueth without thee.

VIII.   Knowest thou the rules and payeth strict attention to him that dealeth the cards as instructions he uttereth

IX.   Never sweateth the small stuff, yet bestow patience and tolerance on thy fellow players, yea, and overlooketh thou the flaws of thine host

X.   Knowest thou the fundamental precepts of Friendly Poker and helpeth in the enforcement of the law and in suggesting of improvements

Scheduling and Invitations

Scheduling the games and managing the attendance can be a bit of a challenge. Some suggestions for making this a smoother process for your game appear below.

Frequency—The group of players that belong to your regular game, including yourself, will dictate the frequency with which you can schedule your games. People have crazy schedules these days, but I have always been disappointed that I couldn't somehow squeeze more games onto the calendar. In grad school, we had classes Monday through Thursday, which made Thursday night the perfect time for a poker game for a group of students. While school was in session, I was able to play every week.

Later, at my first job, a group of work colleagues would play in the break room on paydays, every other Friday evening right after work. The company provided a natural pool of players, a convenient location, and a natural schedule that was easy to keep.

Obviously, you can only schedule the games as frequently as your regulars are able to attend. So, if you want to play often, find a group of folks who match your interest in poker and your degree of free time. Or if that still is not often enough for you, try to "belong" to two or three regular games.

Which Night of the Week?—I have always found it easiest to schedule games on Friday nights than any other night of the week (with the exception of grad school where Thursday night was essentially the beginning of the weekend for the students). But I have heard about other games that are played on Saturdays and still others played on weeknights. It is simply a matter of when you can get the most able and willing players. If you have players that have to travel an hour or more to get to your game, it will be difficult to play on a weeknight. Their travel time will prohibit them from starting early and will ensure they have to leave early to be ready for work in the morning. On the other hand, if everyone in your game is local, if your location is very convenient to where they all work, and if you can start immediately after work, you might be able to keep a regular game going on a weeknight.

How to Find Players—I wish it were easier to find good players. There seem to be enough to play regularly if you work at it, but not so many that it is easy to play as frequently as you may like. Obviously, if you are good at socializing in general, and you are the type who knows hundreds of people personally, it may be easier for you to find players than it is for those of us who are a bit less of a social butterfly. Your job is complicated by the fact that for every 10 people you find who express interest in playing poker, only a couple will work out to be truly compatible with your game. The others will only want to play a few times a year. Or they will be looking for a drinking and cigars party, not a poker game. Or they will be painfully slow at making decisions and painfully bad at it too. So you have to find a large number of potential players in order to find the good ones that become regulars or semi-regulars. Here is a list of sources that I have found productive when trying to find players:

- Colleagues at work or school (note, however, that it is not always comfortable to play with one's boss)
- Neighbors (but watch out for folks who express interest and come to a few games, only to reveal later that they don't like poker much, but they wanted to be neighborly)
- People from community groups such as church, little league, Boy Scouts, the country club, the

Rotary Club, and the like. You just have to ask the ones you know best if they ever play poker.

- Family members—brothers, uncles, nephews, and in-laws

- Your tax guy, financial advisor, barber, lawyer, accountant, mechanic, or anyone else you know pretty well from regular interactions over time. They might play and they may well know other folks who like to play.

- People who might be referred by your friends and family. I have been playing for almost 20 years with a guy who happened to be a neighbor of my sister 20 years ago.

- Regularly ask your players if they know of other good players who would fit in with the game. Your players will likely have played in some other game before they began playing with you. They may well be able to refer a good player to you.

Number of Players Needed on Your List—You will need substantially more players on your invitation list than you can fit around your card table. Simple math will tell you that the desired number of players for a given evening must be a product of your average frequency of attendance multiplied by the total number of players on your invitation list. If, on average, your players can make the game about half the time, and you want to play with six players, you will need about 12 on your invitation list. The math is a major reason why you want players who are as reliable as possible. The more players you have who can make it 90 percent of the time, the fewer total number of players you will need on your invitation list.

Of course, standard deviations sneak in there, too. A couple of players might make every game and a few others might only make it 10 percent of the time. Furthermore, there are seasons (mid-summer, and November 20-January 2 to name two) where it is harder to get even your more regular players to attend. So the math says you want to have even more on your invitation list than the simple average attendance rate would dictate if want to avoid going pokerless on game night.

The other way to work the problem is to let the frequency vary to match the number of true regulars you have on your list. In other words, if you have six regular players, you simply play as often as those six can get together, rather than have several other alternates on your list to fill the seats when your regulars cannot make the game. The downside of this approach is that people's schedules can change. Everyone may have agreed well in advance on a date for the next game, only to have a couple of players have "things come up" before then that make it impossible for them to play. Without alternates and overbooking, you are out of luck until the next time the six schedules have a common opening.

My recommendation is to have 10-16 players on your invitation list. If a player cannot make it to at least a quarter of the games, then drop him from the invitation list and find another candidate. If your players are all pretty regular, you might do with only 10 on your list. If your players are hard to schedule, increase your list until you have no trouble holding the game regularly.

Invite the 10 players who come the most frequently first. If you do not fill your table, then extend the invitation to the rest of your list. If you get too many players for your available seats, consider playing with two tables or just hand out the seats in the order the replies were received.

> **From "The Sting":**
>
> **Doyle Lonnegan:** Mr. Shaw, we usually require a tie at this table... if you don't have one, we can get you one.
>
> **Henry Gondorff:** That'd be real nice of you, Mr. Lonniman!
>
> **Doyle Lonnegan:** Lonnegan.
>
> [*Gondorff burps in response*]

Invitations—Invitations and scheduling have become a lot easier with the advent of e-mail. It used to take more time and effort to make multiple phone calls before nailing down the game and confirming the attendance. Even with e-mail, however, you are likely to suffer the slings and arrows of slow or unresponsive invitees. The most efficient and least confusing procedure that I have evolved over time is described below, but you should embellish or adapt it as befits your gang and your circumstance.

1. Divide your total list of potential players into the "regulars," who attend almost every time, and the "occasional," who can only make it less than half the time you hold a game.

2. Pick two dates, typically a week apart from each other, that you would be able to host a game.

3. At least two weeks in advance of the first date, but no more than four weeks in advance, send out the invitation e-mail to the "regulars." People's calendars are uncertain and people tend to ignore e-mails about

things more than a month away. But people need at least two weeks' notice to reserve the date so other plans are not made.

4. In the invitation e-mail, specify both dates being considered. Reiterate the location and starting time even though these may never vary for your game. Request that folks respond by giving you their availability for both of the two dates—make it clear you will be choosing one of those two dates. You are not asking for a preference (although they can give you that if you like), you are looking for two distinct answers. "Can you play on Date 1? Can you play on Date 2?" Include a reminder that seats are handed out in order of replies received.

5. Track the responses coming back. As soon as you get five "yes" responses for a particular date, you are good to go. (Remember that you are playing too, so that makes six total players.)

6. If you have fewer than five "yes" responses after 2-3 days, and are still missing responses from some folks, send out a second notice—a glorified nagging e-mail—to collect the missing responses.

7. If you do not get five "yes" responses by Day 4, then send the initial invite e-mail to the list of "occasional" players. Repeat the process of nagging e-mails until you have sufficient numbers of responses to decide if the game is a go or not.

8. As soon as you have the five "yes" responses (or even four, if you think that those four plus yourself will make a great game), then send out a confirming e-mail to everyone announcing the now chosen date of the game, declaring that the game is definitely on,

and listing the five or six players who have confirmed seats (including yourself). Do this step even if you want to continue to nag or invite "occasional" players to see if you can get to seven or eight players. It is important to send this "Game On" e-mail to all the regular invitees for two reasons. First, you want your players to know the game is definitely on, not just tentative. And secondly, someone who said "no" will occasionally have his schedule free up at the last minute. It is a sad thing, indeed, when you end up playing five-handed poker only to find out later that one of your regulars could have joined you after all but did not know that the game was on.

Remember to write your invitation e-mails as invitations. They need to be *inviting*. You are trying to encourage your players to want to come join the game. I like to include famous poker quotes at the bottom of the e-mails to whet the players' appetites and motivate them to reply quickly and make sure they have a seat. Your "Game On" e-mail is an opportunity to get people looking forward to the game in advance. Perhaps it might spur some trash talk among those confirmed to play. Perhaps it will further motivate those who have not yet cleared their calendars and requested a seat. The e-mails are all opportunities to enhance the overall atmosphere and "feel" of your regular game. They do not need to be fancy poetry or novel-length treatises. But you should make them fun and, to the degree possible, motivating.

I have included a list of famous poker quotes as an appendix so you can feel free to lift quotes from there if your imagination fails you.

From Rounders:

Mike McDermott: In "Confessions of a Winning Poker Player," Jack King said, "Few players recall big pots they have won, strange as it seems, but every player can remember with remarkable accuracy the outstanding tough beats of his career." It seems true to me, cause walking in here, I can hardly remember how I built my bankroll, but I can't stop thinking about the way I lost it.

Mike McDermott: I feel like Buckner walking back into Shea.

CHAPTER 4

The Best House Rules for Friendly Poker

THERE IT IS. Another bold claim. What makes my rules the best? They just are—can't you just trust me on this? No? OK. I will give you a list of what I believe are the best rules, complete with extensive notes that provide my reasoning for why this specific rule is better than some common alternatives you may have previously encountered. That way you can judge for yourself whether my recommended rule is, in fact, the best for you and your group.

Most folks assume that as long as the ground rules are clearly understood by everyone before the game starts, it does not make much difference what the exact specifics are. Maybe at one house, an Ace cannot go low in a straight, while in another, it can. As long as the rule is spelled out ahead of time, isn't one rule as good as the other?

Not really. The rules exist within the general context of the individual hand being played, the context of the entire night of poker at that sitting, and the overall context of what players may know about poker from outside your regular game. The rules can be in harmony with each of these contexts or they can be at odds with them. Harmony leads to better player satisfaction than discord. The trick is to think through the nuances of context and select the specific rules that will keep everything in harmony. Or if you don't like thinking that much, you can just take my word for it. I have done *way* too much thinking about all of this over my lifetime.

Many of the previously published sets of rules, for example, were written mostly to decrease the chances of anyone cheating or being perceived as a potential cheater. That is very important when playing with strangers where being cheated is a real possibility. But it is not such an important factor when playing with regulars who are your friends or neighbors or work comrades. You basically trust these folks. And the stakes and the regular nature of the game make it unlikely they would be cheating you without being detected anyway.

Keep in mind that the fundamental purpose of your regular game is to maximize player enjoyment and camaraderie. The object for each player, as mentioned earlier, is to have fun, compete, and show off. It follows that the rules of each hand, and the overall "house rules" that apply to all hands, must support these objectives.

Basic Principles Behind the Rules

There are some basic principles that underlie the optimum set of house rules. All other things being equal, the house rule should:

1. Reinforce the 'Friendly' Nature of the Night

It is essential that the rules, where possible, support the concept that this is a 'friendly' competition. The entire object of the evening is to have fun, enjoy the camaraderie, and show off. This principle must take precedence over all others, otherwise your friendly game can get ugly pretty quickly. It is imperative to keep disputes to an absolute minimum and to avoid situations that may cause one player to resent another or to feel that other players have ganged up on him. The 'consistency' and 'simplicity' principles mentioned below are critical, in large part, because they support the avoidance of disputes and thus reinforce the 'friendly' nature of your evening.

2. Emphasize Skill over Luck

Most competitive game players enjoy games that require more skill versus those that depend almost solely upon chance. Players want to feel that the quality of their play affected the outcome. Games that are 100 percent skill such as chess attract a devoted following and are worthy pursuits. On the other hand, the fact that there is no luck involved whatsoever can be burdensome. If a player loses, it has to be the result of their own mistakes or their opponents' superiority. That can be less than enjoyable for many folks, whether they are winning or losing.

Games that are 100 percent luck, however, are extremely boring. It is simply no fun for people to hope for the best with no opportunity to affect their outcome. There is no sense of achievement if they happen to win. And how can you use your victory to show off, to pump up your self-esteem, and to gain your defeated enemies admiration (i.e. gloat) if your victory was completely due to luck?

So the most enjoyable games to the biggest number of players are games that include at least some element of chance. Winners can feel proud of their achievements and losers can feel they were up to the task, and with a break here or there, they might have prevailed. Both want to play again.

Poker, like every other card game, already incorporates a significant degree of chance or luck by virtue of the cards themselves. Oh sure, if you want to play thousands and thousands of hands against the same opponent, you can ensure that the random chance evens out over the long run and you can see the game as pure skill. In the long run. But, as observed by the famed economist John Maynard Keynes, "the long run is a misleading guide to current affairs. In the long run, we are all dead."

In a single night of poker, especially with a variety of different games being played, we do not remotely approach enough hands to ensure that the lucky and unlucky breaks are perfectly balanced out. Therefore, over any hand of poker and over any night of poker, a significant element of chance and luck remain in play.

So, in poker, we are already guaranteed that there are sufficient elements of chance in the game. Given that guarantee, players prefer sets of rules and types of poker games that reward skill as much as possible. Therefore, a main objective of our House Rules must be, wherever possible, to support or increase the skill factor and mitigate against 'dumb luck' deciding the outcomes.

Note, however, that increasing the skill factor does not mean requiring, *by rule,* that players can't do stupid things. Take, for example, the 'house rule' about whether a Five-Card Draw player can draw four cards if he is holding an Ace. Generally speaking, drawing four cards to an Ace is not a particularly smart poker move. The player probably should have folded before the draw if taking four new cards was his best option. A house rule that prohibits drawing four cards to an Ace might prevent a poor player from making a bad poker move. But that rule would not allow the play of the game to reward smart moves versus bad moves. Rather, it would eliminate one opportunity for skillful play to be rewarded and bad play to be punished. The house rules should not prevent bad moves. They should enable rewards and punishments to happen as a consequence of the different plays.

3. Emphasize Simple over Complex

One of the least enjoyable activities in any poker game is the ritual of explaining or re-explaining the rules of a hand, the house rules, the sequence of betting, the values of the chips, the rules of poker in general, or any other kind of general instructions multiple times per hour or per night to those players who lose track or who have not yet mastered them. Neither the folks doing the explaining nor the folks needing the explanations particularly enjoy their role. Who wants to ask for help? And who wants to explain it to him for the fourth time tonight?

A second unenjoyable activity is trying to sort out what to do when a player plays his hand wrong due to misunderstanding of the rules. Someone has to sort out whether the player was properly apprised of the rule before making the mistake (in which case, tough luck for him) or whether the rule was confusing or not well communicated to him (in which case he would seem to have an argument for a compromise resolution). Any solution to a rule misunderstanding can leave one or more players feeling embarrassed, sheepish, angry, or screwed out of some money that should have been theirs.

Where possible, make the house rules simple so they can be easily learned and easily remembered.

It may seem ironic that in an effort to "emphasize simple over complex" it is taking me several pages to describe house rules that in many poker games are covered in 60 seconds at the beginning of the night. But sometimes simplicity can be complicated. Actually, the house rules themselves are very straightforward. The complexity presented here is only for those who wonder *why* the rule is the rule. The "why" can get pretty subtle, and sometimes can only be truly appreciated through experiencing various scenarios over thousands of games.

Furthermore, I can guarantee you that if you walk into a strange game and they only take 60 seconds to describe the house rules, you will be discovering many unmentioned rules over the course of the evening, and that can be costly and frustrating. That completely defeats the objective of game, remember? (Have fun, show off, and feel good, in case you forgot.)

4. Emphasize Consistency

For the same reasons you want the rules to be simple, you need them to be consistent. It makes them easier to explain and easier to remember. Just as importantly, it makes them easier to apply. No set of rules can cover all contingencies. Some gray-area event will occur, and it will have to be arbitrated, or a new player might be told one rule but not another. A consistent set of rules allows the players to extrapolate more easily. If Aces can always go low in a straight, a player can make the assumption that in any new game being dealt, whether the dealer mentions it or not, the Ace can go low in a straight. If the house rule allows each dealer to set that parameter and if every game is different on that point, what does a player do with an A-2-3-4-5 when the dealer has forgotten to specify the rule for this particular hand?

The optimum rules will set as many internally

consistent, general rules as possible to reduce the amount of confusion and explanation that has to occur before every deal. And, if there are no compelling reasons to the contrary, the optimum house rules will be consistent with commonly practiced house rules that players may have learned elsewhere and with the rules and practices used by the casinos. This will help avoid confusion and explanation. But the key phrase in this paragraph is "no compelling reasons to the contrary." In some cases, there actually are compelling reasons why the optimum rules will differ from the rules for casinos, televised tournaments, and non-friendly games.

5. Emphasize Speed

The pace of the game is a very important factor to overall player enjoyment. It is generally not a good idea to try to push players to make individual playing decision faster (this just causes poorer play and resentment in general). But it is very important to reduce the amount of dead time between decisions, deals, or determining whose turn it is.

Some house rules can have an impact on the pacing of the game. All other things being equal, you want rules that allow the pace of the overall game to move faster.

A Word about High-Low Games and Split Pots

Your friendly poker game is likely to include a fairly high percentage of High-Low or other "split pot" games like *Chicago*, or *727*. There are several reasons for this phenomenon, but the most important ones are that split-pot games keep more players in each hand longer and produce more "winners" per night than the single pot games. Since the goal of friendly poker is showing off and having fun, many players will choose split pot games when it is their turn to deal.

The house rules presented here cover the complications of the high-low games and simplify and enable the "declare" (when players reveal the half –pot for which they are competing, the final betting after the declare), the showdown, and the division of the chips to the two halves.

These are very important rules that have a big impact on player enjoyment of the high-low games. If you have already played high-low, or split pot poker, you may be familiar with different approaches. I urge you to use the rules described here. A great deal of time and experience has gone into these rules, and what may seem like a minor tweak to the way you have done it in the past can have a significant impact on player enjoyment of the game.

Some of the important conclusions presented here include:

- The benefits of having players "declare" which half they are contesting rather than just "fall into" a win by happenstance

- The importance of the last bet coming after a clear declaration, so contestants know who they are up against.

- The importance of "simultaneous declaring" so no random benefit falls to the dealer or other player would might otherwise see what everyone else is doing before committing themselves.

These recommended rules include an extremely entertaining alternative to the standard rules of declaring. This alternative involves dividing the pot in half, and then allowing all players a betting round against the high half-pot to contest for high, and another betting round against the low half-pot to contest for low. Players who 'fold' on the high round, can still compete for the low and vice versa. I believe this is a unique approach that has not been previously published and is therefore not yet widely used. But it is an outstanding approach for adding skill, intrigue, and fun into the split-pot games.

All of these rules and their rationales are explained in detail below.

> "I don't mind getting beaten by a good player, and I don't even mind getting beaten by a bad player, but I can't stand getting beaten by a bad player who thinks he is good."
>
> —*H.L.B. Tunica*

The Best "House Rules" for Friendly Poker

Cards and Card Values

1. Cards and Card Values

   a. Aces can always go high or low.

      If the Ace cannot go low, the rank of cards begins with the 2. That seems at least inelegant, since ranking and counting normally begin with 1. I have found it extremely rare to be in a game where A-2-3-4-5 is not a straight. Consistency with the outside poker world and its standards demands that the Ace can go low in a straight. If that is the case, then, absent some compelling reason to the contrary, for the sake of simplicity and consistency, Aces should always be allowed to go high or low. While there has been a bit of surprise from half of the 'Chicago' and 'Low Hole' players in my game that Aces are allowed to be declared the low spade or the low pair, I feel it is less than the confusion that arises if Aces are allowed low in some games but not in others.

b. Aces can go low even in 'Chicago' games or 'Low Hole Wild' games.

    This rule supports the principle of consistency and it also creates more diversity of hands since a player with an ace in the hole has a choice on whether it will be used as his low wild card or if another hole card will be wild.

c. Aces can go low in a straight or straight-flush (A,2,3,4,5 is a straight)

d. A pair of aces is always a pair, but in a declared low hand, it can be the lowest pair

    This provides consistency with other house rules. If an ace can go low in a low hand, why can't the pair of aces be the lowest pair? Also, this rule adds more chance for going both ways with a pair of aces in some games.

2. A wild card can be used as any card in the deck

a. A wild card can be used to fill flushes or straights

b. A face-up wild card in a stud game is assumed to be an Ace or to pair up the player's highest other up-card when determining who bets first. (If on the first round of up-cards, the player to the dealer's left gets a wild card, and the next player gets an Ace, the first bet is made by the wild card, which is assumed to be the "first ace."

Hands and Hand Values

3. There are only five cards in poker hand. A sixth card is never used as a tie-breaker, to form a third pair, or to add a high card, etc.

4. The suits have no values. A spade royal straight flush is an exact tie with any other royal straight flush.

5. The use of wild cards versus 'natural' cards is not used to break ties.

6. The rank of standard poker hands is as follows:

   a. Five of a kind (requires at least one wild card)

   b. Straight flush (a 'Royal' Straight Flush is simply the highest ranking straight flush)

   c. Four of a kind (four of the same rank—J,J,J,J,6 for example)

   d. Full House (three of one rank, two of another— 9,9,9,4,4 for example)

   e. Flush (five of a suit)

   f. Straight (five consecutive ranks—3,4,5,6,7 for example) A straight cannot go 'around the corner'. (Q,K,A,2,3 are not consecutive and that hand is not a straight).

   g. Three of a kind

   h. Two Pair

   i. One Pair

   j. Highest Card

7. Tiebreakers are as follows:

   a. Five of a kind—higher rank wins (five Kings beats five Queens. If two players have five of the same rank, they split the pot—it happens occasionally in community card games with wild cards)

   b. Straight-Flushes, and Straights are compared based on the highest card they contain. If both hands have the same high card, they split the pot.

   c. Flush—High Card wins—if both have same high card, second highest card is compared and so on. If both have same five cards, pot is split.

   d. Full House—the set of three is the tiebreaker (3,3,3,4,4 beats 2,2,2,K,K). If both have the same ranks for the set of three, the hand with the higher pair wins. Identical hands split the pot.

   e. Three of a kind—the higher set of three wins. If two players both have three of the same rank, the highest fourth card wins, and so on. Identical hands split the pot.

   f. Two Pairs—The highest pair is the tiebreaker. J,J,2,2,3 beats 10,10,9,9,A. If the highest pair is a tie, then the second pair is compared. If still a tie, the fifth card is compared. Identical hands split the pot.

   g. One Pair—Highest pair wins. If tied, the highest third card, and so on.

8. Non-standard, game specific hands:

   a. Some so-called poker games allow nonstandard hands or ranks of hands. (For example, in 727, the closest to seven points splits with the closest to 27 points. In the 'Chicago' games, half the pot goes to the highest or lowest spade in the hole.) If a dealer chooses to play such a game, the precise definition of what hands can be used to win a pot must be explicitly called and defined by the dealer ahead of time.

*Keeps the game friendly. There is no standard for these nonstandard hands, their tiebreakers, etc. Avoid hard feelings by getting it clearly defined up front. It also helps if the table, not just the individual dealer, **defines the criteria and definitions once for all times that game is played**. Having subtle rule changes for each dealer for basically the same game is a recipe for players making mistakes, dealers forgetting to clarify and the table ending up trying to arbitrate a big misunderstanding.*

b. Nonstandard hands can be added to more traditional games like Five-Card Stud to liven them up a bit. A blaze (five face cards) might beat three of a kind and lose to a straight, for example. Or a four-flush or bobtail straight might beat any pair, but lose to two pair. These hands must be called and defined by the dealer in advance, and if other dealers decide to use them in their games, their definitions should remain constant.

These odd hands add some interest to simple games like 5 card draw or 5 card stud, which otherwise would not produce enough good starting hands to keep players in the game. The wide variety of more complicated games accomplish the same purpose—add more interest, keep players in, etc.

So it is unlikely in today's games that you will run into anyone playing the simple games with the expanded odd hands.

9. Rankings of Low Hands for High-Low or Lowball Poker

   a. A "low" hand is simply the worst poker hand. Its relative value in a low game can be determined by applying the standard rank of hands backwards.

   b. The best low hand is the worst poker hand possible—a 6 high. Specifically a 6,4,3,2,A not in suit and with the A declared low.

      This follows from the rule of consistency with widely accepted standards AND from internal consistency with other poker game rules. Some casinos and card rooms playing low-ball (low only) games call 'the wheel' (A,2,3,4,5) the perfect low, and some home games say the A must be high so the 7.5.4.3.2 is the perfect low. But in a high-low game, as opposed to strictly low-ball, a straight should be a straight. Consistent with the fact that a pair is a pair. If you are going to disregard straights in low-ball, there is little reason that AAAA2 would not be the lowest hand. It is inconsistent to say that some standard poker hands (a straight or a flush, say) don't exist but that pairs or trips do. If you want to say that Aces are always high in every game, every situation, then you could make a better argument for the 'perfect' being 7,5,4,3,2. But then you lose the intrigue and interest that arises from having the Ace be unpredictable in an opponent's hand. It has been extremely rare in my experience to see a low game where the A cannot go low in a straight. So, even though it would be consistent to say aces are always high, it would be at odds with the outside poker world. If aces can go low at all, ever, they should always be allowed to go low, so no one gets confused.

c. (A,2,3,4,5) is a straight. It cannot be called an A-high

Provides consistency with widely known poker standards. Even in the lowball clubs that play A-2-3-4-5 as the perfect, it is not an Ace high. It is a 5 high with straights being ignored.

d. If all five cards are of the same suit, they are a flush.

Provides consistency with widely known poker standards. Although some card rooms playing lowball will ignore flushes, this is an anomaly, and only applies to lowball (as opposed to high-low). Furthermore, it makes no sense to ignore flushes, but not ignore pairs. So this rule also provides internal consistency with the other poker rules. A pair is a pair, a straight is a straight, and a flush is a flush. This is especially true in games where "cards speak" (i.e. the player does not have to call his hand correctly, the cards themselves are evaluated by the table after the showdown.

e. A straight or a flush can be played low, but it is a counted as a straight or a flush and is, therefore, generally a terrible low hand. A pair can be played low, but, again, it counts as a pair and will be beaten for low by any hand with no pair.

Players often make the mistake of thinking a straight cannot 'go low'. There are times (for example, when all remaining players in a high-low game have high hands showing) when it makes perfect sense to play the straight low. If one of those apparent flushes turns out to be a busted flush, however, and that player also goes low, the straight will lose the low half. Now, about pairs: I cannot think of a reason why, if Aces can go either way, a pair of aces wouldn't be lower than any other hand containing a pair. It is arbitrary to assume that a pair of aces always must be considered the highest pair. On the other hand, allowing a pair of aces to be either the highest or the lowest pair is a logical and useful extrapolation of the commonly accepted practice of allowing aces to go either way. And it adds significant interest and intrigue in 5 card high-low games where an ace showing can be paired with an ace in the hole and STILL win both the high and low halves.

    f.   If two low hands both have the same highest card, the tiebreaker is the second highest card in the hands—with the lower second-highest card winning. So a 8,6,5,4,3, wins a low hand against a 8,7,3,2,A.

Betting Rules

10. Each round of betting typically begins with the player showing the highest cards face-up. In any game with no cards showing, (5 card draw, for example), betting begins with the player on the dealer's left.

11. Betting proceeds clockwise around the table. Always.

12. The second and all following betting rounds in a game

with <u>no up cards</u> begin with the "last raiser". This is the player that made the last raise in the previous betting round. If there were no raises in the previous round, then this is the player who made the first bet in the previous round.

Someone has to bet first. Since , in a home game, you are not playing the same game over and over and over, it makes little sense to have a rotating 'big blind' or 'little blind' defined. Having the last raiser make the first bet on the next round ensures that the burden of acting first is distributed in a rational and easy-to-determine manner. It also allows some skill to come into play when considering whether to raise or not on an early round. Do you want to act first in the next round or do you want to lay back? The alternatives to "last raiser bets" are not as good. If you make the player to the dealer's left begin every round, there would be some positional advantages and disadvantages for he and for the dealer (who gets to always act last.) If you try to rotate who goes first throughout the betting rounds of the game, you will spend a lot of time figuring out whose turn it is to bet first since people folding during the game change the simple order.

13. There are a maximum of three raises in any round. However, at any point (even in the middle of a betting round) that only 2 players remain in a game, there is no limit to the number of raises for the remainder of that game.

The three raise limit is meant to prevent a player from being 'whipsawed' by two aggressive betters who get into 'who can top this' kind of pattern. The third player can never know when that string of raises will

*end and therefore has no good way to control his risk.
But once it is down to only 2 players, any player can
end the raising by simply calling. So they do not need
the protection of the 3 raise rule. It adds to the skill
required if the last two remaining players each have
at least one opportunity to raise each other once they
know it is now mano a mano.*

14. A check counts as a bet of zero, so a bet after a check
    counts as a raise. A fold does not count as a check or
    a bet. If the player "under the gun" (first better of the
    round) folds, the player to his left, not the high hand
    now showing, is the new first better.

    *A fold not counting as a bet is standard with poker
    convention as is the initial bet passing to the left at that
    point. If the first bet after a check is not counted as a
    raise, it would simply create one more raise possible
    in that round. However, knowing this, the player who
    would have checked (either to reduce the potential for
    multiple raises or to pretend he wants to reduce the
    possibility for multiple potential raises) will instead
    just toss in the lowest denomination chip. So the net
    result of not counting a check as a bet is that the pot
    is increased by exactly one minimum value chip per
    remaining player. This is immaterial to the value of the
    pot at the end of the game, but it does require more
    time for the players, more minimum value chips to be
    available, and more time to split up the pot in a split
    pot game. The casinos avoid this bother by increasing
    the minimum bet or raise to higher levels as the hand
    progresses. However, this is not a satisfactory solution in
    a home game where 15 completely different games will
    be played throughout the evening. It is difficult to set
    a single parameter for progressively increasing betting*

amounts that works across a multitude of different games. And it is confusing to try to have different sets of progressively increasing betting amounts depending on which game a dealer calls. So in the interest of simplifying the betting rules, and in the interest of saving the time and bother of throwing the minimum value chip in for a player who would have just checked, it is better to just call the check a bet of zero and a bet after a check as one of the three raises. Note that high low split pot games, which are extremely popular in home games, often result in one player being very confident he will win one half and 2 or 3 players with a good chance, but not so much confidence they can win the other half. The confident player will want to bet high, but the others, who are not even competing with the confident player, will feel they should stay in and will often 'soak up a raise' with a minimum value chip. So there will already be numerous minimum value chips going into the pot

15. The total amount of a bet, call or raise must be specified in one statement and added to the pot in one motion. String bets ("I'll see your dollar . . . and raise you one . . . two . . . three dollars more) are prohibited both in announcing the action and actually placing the chips into the pot.

   Placing the chips into the pot in stages will delay the game and make it difficult for the other players to verify that the correct amount has been, in fact, contributed. Furthermore, the competing players will justifiably believe initially that the "string" better is betting only the first amount he announces or places in the kitty. The subsequent player(s) may announce their call or raise or throw their chips in before the "string" raiser has finished his little dramatic production. In that case, the string better has caused an error in the hand. Information on future calls or raises has been provided out of turn. Prohibiting "string bets" speeds up the game, reduces errors, and provides consistency with casino and most home game practices.

16. A standard maximum betting limit for a single bet or a single raise (the "standard-limit", say $2) is in effect for all split pot games. A much higher limit (the "max-limit", say $10) is in effect for any single winner game. Of course, if three or more players remain in a single pot game, two or more of them may raise the max-limit causing the third or fourth player to have to decide on whether to take the risk of calling a bet that is twice or more times the max-limit.

See the section on setting the appropriate stakes for more information. In short, the dynamics of high-low and other split pot games are much different than the dynamics of single pot games. In a one-winner game, you want to have high enough maximum bets to allow for a meaningful bluff to cause fear in the opponents. But in a split pot game, you don't want a player to realize half-way through that he is the only possible low hand winner and start to bet or raise huge amounts to the obvious detriment of the remaining competitors for the high hand. Nor do you want a big bluff aimed at an opponent for the high half to force the poor guys going low to get out of the game. If the limits are too high in a split pot game, you will find that many games end early on a big bet, and if even if that bet is called, the two players in for that much money will almost always go for different halves of the pot rendering the entire game meaningless as they each recover their big bet and split the pittance contributed by the others before they were forced out.

17. The higher limit ("max-limit") also applies to all games that contain a forced "match the pot" feature including games with a "match the pot if you lose" feature. If, in one of these types of games, a single pot exceeds the max-limit, arrangements are made (split pots across two subsequent hands, or reduced penalties for losing, etc.) such that no player can be forced *without option* to match more than the highest-limit bet. .

    Regarding pot-matching games, it is important that no one be forced without the option of folding to 'match the pot' or 'pay the price' if the price is higher than the max-limit. The max-limit is there to protect your friends from losing more than they can comfortably afford. It is also there to protect your game from having five or six hours of good competitive poker overridden by one stupid hand. And finally it is there to prevent guys from going broke in their first hour and having to sit out the rest of the night, leaving the rest of you short-handed. Simply set the penalty or pot-matching to be limited by the max-limit. For some games like Guts or Forty-four, additional rounds are played if the pot was matched and the pot can double or triple if more than one player has to match. In these games, you can reduce the 'matching' price and/or you can split the pot into parts that are less than the max-limit and play each of those smaller pots in separate rounds.

18. Any split pot game, by definition, becomes a single-winner game if all remaining players have declared the same way or if there are no possible qualifying hands

for one half of the pot. At that point, all remaining bets are subject to the higher limit that applies to single-winner games.

Once a split pot game becomes a single winner game, switch to the single-pot betting limits since they fit better. Big bluffs are a necessary part of the single-pot game. Note also that if only two players remain AND it has become a single pot game, there are no longer limits to the number of times they can raise each other.

19. A player may 'play light' to complete a hand if they have no chips remaining. The player pulls the amount of any remaining bets or raises for the game out to one side of the pot to create a stack that keeps track of what he owes. If the player wins the pot, he takes all the chips, including the 'lights' stack. If he loses the pot, he must immediately purchase chips from the bank to match the 'lights' stack and give these chips, and the 'lights' stack to the pot winner.

This is consistent with widely known poker standards for home games and is really a help in speeding up the pace of the evening. For a decent sized pot, there is a good chance the player pulling light can avoid the time and trouble of purchasing more chips from the bank by winning the pot. If he loses, it takes no more time to buy chips after the deal than it would have taken during the game. And if he splits the pot, the shortcut in the next rule will make dividing the pot quicker than it would have been had he been forced to buy more chips instead of playing light.

20. If a player, 'playing light' ends up winning one half of a split pot game, the stack of 'lights' goes to the other

winner and the two players split the chips remaining in the pot. (This is simply a math shortcut—it is exactly the same as the 'light' player buying chips to pay off the light, putting the new chips and the 'lights' stack in the main pot, and then splitting the main pot.)

The math is pretty simple, although players always do a double-take when told the big stack of lights go to the other winner. Say there is supposed to be $20 total in the pot. But player A has played light the last two bets and so he has not yet contributed the $4 that those bets should have cost him. So he has a stack of $4 pulled out and set aside from the pot as a counter for that debt. That means that the pile of chips left in the middle of the table is missing Player A's $4 and it is missing the $4 that is being used as a temporary marker of Player A's debt. So the pile of chips in the middle only has $12. The light stack is $4. And Player A owes $4. Now player A and B end up splitting the pot. Both should get $10. The $4 light stack goes to Player B, and the $12 in the middle is split evenly. Player B got his $10. Player A only ends up with $6 in front of him and says, "That can't be right!" But it is. Player A received $10 from the pot but had to pay off his $4 debt. Or, stated another way, Player A could have pulled $4 from his pocket, bought $4 in chips and thrown that $4 into the pot and returned the $4 light stack to the pot. Once he does that, the pot is back to $20 and he will get his half—$10. So he would have $10 in chips in front of him, but $4 less in his pocket. He still ends up with $6. The math works. It just takes players some time to get used to it.

The Showdown

21. If two or more players remain in the game *after all betting is complete*, all players, even the losers, must show all their cards at the "showdown". This is true even in a high-low game or other split pot game with only one player going each way.

    This rule provides consistency with casino poker standards, adds interest for the other players at the table and avoids the 'who shows their cards first' debates. The unfortunate notion that a player reaching the showdown can simply muck his hand if he sees the fully revealed winning hand of his opponent is simply wrong. The winner paid to see the loser's cards just as the loser paid to see the winner's.

22. "The cards speak". All at the table, whether in the game at the showdown or not, are free to point out the best value of a players hand, even if the player himself has miscalled it higher or lower than it actually is. The cards themselves, not the player's interpretation of them are the deciding factor in determining the winner.

    This seems to run counter to the principle of favoring skill over luck. After all, the opposite approach, 'players speak', would demand that the winning player call his hand correctly and know what he has. Surely, that would better reward skill. Let's consider an example: A player gets to the showdown in a 7 card game and announces that he has 3 of a Kind, not noticing that his hand also contains a straight or a flush or even a straight-flush. To Darwinistically apply the principle of emphasizing skill, the rule should state that he takes the consequence of his miscalling his hand, and now it

178

only counts as the 3 of a kind he declared. And there is a powerful skill-based argument to be made for this approach.

However, there are other subtle ramifications of that approach that outweigh the goal of rewarding skill over luck. If the player must always call his own hand, two bad things happen to the overall evening of cards. First, play will be slowed down as more cautious or compulsive players check and recheck their cards before announcing what they have. This slower pacing will be felt acutely at exactly the most dramatic part of each hand—the showdown. So the 'Cards Speak' approach improves the pacing of the overall evening.

Even more importantly, the 'Players Speak' approach has a big negative impact on friendliness and fun atmosphere. Why? Because when "Players Speak' is the rule, any comment by the dealer or any other player about anybody's hand can be seen as helping that player to the detriment of others currently in the hand. This can be the source of bitter disputes and resentment. Here is an example:

Alan, Bruce and Chris are the last players left at the showdown in a big 7-card stud hand with deuces wild. The pot is very large as there have been several maximum bets. Bruce, in fact is pulling light and counting on this pot to save his evening. All bets are in and all three players lay down their hands at the showdown. Bruce has a straight to the Jack. Alan has a lower straight. Chris has three kings and five clubs. Just as Chris starts to declare "three kings," Alan, looking at Chris's cards says "aw crap, Chris, your flush beats my straight." At which point Bruce, desperately needing this pot, gets very angry. Had Chris finished saying "three kings", Bruce could say "hey, players speak, my higher straight wins!" Instead Chris hears Alan's comment and manages to declare his flush, thereby beating Bruce and taking the pot. Bruce feels that Alan cost him the pot.

While this exact scenario seems like it would not happen very often, let me assure you that it happens much more frequently than you would think. And there are countless variations on the theme that also happen frequently. I have seen players get angry when another player makes an innocent remark like "3's are cheap" after seeing a third 3 appear on the board. Pretty soon any comment of any kind about the cards on the table, even the poor dealer saying "4, no help . . . 7's a pair . . . Jack, possible straight", etc. can be criticized for helping one player and hurting another.

When playing in a game where "players speak", there will only be a couple of times in any evening when a player miscalls his hand AND it changes who wins the pot. But there will be hundreds of times throughout the evening when players want to comment on the hand in play, make a joke, give wanted or unwanted advice, etc. It is far better to keep those hundreds of comments coming and keep the pace of the game moving more quickly by using the "cards speak" rule.

Also, casinos almost universally use the "cards speak" rule so it is more consistent with the outside poker world. And finally, it is much easier to teach new games to players if helping them interpret their cards is acceptable and expected. The home game often has players learning new games. It is important that teaching be quick, easy and painless.

Split Pots—Declarations

23. A declaration is required in *all* split-pot games (Chicago, 727, hi-low, etc.)

    This rule emphasizes the skill component and avoids the pure-luck result of a winner accidently winning both halves while he was only playing for one. Furthermore, this rule requires a much more skillful decision on whether to declare for both at the risk of a sure thing. Finally, it rewards the skillful player who can remember the individual betting pattern of each player during the hand, and not just the lead better—in the end, he is making his stay or fold decision based upon finally knowing which subset of players were actually competing with his hand and his half. See the rule on betting after the declaration below.

24. In high-low games and in all other games with split pots, players shall "declare" which half or halves of the pot they are pursuing after the last card is dealt and before the final round of betting. The declaration shall be simultaneous, with each player placing his hand under the table and coming up with a closed fist. All hands are opened simultaneously. No chips in the hand means the player is going low. One chip means he is going high. Two chips means he is going both ways.

    Assuming there will be a declaration (see the rule on declarations, above) there needs to be a consistent standard on whether, after the last card, the sequence is bet-declare-showdown, declare-bet-showdown, or bet-declare-bet-showdown. The preferred approach is declare-bet-showdown. Two bets after the last card, with no new card information is a bit excessive, so bet-

181

declare-bet-showdown is unnecessary. A lot of groups I have played with use the bet-declare-show method. But this is a lost opportunity for more skill to be applied and rewarded.

The "declare" provides significant information to the table and a post-declare betting round provides significant opportunity to use that information to sweeten the pot or to bluff or to hedge your last bet, etc. If the showdown comes immediately after the declare, there is no betting round opportunity to use this new information. Furthermore there is no opportunity to bluff that you are going to go high when you have a possible low straight or flush showing. Look at it another way: If there are no 'surprises' in the declaration itself (that is, all the low-looking hands go low, all the high-looking hands go high, and no one goes both), then it makes little difference whether your last bet was before or after the declare. But, if there are any surprises, you certainly want a round of betting to take place to 1) give the surprising hands a chance to exploit their surprising move and 2) prolong the suspense before having the surprises fully revealed at the showdown.

In general, a 'surprise' declaration can fundamentally alter everyone's assumptions. A weak competitor for low might suddenly find himself the only low. An early raiser who fancied himself the only high competitor might suddenly see that there is a straight or flush (or bluff thereof) that must be overcome. And if anyone has gone both ways, all the other players now have to consider the possibility that the "both way" player might be beaten on the other half of the pot and be out of the competition altogether. To go directly to a showdown is a waste of all this intrigue and the potential application *of skill. So put that last bet AFTER the declaration, not before.*

25. Any player going both ways must win both ways outright. If that player loses or ties for either or both halves, he is out of the game and his hand is not used in any way to determine the outcome of the showdown of the remaining players. (This means, for example, that a player who is beaten for the high hand by a player going both ways, can still win the high half if he stays in through the final bet and one of the low hands beats the hand of the player who went both.)

If a player could declare for both halves, lose one, and still win the other half, then everyone would go both all the time. There would be no risk involved. The win outright (and not tie) rule comes from the desire to make it difficult and gutsy to take both halves. In high low stud, with most cards exposed, a tie for low can be reasonably foreseen as a distinct possibility by a player going both ways. And he should have to plan accordingly. Also, if a tie was allowed when going both ways, it would lead to first splitting the pot, then splitting the tied half-pot. This splitting the pot business gets tiresome for the non-winners to watch.

Now for the more difficult question. Why not reward only the guy who beat the player who went both ways? If player A goes high with a straight, player B goes low with a 7-4-3-2-A and player C goes both ways with a flush and an 8-4-3-2-A, why should player A get to take half of the pot? He would have been beat by the flush if player B had not heroically defeated piggy player C for the low half. Good question. And a close call. I have played in games that handled it each way. I think each way can be defended.

Here is how I look at it, though: A stroke of good (mostly unearned) fortune has befallen either Player A or player B. If C's hand is out of consideration, then A (the straight) has picked up half a pot (instead of 0) just because C got piggy. If we did the rule the other way, and C's flush was used to put A's straight out of the game, then player B (the winning low) would pick up the high half-pot (in addition to the low half he won outright) just because C got piggy. Someone is going to get lucky and we want the rule to reward the more deserving of the lucky players.

Player B was playing for low all along, with no expectation that he would win the high half. He played the whole game for the low half-pot. Furthermore, he wins the low half-pot he contested the whole game no matter what rule is used. So awarding him the high half too seems more arbitrary and more of a windfall. A luckier break.

Player A was at least playing for high all along, contesting for that half- pot. He wins nothing at all if Player C's hand is used to disqualify him. It seems less like a windfall and less "out of left field" for him to get the high half that piggy C has forfeited.

It is a pure gift from the heavens. Do you want to give it to the player who never fought for it and who is already raking in the half-pot he just won? Or give it to the guy who was fighting for it and who otherwise gets nothing? I favor the latter.

Alternate form of Declare, allowing Max-limit bets

26. Rather than using the "simultaneous declare" with chips in the closed hand as described in rules 24 and 25, the pot may be split into two halves *before*

the declare happens. In this approach, the players each put a "high" marker and a "low marker" in front their cards. Half of the split pot is put aside as the "Low Half" while all players contest for the "High Half" which is left in the center of the table. There is a betting round for the high half of the pot, using the max-limit since the high half will be a single winner only. Players do not declare high or low, they simply bet, call, raise or "fold" as they contest the high half. A player who "folds" for the High Half simply removes his "high marker" from in front of his cards. He does not muck his hand, because he may still be in for the "Low Half" when it is time for those bets. When the final "High Half" bet is called (or when all but one player have conceded the High Half), the High Half of the pot is moved to the side, (without the showdown yet to see who has won the high half), and the Low Half is put in the middle of the table.

Another round of max-limit betting takes place, this time for the Low Half of the pot. Players bet, call, raise or "fold" until the final bet for the Low Half has been called (or all but one player has conceded the Low Half). A player who concedes the Low Half does not muck his cards unless he already conceded the High Half, too. He simply removes his "low marker" from in in front of his hand. When the final betting round for the Low Half is complete, players that stayed in for the High Half have their showdown and the winner takes the High Half of the pot. Then the players who have stayed in for the Low Half have their showdown and the Low Half of the pot is awarded to the Low winner.

It is very important that the players use the high

and low markers in front of them to keep track of who is still "In" and who has "folded" for each half of the pot. Instead of mucking their cards to indicate his folding from either half of the pot, the player should retain his cards (which he may intend to use to compete for the other half pot) and simply take the appropriate marker off the table. Players are free to compete for either or both halves of the pot, and are allowed to win one half and lose the other (There is no penalty for "going pig" and losing or tying for one for one of the halves.)

This rule, while requiring a bit of learning and the use of some additional game markers, provides single-winner betting approaches and betting limits to be applied to what are traditionally split-pot games. It also allows for more significant bluffing and more potential misdirection during the final betting for the two halves. A player with no hope of winning the high hand, might make a bet on the High Half to misdirect his Low Half competition. A Player competing for the Low Half must read the betting on the High Half to determine who might be competing with him when it is time to bet on the Low. It took my group of regular players four or five hands using this system before they unanimously and enthusiastically made it the standard approach to every split pot game we play. The early bets, as the hands are assembled, are made at the lower limits applying to split pot games and contribute to both halves of the pot. But once the hands are complete, the real bluffing and misdirection occurs in the much more direct and higher stakes protocol of single pot games, with all bets contributing only to the relevant half of the pot for each player.

27. In any game, if one of the remaining contestants offers to "split the pot" with the other(s) at any time during the game, then that offering player is obligated should his offer be accepted. The other player(s) are under no obligation to accept but may do so at their discretion. If all remaining players agree to split the pot rather than play through to a show-down, the pot is split. If one or more players do not agree to the split, then the offer is null and void and the game continues. The player who made the offer to split is no longer obligated to split but can re-offer later in the game or can accept or reject another player's offer to split later in the game. Note that offers to split can be made in high-low games, but only pertaining to the entire pot. No offers can be made to split the "low half" or the "high half" of the pot.

This rule is controversial, with purists feeling that it is wimpy and antithetical to the win or lose nature of poker itself. However, there are a few common uses for it and some very interesting but less common uses. The common use for this rule is in a high low game where it becomes obvious after a few cards that the only 2 remaining players are going for different halves of the pot, it saves a lot of time to end the game early and split the pot. All future cards and bets in that game are not going to change the outcome any—the two players are going to split at a showdown, so why not make things faster? The reason the offeror is obligated is to prevent him from making an offer just to gain information based on the answer and then back out of the offer and use the information to his advantage. (By the way the 'low' player with a chance at a straight is wise to turn down an offer to split from an obviously high hand—it is quite possible to trick the high hand into fearing your straight so much that they take their hand low and you win the whole pot. Of course, it is also possible to make your straight and win the high or to make your straight and lose to a full house!)

The less common, but quite interesting, use for this rule is a consequence of having a maximum betting limit in a single winner game. Once there is a very large pot on the table, and 5 or 6 out of 7 cards have been dealt to the two remaining contestants, it is very likely that the pot odds will keep both players in until the end even if one player is betting the maximum amounts. If both players recognize that their hands are of about equal value, and that with no way to use betting to force the other out, the only determining factor for the hand will be the dumb luck of the last card or two, they may prefer to split the current pot rather than risk the pot on the dumb luck of the last two cards.

There comes a point in some hands when there is simply no skill play that can provide any edge. To avoid the hand being determined by pure luck, the players may prefer to take half a loaf now. There is no reason to prohibit them from doing so. It is a move designed to minimize the impact of luck on the financial outcome for those players, so it is in line with the principles of the game. No one who has folded, regardless of how loudly they howl about the low masculinity index of the 2 remaining players has any stake in the pot on the table. And it speeds the game up to boot.

Picture a televised world series of poker event. The final table. The two chip leaders are substantially invested in the pot. One is all in. The other has only a few chips in front of him. Four cards are on the table, the 9 and 4 of clubs and the 9 and 4 of hearts. Since one player is all-in, the hole cards are shown. Player A holds the K-10 of clubs. Player B holds the K-10 of hearts. The winner will have all but won the title. The loser will be out of the game or all but out of the game. The dealer prepares to flip the final card. The river. The cameras are poised. The audience holds its breath. But wait. . . .

Player A points out just how remarkably stupid it will be to have a skill tournament decided by a simple stroke of dumb luck. How silly. If the game is really about skill and not dumb luck, says Player A, they should just split the pot and keep playing so they can find the hands where skill can and will have an impact. So they can find out which of them has the most SKILL. Which is the BETTER player. If they let the dealer lay that final card they might as well have flipped a coin for the championship. The World Series of Coin Tossing.

Player A is right, of course. And the hands do not even have to be exactly 50-50. In a game where you want skill to be a deciding factor over a night of 100 poker hands, do you want 50% of your financial outcome to be decided by a 48-52% draw of a single card? If the odds are pretty close to 50-50, and if skill can no longer be reasonably applied to that hand, it should be legal and even encouraged to split the pot and look for other hands to exploit your skill advantage.

And that does not even take into account all of the skill that comes into play when you have to decide to accept an offered split. Or when you should offer one. The "Wanna split?" rule has been in effect in my games for over 25 years. It is only used an average of once or twice an evening. Sometimes not at all. But it adds intrigue and interest when it is used. It is a rule that itself requires skill to know when and how to use it. And despite the complaints of the purists, it is a rule that works and should be kept.

One of our regular players, let's call him Zach, vowed never, ever to accept a split that I offered. Mostly this was because he was convinced I only offered a split when I was afraid my hand was too weak to win and that I used it to get less confident players to chicken out when they should have stayed strong and taken me down. There was some truth to his belief. But I was in a very large pot with Zach one night when the outcome of that particular hand was going to decide whether we were winners or losers for the whole night. The game was baseball with 3's and 9's wild. After the 7th card, I tossed in the maximum bet, guessing he would call me with such a large pot. Which he did. And just before the showdown, knowing I was obligated if I offered, I quickly said, "Do you want to split?" He did not even hesitate, he just said "No, let's see 'em." I said "Five Aces" and laid them down. Now, maybe Zach stuck to his convictions and would still never ever split with me again. So maybe the theatrics of that ridiculous offer to split a sure winner was wasted on Zach. But there were five other regulars at the table, too. And all of them had to know that occasionally I offered to split when I had good cards, too.

At its heart, the offer to split is simply making the other player wager half the pot that his hand is better than yours. He can accept and instantly win half the pot, or he can risk that half, hoping to win the whole thing. It can be an awesome move to make when you fear you are at or below 50-50 to win, but the max bet does not allow a sufficient bluff to force out the competition. If the regulars in the game get accustomed to it, it will add intrigue and skill to the game. But be aware that the purists hate it like hell.

Miscellaneous

28. Some games (where players can choose to pass on cards dealt to them or to trade in cards in turn at the end) have a built-in "dealer advantage" (due to the opportunity of the dealer to act last on key decisions). For all such games, each round of dealing shall begin with the high hand showing, so the player actually dealing the cards does not have an unfair advantage over any other player.

   The dealer having a built-in advantage works against the principle that skill, not luck, should be emphasized. This simple adjustment eliminates that problem and further balances out the luck by having the player with the best cards showing suffer the disadvantage of acting first.

29. Chips may only be purchased from or sold to the bank, not from or to another player. One player, generally the host, acts as banker for all transactions.

   There are a few good reasons for this rule. First, it is an absolute must if you are going to keep the accounting straight in any game where "poverty poker" is in place (discounted or bank-loaned chips). Secondly, it ensures that a big winner has the chips in front of him and cannot hide his good fortune. Players really hate it when the winner can sell chips to the loser and stash the cash in his pocket ("rat holing"). A large part of the emotion of the game is to root against the winner and deny him any sympathy for bad beats, etc. Third, it encourages the winning players to play a bit looser, because they have more chips in front of them and are not trying to ration remaining chips to last several hands. And lastly, it keeps the banker (you, typically, the host) in a position of a bit more control over the game, thus strengthening your position as the rules arbiter, etc. It does require that you have more poker chips in your set, however, so see the section on how many chips and how many chip colors will be sufficient.

30. Dealer antes for all players at the table. Generally, the ante is no less than one minimum value bet per player and no more than twice that. If a particular game (Guts or Acey-Deucey, for example) requires a larger opening pot, the dealer antes the standard ante amount first and then each player contributes equally to build the starting pot to the desired level.

This is a rule that comes purely from the desire to keep the pace of the game moving. It avoids the petty and endlessly repeated bickering over "who's not in?" And it reduces the number of minimum value chips you need to have on the table which also speeds up the game by making banking easier, and splitting pots faster. You could always simply play with no antes to achieve these benefits, too, but the game really requires something to be at stake right from the beginning.

I have heard players say that they have nothing 'invested' in a pot if the dealer does the antes for them, but this is not really true. If the ante is a quarter per player, you have essentially contributed a quarter to the pot at the ante whether it was your turn to deal or not. You only get to play on the dealer's ante because you are that much closer to your turn to ante for everyone else.

And that eventual ante is an obligation that is built bit by bit as the deal comes around to you.

And, in any case, money in the pot is 'sunk cost'. There is no 'investment value' in money contributed to the pot and it is very poor play to consider that money an investment that must be somehow protected. The money in the pot belongs to the pot, and is no longer yours in any way. Your decisions are about whether future contributions are worthwhile based upon your likelihood of winning what is already in the pot and what will eventually be in the pot. The notion of being 'invested' in the pot by prior bets is misunderstood if used as a rationale for further decisions.

31. Fast games (6 cards or fewer given to each player, single pot winner) may be dealt twice in a row by the dealer. If the dealer chooses this option ("Two Times"), he puts up half the ante for each of the two deals.

   This rule allows the simpler faster games to work their way into the rotation. Often a few dealers, or even most dealers at the table will become enamored with some of the games that take the longest time to play, such as Anaconda or other complicated high-low games. A player who really likes 5 Card Stud more than any other game, may find himself playing 5 Card Stud for 2 minutes when it is his deal, followed by five more complicated games that take 10 minutes or more to complete. Eventually, over the course of the evening, he will see that he is playing his favorite game 2–3 minutes per hour or only 3-5% of the time. But he is one of six players and fairness dictates that his favorite game should be played for one sixth of the time.

   After a few hours of this, our 5-Card Stud fan will

stop dealing 5-Card Stud and choose a lesser favorite of his from among the long games so that he gets a fairer share of the playing time. This phenomenon is really a shame because it drives some of the best, most elegant and skill driven games out of the rotation. It also cheats the entire table out of one of the key elements of an enjoyable evening—variety. Varying the length of games, complexity of games, and costliness of games, even the skill level of games, is important to keep the players fresh for each new hand. The shorter games provide a needed change of pace, a refreshing break from the longer complicated hands. Conversely, if everyone were biased toward playing only 5 card stud all night, players would benefit greatly from having some variety thrust upon them by at least one more complicated game every few hands.

So our regular poker games have greatly benefitted from the simple rule that the longer games are played once per dealer, and the shorter games can, at the dealer's discretion, be played twice. If playing "two times", both deals must be the same game with exactly the same rules. This ensures that the second deal can begin immediately after the first pot is won, with no explaining what game, what rules, what's wild, etc.

Eligible games for dealing "two times" must be single winner to avoid the lengthy process of splitting the pot between high and low or other multiple winners. The games must be 6 cards or fewer because that is what generally makes them quicker to begin with—one or two fewer dealing rounds and betting rounds. Any game with 'rejected' or passed cards during the deal cannot be considered a fast game eligible for dealing "two times". The decisions on taking or passing cards simply takes too long.

32. An approximate quitting time is determined before the evening begins. When quitting time is approaching, a final round of deals is declared with each dealer getting one more chance to deal before the game ends. Ideally, this will be arranged so that the first dealer of the night is also the first dealer of this 'last round'.

Having the first dealer be the one that begins the last round of the night ensures that everyone has anted equally over the course of the evening and that everyone has had the same number of chances to choose the game.

A quitting time is necessary to avoid hard feelings. There is nothing worse than having the evening's big winner stand up at 10:30 at night and say it is time for him to go home, leaving the game short-handed and robbing the other players of their opportunity to win back some of their losses. Particularly if you are significantly behind and drove 90 minutes to get to the table.

It is also not pleasant to count on the game ending at midnight, and to manage your drinking, your playing, your money, and your energy to that endpoint, only to find that the rest of the table expects to play until dawn. Furthermore, the consequences of playing later or longer than you really should have will be fewer players wanting to come play regularly. It is one thing to give up their Friday evening. It is another thing to blow off Saturday too because they were so tired or hung over from playing until dawn.

The "last round" instead of a specific set ending time provides players with a heads-up that there are only a few more hands. It also prevents the pleading for 'one more hand' which would be sure to come from the losers and which leads to another plea of 'one more hand' when the first 'one more hand' is finished. And it allows players to do a little housekeeping during the last 20 minutes or so of play. They might count and stack their chips to speed up the end of game banking. They may have a cup of coffee before their ride home. They may manage their betting to arrive at a satisfactory end-of-the night result.

Just be sure to begin the final round 15 minutes or so before the generally accepted ending time. If you generally quit around midnight, call the final round when it is the initial dealer's turn and it is any time past 11:45. If you have passed midnight before anyone notices, it is more important to get a final round (or partial round) in, then it is to ensure that the initial dealer begins the final round. People really need that heads up.

33. Any and all misdeals and all other disputes are settled by consensus of all players, if possible, and by the host, if consensus is unavailable. In general, if a deal or a game can be 'fixed' without obvious, and clear harm to one or more players, it should be fixed. Only if the error cannot be corrected, should a misdeal terminate a hand. In general, if betting sequences can be undone and restarted correctly, or if a series of upcards can be taken back and redistributed in their proper order, then that may be considered a fair resolution.

The traditionalists will really cringe at the idea of "fixing" misdeals, but it is the most practical and reasonable thing to do, if it can be done without raising even more arguments. Misdeals have to be handled more strictly among strangers to prevent the possibility of cheating. In a regular game among friends, however, there is little reason to abandon a game in progress and declare a misdeal if the error is relatively minor and the fix is generally agreeable. Even if a subsequent bet after an error or a whole round of betting has occurred, and, thus, players have gained information they would not have had without the error occurring, it is often the best solution to give the players back their last bets, go back and fix the error and then restart the betting over again.

The reason this is a better solution in many cases is that canceling a hand in the middle causes such strong reactions. Those with killer hands are resentful. And everyone in the hand still planned to win it! So everyone feels cheated out of the proper resolution.

Some "fixes" will be easy. If the dealer misses a player while tossing out up cards, but no one has yet made a bet, simply move the cards back a player so they end up where they belonged. No harm, no foul. If someone bets out of turn, simply make him take his money out and wait his turn. It is, however, a slippery slope between 'easy' fixes and more problematic situations. Maybe the last down card of the hand is being dealt and a player is missed. He speaks up, but the player following has already picked up the down card that would have been his and looked at it. Now, what do you do? If you give the skipped player the card that his opponent has already seen, his opponent knows his river card. If you deal the skipped player a new card off the top of the deck and the card that was supposed to be his would have made his straight-flush he is going to be pretty unhappy.

These tougher situations call for careful handling. First, don't let the dealer or anyone else take unilateral action. Make sure the error is described for the table and *any proposed solutions are generally agreed to before they are implemented. Give particular consideration to the player who was potentially harmed by the error. In the scenario above, maybe the skipped player is offered a choice between taking the card his opponent has seen, taking a new card from the top of the deck, or asking for a misdeal. If the others are agreeable, then execute that plan. The players receiving cards in error cannot object if those cards are taken away from them and given to the proper player. They weren't supposed to get those cards anyway. But if the skipped player chooses to take the top card off the deck, the player who received the first card in error is not given a chance to choose. He has received a random card that no one else has seen and, thus, he has essentially been "made whole". It is not a perfect solution, but it is preferable to declaring a misdeal and starting over.*

34. If a player is prompted to fold by a bet or other action that was done in error, then, if possible and practical, that player may be restored. If, however, he has "mucked his cards" (thrown them into a discard pile), then it may not be practical to try to restore his hand when 'fixing' a misdeal. That player should keep in mind that it was partially his own responsibility to keep track of whether all actions prior to his turn were correct.

Restoring a folded hand should be very rare, but it will sometimes be appropriate and agreeable. Most commonly, you may see this happen after the "declare" in a high-low game. One of the only two players going low, for example, might fold and there might even be a bet or two before it is discovered or realized that the other low player cannot possibly qualify low. That player's "low" declaration was an error and he should have folded before the declare and must fold now. If the other "low" declarer still has his cards in front of him, even though he folded, it may be appropriate to allow him to restore his hand and continue the game as he doubtlessly would have as the only valid low declarer. It seems wrong to have the error force him out when there is no real harm caused by restoring him to the game. But again, there must be general agreement at the table, and if a valid objection to that "fix" is raised, it must also be considered. (The high players' objection that now they will have to split the pot with the restored low player is, of course, not, by itself, a valid objection).

35. A misdeal of face-down cards that occurs before the first round of betting should be resolved, if possible, by rearranging any unseen cards to their appropriate players. If some cards were seen, but by the wrong players, it is acceptable to assign those cards to the player who saw them and to deal new cards to the player who consequently needs additional cards. If a card that was supposed to be dealt face-down is flipped face-up by mistake, and if the players are supposed to receive a face-up card in that game before the first betting round, then it is acceptable to leave the exposed hole card as that player's face-up card and deal him a new hole when everyone else is getting their face-up cards. If a face-down card is wrongly exposed, and if a subsequent up card will not be dealt before the first round of betting, and if the player receiving the exposed card has not yet looked at any of his other cards, that player may reject (and have the dealer discard) the wrongly exposed card. He gets the next card from the top of the deck if he

exercises this option, and he flips the exposed card face down and keeps it if he declines this option.

In the cases mentioned above, there is a fairly easy and standard fix that can be applied to save everyone the time and effort of trashing the hand and redealing. Since there is no real downside (at least in friendly games where cheating is not a danger), and it improves the pace of the game and avoids embarrassing the dealer, these 'fixes' should be automatically applied.

In many cases, a gross misdeal of the cards that precedes the first round of betting is corrected by mucking all of the hands and redealing from the other deck. There will be cries of complaint from anyone who sees that their hands held a great opening card or set of cards, but they have no sustainable complaint. They have wagered nothing, nor lost anything to the misdeal, and their great first cards may have only led to a big losing 2nd place finish for them.

36. At any point until the pot is awarded, there may be an unfixable misdeal. The ultimate remedy, if no better one is available or agreed upon, is to end the game, and split the pot evenly among all remaining players. The *potential* for big winnings if the game were not misdealt is not a consideration for resolving disputes. For example, a player holding 4 Aces when an unrecoverable error happens in the game is treated the same as a player holding no pair. Both have contributed evenly to the pot thus far. And the game did not reach the point where the 4 Aces achieved their value.

From "The Cincinnati Kid"

Slade: How the hell did you know I didn't have the king or the ace?

Lancey Howard: I recollect a young man putting the same question to Eddie the Dude. "Son," Eddie told him, "all you paid was the looking price. Lessons are extra."

CHAPTER 5

The West Chester Progressive System for Player Protection— Poverty Poker

Iɴ Cʜᴀᴘᴛᴇʀ 2, I described how Loss Limit systems (or Poverty Poker rules) are very important to friendly poker games. In fact, I repeatedly stated that:

Loss Limit rules are the most powerful tool you have to ensure that your poker game will succeed as a regular, friendly poker game, and that your players will remain friends after the game is over.

I also described the principles behind such systems and some of the advantages and disadvantages of each of them. Finally, I recommended the West Chester Progressive System for Player Protection which is described in more detail here. Once again, I strongly encourage you to implement this system

203

in your regular friendly poker game to ensure that you can both play poker, and remain friends with your regular crew.

Poverty Poker systems are designed to ensure that friendly games remain friendly and that two conditions are met simultaneously:

1. Players, regardless of how far ahead or behind they are for the night, are risking real money on each bet and thus have appropriate incentive to play smart poker

2. Players are protected by a 'safety net' from losses that would be uncomfortably high or that would force them to go home early

These are seemingly mutually exclusive conditions. Poverty Poker systems attempt to reconcile the two conditions in an optimal fashion to protect the friendly nature of the game.

Our system works by partially deflating the net winnings of players who come out ahead to allow the players who are taking the biggest losses to mitigate the cash value of those losses. Here are the specifics:

1. Each player makes an initial buy-in of $40.

2. If a player loses all of those chips, he may subsequently purchase another $40 in chips for only $10 in cash. He also gets a marker at that time indicating a second buy-in. He may do this as many times as needed, each time receiving discounted chips and an additional marker.

3. A player who has made a discounted second or third buy-in may pay off one or more marker at any time during the game by turning in $40 worth of chips along with the marker, and receiving the $10 cash that he paid for them.

4. No player may buy or sell chips to or from other players. All transactions are through the bank.

5. At the end of the game, if there are no outstanding markers, then everyone's chips are redeemed at face value. If there are any outstanding markers, then the chips are redeemed as follows (and in this order):

   a. Any player with one or more markers gets 25 cents for every dollar in chips he holds and he turns in all chips and markers to the bank. (These players have lost their entire $40 initial buy-in and parts of any subsequent $10 buy-in that they cannot now redeem at 4-1.)

   b. Any player (with no markers) with $40 or less in chips gets face value for all his chips. A player with $27 in chips at the end of the night gets $27 in cash. (These players have lost part of their initial buy-in, but they do not further suffer from deflating their chips.)

   c. Players with more than $40 in chips first receive their initial $40 buy-in back at face value and turn in $40 worth of chips. (These players have won at least some money and the deflation will never affect anyone's initial buy-in amount). Then, the winners split the remaining cash in proportion to the chip values they have left over. For example, if a couple of players have markers at the end of the game, there might only be $90 in cash in the bank to cover $120 in chip values held by the net winners. In this case, each winner gets 90/120 or 75 percent of their chip value in cash from the bank.

6. The net winnings are sometimes worth 100 percent of face value. Typically, the net winnings are worth 60-80 percent of face value. I have never seen the winnings deflated by more than half. And because the initial buy-in is redeemed at 100 percent, only the *net* winnings are deflated at all.

The key to this system is to ensure that the initial buy-in is set at a workable level. It must be high enough that only a few players will need a subsequent buy-in and that only one or two players might need a third or fourth buy-in. On the other hand, it must be set low enough that all players can comfortably handle going home losing 150 percent or even 175 percent of that amount on a really bad night.

With two subsequent buy-ins (three total counting the initial one), a player will have invested 150 percent of the initial buy-in amount, and he will have obtained 300 percent of the initial buy-in in chip value. With three subsequent buy-ins (four total), he will have invested 175 percent of the initial amount and obtained 400 percent of the initial buy-in in chip value. The initial buy-in should be set such that it would take a truly horrendous player or a spectacular run of bad beats to cause someone to need more than three buy-ins.

Is this system as simple as using face value for all chips all the time? No. But it won't cost you a player quitting your game at 8:45 because a few bad beats have tapped him out. And it won't cost you hard feelings among folks who will be working together or living in the same neighborhood long after the card game is over.

Is it socialist? Well, it does smack a bit of Marx/Engels— "from each according to their abilities to each according to their needs." But, after all, poker is a pretty heartless, dog-eat-dog, zero-sum, win-lose, capitalist, Machiavellian game at heart.

So maybe a smidgeon of "share the wealth and safety-net the unfortunate" is a good thing.

But before you purists or even Machiavelli followers reject Poverty Poker "on basic principle," keep in mind this fundamental hypothesis of Poverty Poker:

> In the long run, over a year or two of poker nights with the same regular players, the total cash won by the better players will come out about the same whether you use a Poverty Poker system or not.

This is a bit counter-intuitive. One might assume that the better players, who will be the biggest winners over the course of a year, would be hurt the most by the Poverty Poker System. With only net winnings being deflated, surely they will have more deflated chips than anyone else. Wouldn't they be far better off if every chip they won could be redeemed at face value? The answer is no. They would only be better off if two conditions were true:

> IF they won the same number of chips whether or not Poverty Poker rules applied
>
> *AND*
>
> IF those chips could be redeemed at face value.

But would they win the same number of chips? Not likely. Without the Poverty Poker rules mitigating the losers' cash losses, those losers would lose their money faster, reach their tolerance level for money lost more quickly, and quit playing on bad nights. Eventually, after losing too much for them to afford on a consistent basis, they will stop playing entirely. Consistent losers have both a fiscal limit and a pride limit to the losses they can withstand over time. Whether it is in the short term or over the long run, there is a limit to the amount of cash they will contribute to the game. The Poverty Poker system simply paces their cash losses to a level they can maintain indefinitely.

Over time, the winners, among them, can only win the total cash that the losers over time are willing and able to contribute to the game. In a regular game with regular players, the total available cash the losers will contribute in a year does not decrease due to the use of Poverty Rules. One might argue the opposite (see further below).

If a consistent loser leaves the game after a few nights, he must be replaced. If his replacement is a much better player, there won't be as many lost chips for the winners to split going forward. If his replacement is a poor player, the replacement will leave after a few nights as well, and you will need to keep looking for new players.

Are the Poverty Poker rules simply a clever and disguised method for shearing the sheep of more money over the long term and keeping the suckers coming back for more? Not really. The Poverty Rules do keep the losers coming back for more. But they do it by extending the length of time in months and years that it takes them to lose enough to reach a decision to quit playing. And it is precisely that length of time that allows the poorer players to become better players, thereby further reducing their loss rate.

The riverboat card shark, gambler, and con man, Canada Bill Jones is credited with the classic poker truth that "it is immoral to let a sucker keep his money." Most people interpret that as an ironic statement of how Canada Bill, and hustlers in general, define morality to themselves. Another interpretation, however, is that it truly *is* worse for the sucker to be played for small losses over a long period of time than it would be to get beat quickly and decisively. The quick beat down gives him a better chance to recognize his inferiority in one sitting and avoid damaging his pride and maybe his wallet by getting bled drier over a longer period of time.

But that theory envisions a sucker who cannot change, learn, or improve. In the real world, given sufficient interest or motivation, people learn and improve over time. Certainly in your group of regulars, you want to be hanging out with folks who seek to learn and improve over time. And you want to be pushed to be learning and improving too. The quote that applies best here is not about immorality and suckers keeping their money. It is about learning and improving: "Fool me once, shame on you. Fool me twice, shame on me." Anyone you want to spend several hours with on a regular basis will be learning and changing. And that will keep you learning and changing, too, so you can stay one step ahead.

You essentially have a choice in establishing your "regulars." You can force poorer players to quit the game and keep replacing them until everyone at the table is comfortably at about the same skill level (thereby keeping anyone from consistently losing and quitting the game for fiscal or pride reasons). Or, more productively, you can encourage improvement and allow time for the poorer players to improve. Either way, the fundamental theory holds that the net cash lost by even your poorer players over the course of a year is not significantly affected by deflating the chip values.

So, really, in a game of regulars, what it boils down to is this:

- In the longer term, the sum total of cash available from the net losers is entirely due to skill differential among the regular players, is limited by the losers' tolerance for net losses over time, and is essentially unaffected by any chip deflation system.

- Any regular game with regular players will weed out poorer players and thus produce less cash winnings for the better player over the long term as better regulars replace the poorer players.

- Poverty Poker systems weed out poorer players by giving them time to become better players instead of forcing them to quit.

- If your goal is to maximize cash winnings, you want a game that features new suckers every few nights or masochistic serial-losers of whom you may take advantage. Those types of games are not the subject of this book.

> "If you could lose all of your money again... what would you have done differently?"
>
> —*Unknown*

CHAPTER 6

Skills and Strategies

THIS BOOK IS not primarily about poker playing strategies or tactics. There are hundreds of books available already that cover those topics. However, it is important to the overall enjoyment of your game that your players are conversant in the basic precepts of poker strategy and that everyone continues to improve their game. To help the inexperienced players improve, and to raise the skill level of the game in general, you may want to encourage productive discussions of just-completed hands during an evening of poker. Actually, there will be players who need very little encouragement before jumping into questions or complaints about another player's decisions. So the post-mortem conversations are going to happen after some hands one way or another. As the host or participant in a friendly game, you want these conversations to be as useful as possible.

Most post-showdown discussions center on why a player made the decisions that he did throughout the game. Players, particularly those who were fooled and/or beaten want to know how the winner knew to play his hand a certain way. Now, the winner could simply quote the terrific line from *The Cincinnati Kid*, and say, ""Son ... all you paid was the looking price. Lessons are extra." But more likely, and more productively, they will try to explain their strategy, at least a little. (Because it allows them to show off, which as we know is a fundamental objective of games in general and poker in particular). And that explanation provides a learning experience for everyone.

Outlined below are some basic areas of poker strategy that will come up in these post-mortem discussions. Your game will improve once all of your players are aware of these areas of strategy and are able to put them to use. Some of your players will not have a good grasp of these principles and will need to have them explained or at least pointed out. Even if you and your players are advanced practitioners of the strategies already, you may find it helpful to have a significant portion of the strategic picture categorized in this way to help you think or talk about what happened.

Throwing Away the Trash

It is important for players, particularly weaker players, to learn to fold the hands where their starting cards are poor. It is also important for them to learn to fold if a marginal starting hand does not improve with the next card dealt. There are games, particularly wild card games, where poor starting cards are almost impossible to improve into a winner. Yet players will often go along with the first round of bets or two to see if they improve. Encourage discussion about what the stronger players consider minimum hands to have before deciding to stay on the first round of bets.

Building Pot Size

On the opposite end of the spectrum is the early play of strong starting cards. A fundamental poker strategy is to increase the size of the pot with larger bets or raises early in games where your cards look relatively strong. Many players will bet conservatively until they are fairly sure they have *made* a winning hand. The better players will recognize a hand that has high potential of *becoming* a winner and begin to build a pot even before they get the cards needed to realize the potential. If you are dealt A,A in the hole and a matching queen up in a 7-card stud hand, you want to be sure there is money going into that pot right away. A pair of aces alone will almost never win the pot in a 7 card stud game. But your cards have stronger than average potential to *become* the winning hand, so get the pot bigger now. Sure you will lose some where you get nothing on your next four cards. But overall, you will benefit by sweetening the pot with such strong starter cards. So the poorer players, to improve, need to understand and follow this practice.

Understanding Pot Odds

Let's say you are 90% sure that your opponent has a better hand than you. He bets $2 on the last bet of the hand. Should you call his bet? It really depends on the size of the pot. If the pot only had fifty cents in it before the last bet and now has $2.50 in it, then you should not call. You would be wagering $2.00 to win $2.50 with the odds being 9-1 against you. On the other hand, if the pot has $300 in it, you should absolutely call. You are risking $2 to win $300. You are taking a 1 in 10 chance to win 150x your investment. That 10% chance that you have to win is worth $30 when there is $300 in the pot. But it is only worth .25 with $2.50 in the pot. Poorer players sometimes miss this entire concept and will fold out of a very big pot for a relatively small bet.

Evaluating the Strength of a Poker Hand

There are at least four levels of analysis used by the better players to evaluate the strength of their poker hands. Do not think of these levels as a progression that the players pass through once as they get better and better. Rather, these levels are all active for all players during all hands. (It sort of reminds me of Maslow's Hierarchy of Needs. We don't progress once from seeking physical need fulfillment to seeking self-actualization. Instead, we may be driven at any time by any of the levels of human need depending on our circumstances. But if you have never had to learn about Maslow's Hierarchy that may not a very helpful analogy). During the play of any hand, a player should always be aware of how strong his hand is or might be, based upon at least four different comparisons.

Level 1: Your hand versus the <u>average winner</u>—If you are holding a pair of Kings in a Five Card Stud Game with no wild cards, that is pretty good. The average winning hand in Five Card Stud is a high pair, maybe Jacks or better assuming a table with six or seven players. But if you have only a pair of Kings in a Seven Card Stud game with deuces wild, it is a terrible hand. The most basic level of evaluating your hand is to know how it compares to what it typically takes to win that game.

There are too many variables involved to be able to definitively calculate the exact average winning hand for every variety of poker game. For any distinct game, the hands will be higher on average if there are more players at the table, and will also be higher if more of the players stay in the game until the end. Statisticians have come up with the probabilities of getting particular poker hands based upon a straight deal of x cards to y players, all of whom stay to the end. These analyses can be used to approximate pretty accurately the average winning hand in basic "5 Card Stud" or "7 Card Stud". But the addition of stronger and weaker than average players, or game elements such as wild cards, choice cards, high-low decisions and the like, or players who fold more or less often than average make it impossible to compute mathematically the precise average winning hand for every game you will play in an evening.

But you can and you should develop your best guess of the average winning hand for each of your games based upon your players and your experiences. The more experienced players should share this information with the newer players to eliminate any up-front disadvantage to the newcomers. And everyone, newcomers and old-timers alike, should always remember as they make their betting decisions, to evaluate their actual hand against this experience-based understanding of what it usually takes to win.

In the description of games included in this book, I have listed what the collective experience of my current regular players tells me is the average winning hand for each game. It should prove a decent starting point for you and your players to apply as you play one of these games. You may want to adjust it upwards or downwards for how many players you have at your table and how likely they are to stay to the end. So, scientific exactitude is unattainable. But these experiential approximations will not be too far off the mark.

Your hand versus <u>what the others are showing</u>—Ok, so a pair of Kings is a strong hand in "Five Card Stud". But before you go betting or raising the limit, you need to check what else is showing on the board. If an opposing player has a pair of Aces showing, the fact that Kings will usually win that game isn't going to help you very much. Furthermore, if no Aces are showing, but three other opponents have lower pairs showing, you have to consider those cards, too. Even without trying to analyze their betting patterns or 'read' their faces, the mere fact that they are all showing pairs means that any one of them might have a hole card that gives them trips or two pairs and sends your Kings down to defeat. In order to know the relative strength of your hand, you have to be able to quickly figure out the potential threat provided by the up cards showing in your opponents' hands.

The first level of evaluation, comparing what you have in your hand with what typically wins the game you are playing is the most basic kind of evaluation and the easiest to make. It also is purely objective—it is an evaluation where you are certain of what you are assessing. You *know* your hand. And you *pretty much know* what it takes to typically win the game you are playing. The second level—comparing your hand to the possible hands of your opponents, based upon their up cards, is also purely objective. You can know with some certainty the relative strength of what they have *showing* and the range of possible hands they *might* have, based upon what you can see on the board. Before you even begin any guesswork or 'reading' faces or analysis of betting patterns, you have these two basic levels of objective evaluation that you need to make (and that you need to encourage all players to learn to make). Do the up cards on the board make it clear that the range of hands for this game will be of higher value than the average game? Or, perhaps they make it clear the hands are lower on average.

While these straightforward evaluations of the hand seem to be a pretty basic step for any poker player to do automatically, you might be surprised how many players skip the second level entirely. Many times, I have asked a player when a hand was over why he didn't know his hand was a lock to win or why he didn't see that his hand was very likely to lose. It had been obvious to me just by looking at the available up cards in everyone's hand. Many times, I have said "the best he could have possibly had was a ….." or, "you could see on the board that he had to have at least….." But players forget to do this surprisingly often. They do so because they are concentrating on some of the next levels of evaluating their cards. They might say, "I thought he was trying to bluff me." Or "I knew he didn't have the straight." But they might have forgotten to realize that they were beaten by the pair that was showing. Or that there were other extremely likely hands much lower than a straight that would be good enough to beat them.

I do not mean to imply that this only happens to new players or inexperienced players. It happens to everyone else, too. All of these methods to evaluate and discern the relative strength of your hand are all active simultaneously in each hand you play. If you pay too much attention to one type of evaluation, you might forget to do the basics.

So, while the next levels of evaluation, described below, may be more sophisticated, and *potentially* add a lot of value to your decision-making, they require more and more guesswork. More art and less science. And much more potential for you to be fooled. And they can distract you so much with their associated mind games that you forget the more concrete basic evaluation steps. Always remember to consider the solidly grounded evaluation of your hand versus the average winning hand and versus the hands showing on the board, even as you also consider the more subjective kinds of evaluations that are described below.

Your hand versus what you believe the others are holding— Now we are getting into the deceptive essence of poker playing. Your job is to try to discern or make educated guesses about what your opponents are holding based upon all of their verbal and non-verbal communications and each of their specific actions and decisions. Did they raise, or did they just call after they got that second Jack? Did they show weakness by soaking up a raise with a minimum bump? Are they breathing more heavily? Are they trying to "sell" you one way or the other? How did they play the hand the last time when they had the big hole cards hidden? How often have you seen them bluff in this situation? On and on and on.

If you are observant and perceptive, you may get an accurate 'read' on whether they have the cards they are representing that they have. You may be able to 'feel' it when they are bluffing or trying to slow-play you into a big trap. They are trying to keep a secret or project a false front. They are trying to manipulate your behavior. Your job is to evaluate what they most likely have, using your perceptions of their behavior to help you make the right judgment. Then, if your cards are good enough to beat what you think they have, take them down.

This level of evaluation is highly subjective, of course. You will sometimes get fooled. And there will be other times when you win despite being incorrect in your 'read' of their actions. You may feel they were trying to bluff you only to find out that they were being sincerely confident because they misread *your* hand. It wasn't a bluff, it was genuine behavior on their part based on an error they made. But there will also be times when you nail it. When you discern what they are doing, and why, and you win because of it. And that is where the fun is. You have displayed superhuman skills. You have ESP. You have seen the unseeable.

This is the fun stuff, and it is easy to spend so much time on this aspect of your game that you forget from time to time to remember the basics. But becoming more skilled at doing all of the evaluations at the same time will make you a better player and make the game much more fun.

The projected image of your hand **vs. what you believe the others have**—Always remember that your hand has an actual value and a perceived value. There are many actions and nonverbal communications that you can employ to create a perception or image of what your hand is. You do this consciously by deciding what image you want them to buy into and acting accordingly. And you do this subconsciously by accidently revealing your feelings about your cards. The opponents will very often be evaluating their hands against the image or perception of your hand that you have created.

You may want to project an image of stronger cards (the normal posture when bluffing), or you may want to project an image of weaker cards (the posture you might take to lure opponents into a pot when your actual cards are unbeatable or very strong). Or you may want to show nothing at all and let the up cards speak for themselves until you decide to project an image one way or another later in the current hand or in a subsequent hand.

Understanding the image you project is the flip side of the deceptive essence of poker mentioned above. That third level of evaluation involves trying to read through your opponents' posturing to determine what they actually have in their hands.

This fourth level of evaluation is understanding the image of your hand so you can determine what your opponent believes you are holding. Only by figuring out what he thinks you have can you consider his actions and decisions to help you make a good guess about what he has.

There are two key components to this fourth level evaluation. First, you must determine what image your cards and your actions to date have projected about your hand. And second, you must evaluate the degree to which your specific opponent has perceived and bought into that image. It is one thing to act or bluff convincingly and to have up cards that perfectly support your acting. It is another thing entirely to gauge the degree to which your opponents are buying into your act or whether they are strong enough players to understand the implications of the hand you are trying to represent. Or even whether they have been paying attention to your beautiful misdirection.

In the movie *House of Games*, David Mamet has one of his characters speak the truth known to skillful poker players everywhere: "You can't bluff someone who's not paying attention." Well, starting with that one, let's create a list of related truths.

You can't bluff someone who:

- Is not paying attention
- Is too stupid to fold
- Is not good enough to know what your bets mean
- Only thinks about their own hand
- Is holding all the Aces
- Has never seen you bet high when you actually have good cards
- Can see the pot odds are too good to quit

Now the first four of these situations arise when your opponent is not able or simply chooses not to properly evaluate his hand against the objectively possible hands you may be holding (the second level evaluation as described above) or when he is not able or chooses not to make an attempt to perform the third level evaluation of subjectively discerning or guessing at what you might have. These situations can be summed up by the old saying, "a wink's as good as a nod to blind man".

But none of these situations relieve you from the need to properly evaluate the relative strength of your hand in light of the image you and the up cards are projecting. It does no good to wink or nod at a blind man, true. But your knowledge that the blind man is acting without knowing that you winked or nodded is an important part of understanding his actions.

Furthermore, blindness is a Boolean variable (can only be one of two discrete values, yes or no). Your opponent's lack of attention, or lack of skill has gradations. Did he totally ignore your hand, or only partially? Is he so bad, he never understands what your bets or cards mean, or is he only bad some of the time? You need to properly assess whether or not your opponent has been at all affected by the image of your hand. And take that assessment into account when considering his actions and making your assessment about what he holds in his hand.

Recursive Evaluations

"Recursive Evaluations" is a rather fancy title for a phenomenon well known to poker players. As you try to figure out what your opponent actually has in his hand, you analyze your opponent's actions and his verbal and non-verbal communications. But, you also know that your opponent is *expecting* you analyze his actions. So your opponent will adjust his actions to mislead you further. However, he *also knows* that you are expecting him to make these adjustments, so he may change his actions back again to ensure that he still fools you. Of course, he knows you will expect that too, so on and on it goes ...

When you or your opponent have an unlimited number of words, facial expressions, or body language components to use in your battle of wits, this recursive loop of analysis can motivate a wide variety of creativity in words and actions. When it comes time to make a bet, however, there are limited choices. You can bet the minimum, bet the maximum, or bet some defined amount in between. Or, if you are the last person to act, you can call and go on to the next card or raise and create more betting decisions. In these situations, the recursive analysis becomes particularly apparent.

If he had a strong hand, he would have raised. But he knows I would think of that, so he may have just called to fool me. But he knows I would figure that out, too, so he would have raised, after all. So I know he doesn't have a strong hand and I should raise him. But wait, maybe he knew that's what I would do, and it's all a trap, so I should just call.

Perhaps you remember the movie "The Princess Bride" where the head bad guy, Vizzini is trying to outsmart our hero, the Man in Black (actually Wesley):

Man in Black: All right. Where is the poison? The battle of wits has begun. It ends when you decide and we both drink, and find out who is right... and who is dead.

Vizzini: But it's so simple. All I have to do is divine from what I know of you: are you the sort of man who would put the poison into his own goblet or his enemy's? Now, a clever man would put the poison into his own goblet, because he would know that only a great fool would reach for what he was given. I am not a great fool, so I can clearly not choose the wine in front of you. But you must have known I was not a great fool, you would have counted on it, so I can clearly not choose the wine in front of me.

These situations will come up in a poker game. And sometimes they will result in very funny outcomes and explanations after the hand is over. The smart players will keep in mind that 'reading' the other player and discerning his motivations are an important part of becoming a better player. But, these 'reads' or 'gut feelings' are subjective and imperfect. The more iterations you go through, guessing what he would do and guessing that he knows what you would do, the further you get from objective facts. That is why you always want to keep one foot firmly planted on the objective and knowable levels of evaluation.

> There's the me I see, and the me you see, and the me I
> think you see;
> There's the you you see, and the you I see, and the you you
> think I see;
> There' s the you I think you think I see, and the you I
> think you'll change to be;
> There's the me you think I think you see and the me you
> think I'll change to be;
> All of this figured out, until infinity;
> But, in the end, my Kings up lose if you have deuces, three.

The Series of Hands, the Series of Games

It is fun, lucrative and ego-rewarding to take advantage of all the great mind games and strategy that you can employ to come out victorious in a poker hand. But it is also important to keep in mind that your real objective is larger than a single hand.

Your real objective is a positive outcome for an entire evening of poker. Or even the optimal outcome for an entire series of poker games over a multi-year period.

Most of the time, the objective of winning the hand, and optimizing performance over multiple years will not be in conflict. Actions you take to maximize your odds of winning the hand will be appropriate to both the short term and the longer term goal. Sometimes, however, this will not be the case. Sometimes, you need to take a short term hit for a longer term payoff.

Stated below are two pieces of poker wisdom that are imperative for good players to know, understand and appreciate:

1. If I don't occasionally get caught bluffing and lose the hand, I am not bluffing enough.

2. If I don't occasionally fold a winning hand, I am not folding enough.

Both of these refer to the importance of always playing for the long term, in addition to the short term. Both statements are encouragement about the wisdom of taking a short term hit if it pays off in the long term.

Every time you get caught bluffing, it causes you lost money on that hand. Yet, if you *never* get caught bluffing, then it costs you a significant amount more in the long term. Why? Because your opponents are not all stupid. They will notice that you never bluff. And once they have this perception, they will never call your bigger bets because they will know that if you make a big bet, you have the good cards. You need to be caught bluffing every now and then if you are going to be able to get anyone to call your bets when you have the winners.

For many players, there is nothing more painful than folding a hand in the face of a big bet and then finding out that their hand would have won if they had only stayed in the pot. This causes them financial pain, and makes them feel like they made a strategic error. Some will even go "on tilt" and play poorly for several minutes or hours until they get over their "error". The smarter player, however, will recognize that folding an occasional "winner" is inevitable if he is playing smart, percentage poker.

If you have a 25% chance to win a $40 pot, but it will cost you $20 to see the last bet, do you stay in? Of course, you shouldn't. Do that four times and you will win $40 once and lose $20 three times. You'll be broke in no time. So, the smart player folds. But one time out of four that he correctly folds in the face of the $20 bet, he will have folded the winning cards! The better player will take that in stride, and not second-guess himself with 20-20 hindsight. The weaker player will immediately berate himself for not knowing he had the winning hand.

If you are a player who tries too hard to win every hand and who very rarely folds a winning hand and gets agitated when he does, the other players will pick up on that tendency. And, when they have got great cards they will be emboldened to bet bigger sums against you, knowing that you are unlikely to fold if you have any chance of winning. When they are up against you, they will have no worries about milking a strong a hand. And, over a series of hands, and a series of evenings, you will come out far behind.

So a good player must keep in mind that his tendencies are noticeable over time. And he should adjust those tendencies to optimize his results over time.

Of course, one of the most pronounced tendencies of good players is that they make good decisions on each bet and in each hand. And, as a good player, even that tendency can be used to your advantage if you feel that the others have picked up on it. Once you are known as a guy who makes the smart play all the time, you are in position to set a longer term trap.

Setting Traps

If you are enjoying basic strategy, the various levels of hand evaluation, and the infinite loop of recursive analysis between you and your opponents, you will recognize the importance and the thrill of setting traps. In its basic form, setting a trap simply means acting in a way that motivates your opponent to take an action that is beneficial to you. An example would be checking or slow-playing an extremely strong hand until your opponent makes a large bet into you. You have trapped his large bet in the pot by luring him in, and now you get to raise him back an even larger amount that it will be difficult for him not to call (because the pot odds will often force him into it, not to mention his ego being afraid of being bluffed out of a big pot).

In its most intricate form, the trap can be a thing of beauty. There are opportunities where making a foolish poker move (raising a bet when you should be folding, for example) can trap an opponent into a particular evaluation of your hand. Your move in this hand, combined with all the moves you have made in every hand you have ever played with him, can convince him to a degree of certainty that he knows what you are holding. And, if you get lucky and catch the cards you need, he will never see that coming, because he is no longer considering that possibility.

Maybe an early raise convinces your opponent that you must have trips or a pair, when all you have is an unlikely flush draw. If you catch the flush one or two cards later, he will be so busy betting against your trips, that he won't even see it. Once you have played a large number of hands with smart opponents, a foolish poker move on one betting round can set up a trap that yields huge results in the final betting round of the hand. But if you have to make several foolish moves on several hands before one pays off, that can get to be expensive.

The trap set by unwise poker moves has less opportunity to be financially successful in games with a limit to the betting. In a no limit game, a savvy player may be able to afford a number of decent size "foolish" bets to set up the one situation where he can trick the opponent into losing everything. When the maximum bet is only a multiple (even a 20x multiple) of the minimum bet, it is harder to cover the cost of the several bad poker moves it might take before the cards land right for you to spring your trap. It is still a lot of fun, however, to consider not just the strict pot odds on winning the hand, but also the possibility that a big score can be made on the last bet or two in the unlikely event that things go your way.

The more intricate traps are also usually limited to games where your opponent sees some of your cards. He has to be "putting you on" a specific hand (concluding that you are holding specific cards), not just evaluating your relative potential strength. In "Hold 'Em" or "Five Card Draw", you could be holding anything so your opponent will be harder to mislead. In stud poker, particularly "Five Card Stud" or "Six Card Stud", your limited number of hole cards leads your opponent to draw conclusions about what they must be and how they must relate to your up cards. That is where a "bad" move can convince him of an erroneous read.

For a terrific illustration of the "bad move" trap, I urge you to watch *The Cincinnati Kid* starring Steve McQueen, Karl Malden, Edward G. Robinson, Ann Margaret, and Tuesday Weld. It is considered one of the best poker movies ever made. And the final showdown involves a beautiful trap move carried out in "Five Card Stud" the perfect game for such traps.

In the more modern Poker classic *Rounders*, Mike McDermott, played by Matt Damon, catches his nemesis, "Teddy KGB" (played brilliantly by John Malkovich) in a similar trap. The *Rounders* scene seems more unlikely, however, since the game is "Hold 'Em" and Teddy KGB has no real reason to fall into the trap, given that he can see none of McDermott's cards. The *Rounders* scene mitigates this unlikelihood, somewhat, by demonstrating how McDermott gets Teddy KGB to go "on tilt" and lose his edge before the final showdown.

"To win a bit of money, make your opponent think your hand is stronger than it is. To win a lot of money, make him think your hand is weaker than it is."

—*Josh Avery*

CHAPTER 7

The Games

S KILLFUL POKER PLAYING can require a lot of patience. Those who play poker strictly for monetary gain have no problem with patience. They are already sacrificing enjoyment for financial achievement. They are "working". They will seek the games and the rules and the environments that maximize their opportunity to profit from their work. But friendly poker playing is about fun and enjoyment. If too much patience is required, it begins to erode the fun factor which is at the heart of friendly poker.

The evolution of Poker, therefore, has gone down two separate tracks. For the professional or money-driven audience of players, the game has evolved towards varieties of poker, and rules and standards that efficiently reward skill and cunning with the biggest monetary payoffs. For the rest of us, who just want to have a good time and to show off with our buddies, Poker has evolved to a collection of games designed to maximize fun and enjoyment of the game.

Skill needs to be rewarded in our friendly games, too, but not at the expense of fun. In the friendly games, skill is rewarded to the extent that it allows for more fun and enjoyment. We are happy to slow down the money transfer with betting limits if it helps increase the enjoyment and fun for all of us. We choose to sacrifice some of the pure relationship between skill and financial performance in favor of a relationship between skill and enjoyment. We are not working. We are sporting. It is the friendly poker game players who have invented wild cards, choice cards, twists, Mariah's, Indian poker, no peek, and every other crazy wrinkle that has ever been created to "liven up" a poker game.

We do it because it is fun. Now, fun for many of us still requires that skill pay off in the final bragging rights of who won the most that night. But there is a spectrum of friendly players that runs from one extreme, where fun is defined as competition and skill, to another extreme where fun is defined as laughter, chance, surprises, and lack of stress. Although most of the suggestions in this book apply to all parts of this spectrum, you will probably recognize that my personal perspective is on the skill and competition end of the scale.

Just as the professional players have their own preferred games, designed to efficiently allocate the money according to their hard work, each part of the spectrum of friendly poker players will have their preferred games too. The wildest, craziest games will be preferred by those who value laughter, stress-free atmosphere, chance, and non-competitiveness. The more skill-oriented games will be preferred by those who pursue their fun through competition and sport. The reason that friendly games are "dealer's choice" and include a number of different poker varieties, is that the players all want to have fun, but all come from different points on the "what fun means" spectrum.

Over time, if you host a regular poker game, you will gravitate towards inviting regulars who are closer to your point on the spectrum. And that will make the game more enjoyable for all of you. But even though your group of players will be more tightly bunched on the spectrum, they will not be exactly the same. So, your players will each favor different games.

There are hundreds if not thousands of different poker games and variations that have been invented and played over the past hundred and fifty years. It is not possible to list every game here due to the large number of games in existence and the speed with which new games are invented. Since there is no official rule book or official compendium of existing games, it is possible that the same game may go by various different names among different groups of players.

Yet, it is important to the quality of your regular poker game that you and your players are aware of the most popular varieties and the basic categories into which almost all games fall. This knowledge will allow you to select a set of house rules that can consistently cover the games you play and almost any new game you learn.

Furthermore, it is essential that your group is familiar with the best games yet invented, so that you can play the varieties of poker that most emphasize skill, fun, camaraderie and showing off. This chapter describes the most popular games, divided into basic types. For each game described, there is a ranking given in several categories:

- Time to Play—from the beginning of the deal to the time when the chips have been raked into the winners' piles.

- Complexity—how long it will take to teach the game to new players, how difficult it will be to master the game's subtleties, how many rules there are to remember and apply, and the number and intricacy of decisions each player will have to make.

- Skill Factor—the degree to which the individuals' skillful play or avoidable mistakes will influence the game's outcome as opposed to the degree the outcome is driven by dumb luck.

- Average Pot Size—the extent to which the game tends to build large or very large pots compared to the other game varieties

- Average Winning Hand—the hand that will win half the time or more. [Ok, so this is more of a *median* winning hand, but who talks like that, anyway?] Note: these "averages" apply to games of 5-7 players. The more players there are, the better the average winning hand will have to be.

- Good Starting Cards—beginning cards that good players will want to have before deciding to call or make an initial bet.

There are no "ideal" rankings for any of these categories. Some people love the simpler games, while others favor the more complex. Some players like longer games while others like the shorter ones. The key to a good night of poker is the variety of games being dealt. Any single game can get tiresome when it played over and over with no variation. That is one of the reasons the "Hold 'Em" marathons are much less satisfying than a real, dealer's choice poker night.

Even as you try to emphasize the skill games and weed out games that are more dependent than luck (and, therefore, inherently boring), you want to have some variety involved. Throw in a game with more of a luck factor every now and then to give everyone a mental breather. If you sense that the last hour has been spent in long and complex games, deal a few hands of 5 or 6 Card Stud to change the pace.

Types of Poker Games

The nearly infinite number of poker games can be grouped into these main types:

- Stud Poker—Games where players receive some concealed "hole" cards, and receive other cards dealt face up. Examples are "Five Card Stud", "Seven Card" and "Baseball".

- "Community Card" or "Board" Games—Players receive one or more "hole" cards and build their hand from these hole cards plus some cards dealt "on the board" for use by everyone. "Texas Hold 'Em" and "Omaha", are examples of community card games.

- "Choice Card" Games—Players have choices during the game to discard or pass cards dealt to them and receive the replacement cards from the deck or from another player. "Five Card Draw" is the most well-known example, but others include "Anaconda" and "Push".

- Double Handed Games—A collection of outstanding new games where players play two hands of "hole cards" simultaneously, sometimes with two sets of dedicated up cards, sometimes with a single set of up cards that go with both sets of hole cards.

- Miscellaneous Odd Games—Otherwise unclassifiable, some of these are hardly even poker. But they are popular anyway, so here they are.

Options that Can Apply to Almost Any Game

The large number of basic games contained in the seven categories above grows exponentially when combined with various options that can be applied to almost any game. Some more popular **options** are discussed below.

High, Low or High-Low

Almost any game can be played high-only, low-only, or high-low. In practice, however, it is unusual to see a wild-card game played high-low or low-only. Wild cards can make it too easy to get a perfect low hand.

Many games are a somewhat boring when played low-only for three reasons:

- Pairs, face cards and tens are pretty useless or damaging in a low hand while any card can contribute to a decent high hand. So there are more hands that wash out early when a king or a pair falls.

- There is really only one target low hand. Flushes, straights, pairs, trips and other combinations that add variety and possibilities to high-only games are taken out of the picture when playing low. The result is that there are fewer interesting or playable hands in each deal.

- It is more difficult to bet in the early rounds of a low-only game. If, for example, you are dealt A-A-A in your first three cards of 7-Card Stud, you already hold a likely winner regardless of your remaining cards. So a bet here (or a bluff after three cards) can make more sense. If you are playing it low-only, the best three cards you can get are A-2-3. It is a good start, but, relatively, it is far less likely to win than the A-A-A in high-only. You just don't really know

you have a good low until you actually hold 5 good
cards.

While some games can be almost as entertaining low-only
as they are when played for high, these tend to be the simpler
games like 5-card draw which, truth be told, are not all that
interesting played high-only either.

The High-Low option, however, can add a significant amount
of intrigue, skill and fun. Unlike Low-only, High-Low adds
possibilities, betting rationale and bluffing opportunities to
many games. It creates a very different game, however, reducing
each winners' take by 50% and allowing more opportunity for
weaker hands to sneak in and swipe half a pot. High-Low is
extremely popular in friendly poker games because it keeps
everyone's hands alive longer, and produces twice as many
winners (albeit at lower total winnings per hand).

High-Low poker demands an additional set of skills over and
above what is needed for regular, high-only poker, including:

- Recognizing when you may be the only player who
  will declare one direction or the other

- Evaluating your cards' potential to improve in
  either direction

- Bluffing into players who may not even be
  competing for "your" half

- "Representing" a specific hand AND an overall
  direction you want folks to think you have

"Twist" Cards

A "twist" card is the opportunity to discard any of the cards
in your hand for a replacement from the deck. Sometimes it
is free to twist a card, other times there may be a significant
fee. Usually a twist is added to a high-low game, but it can

be used in low-only or in high-only games as well. (In a low or high-low game, the twist gives a player a chance to ditch a face card or pair that has ruined an otherwise good low hand). There may be multiple rounds of "twist" cards. A twist is most often added to games where only 5 or 6 cards are dealt to each player.

Wild Cards

Wild cards can be added to any game to liven up the proceedings. Wild cards probably were invented to add some possibilities to otherwise "tighter" games like 5 Card Stud or 5 Card Draw. This desire to add more possibilities to dull games was also the driving force behind the High-Low option, the "Twist Cards", the extra cards in 7 Card Stud, and the oddball hand definitions such as Four-flushes, Blazes, and Kangaroo Straights.

Wild cards are an extremely popular option in poker games and there is nothing inherently wrong with them. Contrary to some traditionalists' beliefs, wild cards can add to the skill level required to play winning poker.

Like most everything else in life, the problem with wild cards comes with lack of moderation. As stated above, a 7 card game has already added significant hand possibilities to the duller 5 card stud. Declaring 8 or 12 wild cards in the deck is overkill. If deuces and jacks are wild in a 7 card stud game, you pretty much have to fold if you are not dealt a wild card in your first three cards (and you really should fold even if you have a wild card and your other two are unrelated) Instead of encouraging players to stay, the wild cards are actually forcing people out!

In a 5 or 6 card stud game, however, declaring deuces wild can add some intrigue without destroying the integrity of the game.

Qualifiers

Qualifiers are minimum quality hands that must be obtained before the pot is awarded for the hand. If none of the players at the end of the game have the minimum qualifying hand, then the pot remains on the table, there may be another round of antes and the hand is re-dealt to anyone who had not folded before the showdown.

Qualifiers can be added to high-low games to ensure that a legitimate hand takes each half of the pot. The qualifier prevents someone from winning one half of the pot simply by guessing that everyone else was going to declare for the other half. If there are no qualifying low hands, the entire pot goes to the winner who qualified for high, and vice versa. If no one qualifies either way, the pot stays on the table and the hand is re-dealt.

Qualifiers can also be added to high-only games to ensure that a strong hand is obtained before the pot is awarded. This has the effect of building bigger pots if the qualifier is not achieved on the initial deal.

Extra Cards or Fewer Cards

Extra cards can be added to almost any game to create additional betting rounds and hand possibilities. This is likely how "6 Card Stud" and "7 Card Stud" were born—simple extensions of the classic "5 Card Stud" poker game. Similarly, "7 Card Stud" can become "8 Card Stud", "Texas Hold 'Em" can be played with 3 hole cards or 6 community cards or both, and so on.

Other games, such as "Baseball" or "Follow the Queen" can be played with fewer than the standard 7cards. I would, in fact, argue that almost all 7 card stud games with wild cards become much better games when played as six card games, without the final down card. This mitigates, to some extent, the overly high values of the winning hands and the overly large impact of the last card being hidden.

237

Stud Poker Games

Stud Poker, particularly "Five Card Stud", is one of the oldest and best known forms of poker. It has been prominently featured in artworks, theater, movies, and television. Its popularity in the visual arts, and among poker players for over a hundred years comes from the combination of exposed cards and hidden "hole" cards. The exposed cards, as they are dealt, give everyone at the table an opportunity to gauge the reaction of the other players and to practice their own deceptive behaviors. The hidden cards provide the all-important opportunity for players to bluff, while enabling unpredictable and dramatic endings for observers and contestants.

"Five Card Stud" undoubtedly led to the vastly underrated "Six Card Stud", and to "Seven Card Stud". These simple Stud Poker games, in turn, led to a wide variety of other stud games employing wild cards and penalty cards. Eventually, the "Community" or "Board" card poker games, such as "Texas Hold 'Em, were developed. These Community Card games are essentially Stud Poker, but with all players sharing the same up cards. Stud Poker also was the genesis for many of the "Choice Card" games and "Double Handed" games described later.

So, in many ways, Stud Poker, particularly "Five Card Stud" is the Granddaddy of modern poker. While "Five Card Draw" is probably just as old and certainly just as much of a classic, it is Stud Poker that begat much of our current set of games and practices.

Five Card Stud

Description:

Each player receives one "hole card" face down and four cards face up. There is a betting interval after each round of up cards have been dealt. The showdown follows the fourth and last betting interval.

Comments:

A classic poker game known to almost all players. With only a single card concealed, all players can try to read their opponents' hands by their reactions to each up card that is dealt. Bluffs are a very important part of this game but are limited by there being only a single hole card for each player. Better players may deliberately make costly "wrong" moves on the first few cards to create false impressions that allow them to set up the possibility for a bigger score in a later hand or with an unlikely combination of 4th and 5th cards.

Five Card Stud was the game seen most often in movies before the Texas Hold 'Em craze of the past ten years. *The Cincinnati Kid*, one of the great poker movies of all time, focused on the game of Five Card Stud, as did the outstanding poker scene in *Cool Hand Luke*, which gave Luke his nickname.

Variations:

Last card dealt face down. Wild cards. Twists (exchange cards after 5 are dealt)

Time to Play:	1—very quick relative to other varieties of poker.
Complexity:	1—very simple and straightforward
Skill Factor:	4—Skill will be a very significant factor in player outcomes over multiple hands
Pot Size:	3—Average pot size (4 betting rounds, but few players stay in for all of them)
Average Winners:	A pair of 10's or Jacks.
Good Starting Cards:	A pair or at least one card higher than anything showing.

Six Card Stud

Description: Played like classic "Five Card Stud" except that each player receives two hole cards at the start, followed by 4 up cards.

Comments: This is probably the most underrated poker game of all time. It is significantly better than Five Card Stud in that there are many more possibilities for hand formation and for bluffing due to the two hole cards. The three cards before the first bet keep more players in the game. It is less arbitrary than Seven Card Stud because it omits the third concealed hole card so if someone catches a lucky winner on the last card, at least the opponents have a chance to see it. Furthermore, with only 2 hole cards, a player cannot pull out a completely hidden full house or 4 of a kind that he lucked into on his last card.

Dealing Notes: Can be played with eight players without fear of running out of cards. The first two cards should be hole cards. The game is much different (and inferior) if dealt one down, four up and the last one down.

Variations: Limitless wild card variations, some of which will be covered separately.

Time to Play:	2—quicker than average relative to other varieties of poker.
Complexity:	1—very simple and straightforward
Skill Factor:	5—Skill will be the determining factor in player outcomes over many hands
Pot Size:	4—Larger than average pot size due to 4 betting rounds with more players in
Average Winners:	Medium two pair, but there is a big standard deviation in this game. An Ace-
	High might take a pot once a night, and there will be an occasional full house.
Good Starting Cards:	A pair, 3 cards 10 and over, 3 cards to a flush, or 3 consecutive

Seven Card Stud

Description:	Each player receives two hole cards, then four up cards, and lastly, a final hole card. There are betting intervals following each up card and a final betting interval following the last hole card.
Comments:	A very common and well-known poker game in its own right, Seven Card Stud is also the basis for many wild card variations. It is more well-known and played more often than the underrated Six Card Stud, probably because weaker players like the extra opportunity provided by the extra and hidden seventh card.
Dealing Notes:	With 8 players, you may run out of cards. This will be pretty rare, however, and can easily be handled by checking the deck before dealing the seventh card. If there are not enough seventh cards to go around, you can, by previously announced convention, convert the game to Six Card Stud, or deal a single seventh card face up in the middle of the table that becomes part of every player's hand. (Casinos routinely use this latter solution and seat 8 players at their Seven Card Stud tables, knowing that the community seventh card is seldom needed.)

Variations:	Limitless wild card variations, some of which will be covered separately.
Time to Play:	3—About average relative to other varieties of poker.
Complexity:	1—very simple and straightforward
Skill Factor:	3—Skill will be a significant factor in player outcomes
Pot Size:	4—Larger than average pot size due to 5 betting rounds
Average Winners:	Two pair, Aces over
Good Starting Cards:	A high pair, 3 cards 10 and over, 3 cards to a flush

Five Card Stud High-Low Twist / One Buck Two

Description:

Played like Five Card Stud, except that it is a high-low game and after the fourth betting round (following the 5th card), each player, in turn, has an opportunity to discard one of their cards and receive a replacement. (The twist). If they discard or twist their hole card, they receive a new hole card. If they throw away an up card, they get a new up card. There is typically a fee charged to those who elect to twist. After the twist, players simultaneously declare whether they are playing for high or low. There is one final betting round and then the showdown.

Comments:

A very intriguing game, since anyone can pair up on their twist card and jump from a low hand to a high one. Furthermore, unlike most high-low games, the winning low may contain face cards or even a pair. Players reveal quite a bit by choosing to twist and by which card they throw away.

Dealing Notes:

The last player to twist will have a decided advantage since they see the cards the other players throw away and receive before they have to make their own decision. So as not to give this advantage automatically to the dealer, the first person to twist should be the last raiser from the previous round, or the high hand showing if there was no raise.

Variations:	During the twist round, you can have folks each choose their discard before dealing any replacement cards. This can be done in turn or simultaneously (at the count of 3, everyone points to the card they will exchange). This will speed up the game a little and reduce the positional advantages, but it will also reduce some bluffing opportunities.
	"One Buck Two" is the same game, but with an additional (second) twist round costing twice the fee of the first twist round. Adds an additional betting round and a great deal more intrigue. Takes a long time, however.
Time to Play:	4—Takes longer than the average game due to twist round decisions
Complexity:	3—Fairly complex, as it involves high-low and twist decisions
Skill Factor:	4—Skill will be a very significant factor in player outcomes
Pot Size:	4—Large or very large pot but split two ways
Average Winners:	Pair of Kings or Aces high. 9 low. With a second twist, figure 2 pair for high.
Good Starting Cards:	Almost anything except an unpaired 10, J or Q.

Six Card High-Low / Seven Card High-Low

Description:

Played like regular Six or Seven Card Stud, except that these are high-low games with the pot being split between the best poker hand and the worst. Players simultaneously declare for the high half or the low half of the pot before the final betting round and showdown. A player can declare "Pig" or "Both Ways", to try for both halves of the pot using different combinations of his cards. A player going both ways must win both halves outright. If he ties or loses either half, his hand is dead.

Comments:

This game keeps a lot of players active since it rewards high hands and low ones. There are more straights and flushes than in regular 6 or 7 Card Stud because players who would have folded low cards remain in the hand going low and occasionally draw a straight or flush as they do so. Better players watch carefully and find occasional opportunities to win half a pot, regardless of their cards, by deducing that all other players are going for the other half.

High Low games are very common and popular in friendly poker games, often accounting for the majority of deals during an evening. Conversely, I have never seen high-low games played in casinos and it is not possible to play high-low games for table stakes. With twice the numbers of winners and with its compatibility with limit poker, the high-low game is a very prominent part of friendly poker.

Time to Play:	3—Splitting the pot adds a few minutes to the high-only versions
Complexity:	3—Fairly straightforward once players understand the rank of low hands
Skill Factor:	3—Skill will be a significant factor in player outcomes. The 6 Card version is a bit more skill oriented since it omits the third hole card, forestalling the rescue of poorer players hoping for a miracle.
Pot Size:	3—Large pot with more players in, but split two ways
Average Winners:	7 Card: 2 Pair, Aces up high (but watch for low straights), 8-6-x-x-x for low
6 Card:	Medium 2 Pair for high, 9-6-x-x-x for low
Good Starting Cards:	High pair, 3 cards 10 and over, 3 to a flush, 3 consecutive or 3 below a nine

Baseball

Description:

Played like Five, Six, or Seven Card Stud, but 3's and 9's are wild and if a 4 is dealt face up, the player gets an extra hole card. 9's are free, as are 3's dealt in the hole, but there is a heavy fee for an up 3 if the player chooses not to fold.

Comments:

A well-known poker game in Seven Card Stud format, "Baseball" is actually a much better game played as Six Card Stud. With 8 wild cards in the deck, and extra hole cards, the hands are very high, and the winner often has two or more wild cards in the hole. Playing with 6 cards makes the 4's more valuable, reduces the overly high hand values to where a flush or straight can sometimes win, and significantly reduces the chances of multiple concealed wild cards which makes the 7 card variety so crazy.

Variations:

If a player folds rather than pay the penalty for an up 3, the 3 is given to the next player in turn who faces the same decision. A hole card 4 can be turned face up for a fee and the player receives an extra hole card.

Dealing Notes:

The dealer must pause after dealing a 3 and force the player to make the pay or fold decision before continuing the deal. Players getting a 4 dealt face up get their extra hole card at the end of that dealing round. In the variation where the 3 can be passed, if the dealer folds rather than pay for a 3, the 3 is dead.

Time to Play:	3—About average relative to other varieties of poker.
Complexity:	3—fairly complex until all are familiar with the many rules
Skill Factor:	2-3—Skill is a factor but wild cards cause big and arbitrary swings, especially with 7 card hands.
Pot Size:	4—large pots due to multiple rounds, fees for 3's and single pot winner
Average Winners:	7-Card: Low straight flush, 6-Card: Full house
Good Starting Cards:	7-Card: Medium trips OR a wild card and 2 high or straight flush cards
	6-Card: A wild card or a high pair, or 3 cards to a straight flush

Follow the Queen

Description:

Played like Five, Six, or Seven Card Stud, but Queens are wild. If a Queen is dealt face up, then the next up card and all like it are also wild. However, if a subsequent Queen is dealt face up, then the card following the previous Queen is no longer wild, and, instead, the card that follows the latest Queen is wild. If the last up card in the game is a Queen, then only Queens are wild. So, if a Queen is dealt in the first round of up cards and the next card dealt is a 7, then Queens and 7's are wild. But if a second Queen comes up in a later round of dealing and is followed by a 9, then 7's are no longer wild, but Queens and 9's are now wild.

Comments:

Although most often played in Seven Card Stud format, "Follow the Queen" is actually a much better game played as Six Card Stud. With 8 wild cards in the deck, the hands are very high, and the winner often has two or more wild cards in the hole. Playing with 6 cards reduces the overly high hand values to where a flush or straight can sometimes win, and significantly reduces the chances of multiple concealed wild cards which makes the 7 card variety so crazy. The fact that the wild cards can change makes the game rather arbitrary.

Variations:	This game can be played with only the cards that follow a Queen being wild, not the Queens themselves. This makes the game a bit less crazy, but it is still difficult to know how to bet when the wild card is unknown. Fees can be added for wild cards and increased with every Queen dealt.
Time to Play:	3—About average relative to other varieties of poker.
Complexity:	3—fairly complex due to the changing wild cards
Skill Factor:	2—Skill is a factor but wild cards cause big and arbitrary swings, especially with 7 card hands, and skill is difficult to apply when the final wild cards are unknown.
Pot Size:	3—Average sized pots unless fees are applied
Average Winners:	7-Card: Low straight flush, 6-Card: Full house
Good Starting Cards:	7-Card: Medium trips OR a Queen and 2 high or straight flush cards
	6-Card: A Queen or a high pair, or 3 cards to a straight flush

Low Hole / Roll Your Own or Mexican Stud

Description: **"Low Hole"** is played like Five, Six, or Seven Card Stud, but the lowest hole card held by a player (and all others like it) are wild for that player. In **"Roll Your Own"**, each card normally dealt face up to players, is, instead, dealt face down, after which the players choose which hole card to turn face up for that round. In the 7 card version, the last card dealt (the third hole card) can change a player's wild card if it is lower than the other two hole cards. For that reason, players may, for a fee, choose to receive their 7th card face up.

Comments: Everybody gets a wild card! And many players, especially in the "Roll Your Own" variety, will end up with a pair of wild cards. **"Low Hole Roll Your Own"** is more popular than simple **"Low Hole"**. In "Roll Your Own", a lot can be communicated by which cards players choose to turn up. While there will be more players with two cards wild, it will be rare for a player to have three wild cards in their hand, particularly with only 5 or 6 cards. Keep in mind that a player with 2 wild cards cannot make a full house without really having at least 4 of a kind.

Time to Play:	3—About average relative to other varieties of poker.
Complexity:	3—fairly complex due to the changing wild cards
Skill Factor:	2—Skill is a factor but wild cards cause big and arbitrary swings, especially with 7 card hands.
Pot Size:	3—Average sized pots unless fees are applied
Average Winners:	7-Card: Four of a kind. 6-Card: High flush. 5-Card: Trips.
Good Starting Cards:	7-Card Roll Your Own: a pair or 3 straight flush cards.
	6-Card Roll Your Own: a pair or 3 to a flush
	5-Card Roll Your Own: a pair or an Ace or King up.

Other Stud Games

There are a large number of other stud games that differ from those described previously only in which cards are wild or in slight variations of the dealing. Here are some of the ones you may run into:

Woolworths: 5's and 10's wild. (Woolworths was a 5&10 store, get it?)

Dr. Pepper: 10's, 2's, and 4's wild. (Apparently Dr. Pepper had an ad campaign that featured the time <u>ten to four</u> in the afternoon as "Dr. Pepper" time. With 12 wild cards, 5 aces might only get you a tie!)

Kankakee: The first up card (and all others like it) to each player is wild for that player.

Shifting Sands: Played like **"Roll Your Own"**, except the first card turned up by each player (and any others like it) is their wild card for the hand.

Chicago: Also called **"High Chicago"**. Half the pot goes to the best poker hand, the other half goes to the highest spade dealt in the hole. In **"Low Chicago"**, the pot is split between the high poker hand and the lowest spade dealt in the hole. In some forms of **Chicago**, the pot is split three ways among the high hand, the high spade in the hole and the lowest spade in the hole. In yet other versions of **Chicago**, players need *both* the high hand and the spade in the hole to win or the game is redealt.

Black Mariah: The game does not end until a player has BOTH the best poker hand AND the Queen of Spades.

If no player has both, the pot remains in the table and the hand is redealt. In a variant, that is also called "Black Mariah", the Queen of Spades is not needed to win, and, instead, if the Queen of Spades is dealt up to any player, the game ends and is redealt.

Sequence: If a two is dealt face up during the game, then twos are wild. If, after a two is dealt face up, a three is dealt face up, then twos are no longer wild and threes are wild. And so on . . .

"Community Card" Games

"Community Card" games are very similar to Stud Poker games. The key difference is that, after receiving their hole cards, players do not receive their own dedicated up cards. Instead, several up cards are dealt in the middle of the table (or "on the board"), and each player uses some of his hole cards and some of these shared "community" cards to form his poker hand.

Community Card games allow for many more simultaneous players since everyone shares the up cards. While a game of "Seven Card Stud" can be dealt to a maximum of 7 players at a time, for example, a single hand of "Texas Hold 'Em" could theoretically be dealt to over 20 players, if there were a table big enough to accommodate them.

A common characteristic of Community Card Games is that the strength of the hand it will take to win will vary significantly according to the quality of the shared cards that are dealt on the board. In a hand where the board features wild cars or pairs or three or four of a suit, it will take a much stronger poker hand to win. If the cards on the board are unrelated to each other, a weaker hand may prevail.

One potential negative feature of Community Card games is

that all of a player's dedicated cards are hidden. This provides a lot less information to the other players as the hands develop. In Stud poker, after the first hole card(s), you see each player react to the additional cards that fall into his hand. A hand can begin to look like a straight, or look like a flush, or maybe it contains a pair, so it looks like it may be trips, etc. The visibility of some of the player's dedicated cards gives him the opportunity to represent particular hands. And it allows the other players to rule out some combinations for him and to narrow their interpretation of his hand to a few options. Conversely, in Community Card games, if the board makes a straight or a flush a possibility, then *everyone* might have a straight or a flush. In a sense, everyone has the same range of possible hands.

In a "Hold 'Em" game among professionals or experts, you might be able to draw specific conclusions about an opponent's hole cards based solely on their betting patterns. But in a home game or a friendly game, where skill levels are all over the place, where there are limits to the betting amounts, and where no one specializes in a single variety of poker, there is very little way to draw such specific conclusions based only upon their betting pattern. You are left with a more limited guess as to whether the opponent's hand is strong or weak. The up cards in Stud Poker, or the number of cards drawn in Draw Poker, or which cards are passed or discarded in the "Choice Card" games which will be discussed in the next section—all of these provide opportunity to evaluate a player's actions and discern something specific about his down cards. But all of those potential clues are missing in the Community Card games.

Still, Community Card games are very popular among home players. I suspect some players rather like the simpler evaluation of strong vs. weak that the Community Card games leaves everyone. It may seem more straightforward and direct and less about the bells and whistles and fancy complications.

Limit Texas Hold 'Em

Description:

Friendly poker conventions do not support no-limit games for reasons detailed elsewhere in this book. However, people still like playing "Hold 'Em" and it can fit into your friendly poker game if it adheres to the same betting limits as the rest of your games. Just like on TV, each player receives two hole cards followed by a round of betting. Unlike on TV, since you won't be playing hundreds of hands in a row, it is not appropriate to have the blind bets. Just let the person to the dealer's left bet first on the first round, and he or the last raiser can lead the betting on subsequent rounds. A "flop" of three community cards is dealt next, followed by a betting round, a fourth community card ("fourth street") a betting round, the fifth community card ("the river") and the final bet.

Comments:

You will need to reinforce that, no, the house rules are not suspended so that you can comply with World Series of Poker betting rules. Texas Hold 'Em is just another variety of poker and it will be played consistently with every game you play. Obviously, with betting limits, it is harder to force everyone out with a big bet. Just play it like all the other games.

Dealing Notes:	There is no need to "burn" a card before dealing the community cards. That is mostly casino flash, and some anti-cheating protection that your friendly game should not require. Burning the cards doesn't hurt any, but do not get dragged into debates about whether not burning a card caused a misdeal. The first card turned up is the valid upcard whether a card was burned first or not.
Variations:	Hold 'Em is an intriguing game to play high-low.
Time to Play:	2—A little faster than the average game, even though players see 7 total cards
Complexity:	1—Very simple and straightforward
Skill Factor:	3—Skill will be a very significant factor in player outcomes
Pot Size:	3—Average pot size (4 betting rounds, but few players stay in for all of them)
Average Winners:	Two pair including highest board card—better if board has pairs, straights or flush draws
Good Starting Cards:	Pair, Ace, face card suited, suited connectors

Omaha

Description:

"Omaha" is very similar to "Texas Hold 'Em". However, each player receives four hole cards instead of two. The five community cards are dealt exactly as in "Hold 'Em". The players, in the showdown, must use exactly two of their four hole cards combined with exactly three of the five community cards.

Comments:

The extra two hole cards inflate the hand values. But the restriction to using exactly two of them deflates the hand values, as a player loses several possible combinations. To make a flush or a straight, a player must have two of the cards in his hand and three on the board. Players find it difficult to evaluate their completed hand properly, much less calculate odds of improving between the flop and the river.

Variations:

Omaha is often played high-low and, if a player goes both ways, he may use different hole cards and community cards for his high hand than he uses for his low. But each hand must contain two hole cards and three community cards. Ties (which cause a player going both ways to lose all) are common since only two of the cards are unique to the players' hand.

Time to Play:	3—About average relative to other varieties of poker.
Complexity:	4—Fairly complex due to the tricky rule on exactly 2 hole cards being used
Skill Factor:	4—Skill will be a significant factor in player outcomes
Pot Size:	3—Average pot size (4 betting rounds, but few players stay in for all of them)
Average Winners:	Trips—better if board has pairs, straights or flush draws
Good Starting Cards:	High Pair, 3 cards 10 or higher, two good sets of connecters

Cincinnati

Description:

Each player gets five cards face down. There are five community cards dealt as well. Each player makes their best hand using any combination of hole cards and community cards. In the wilder version of this game, there are six betting intervals, one after the hole cards and one after each community card is exposed. In slightly more conservative versions, the number of betting intervals is held to four by exposing the community cards as in "Hold 'Em" with a flop of three, then a fourth and then the river. It can also be played with a flop of two, then the third, then a final flop of two.

Comments:

Hands are very strong, since there are ten cards to choose among, and stronger still if the board contains pairs or trips. This game builds a big pot.

Dealing Notes:

It is important to decide ahead of time and announce how many betting intervals there will be and how the community cards will be exposed.

Variations:

Can be played with different number of hole cards or community cards. This game lends itself to high-low with different combinations of cards being allowed for players going both ways.

Time to Play:	4—Takes longer than the average game if six betting intervals are used
Complexity:	2—Fairly straightforward
Skill Factor:	2—Skill will be a factor but bad beats will occur as too many players will stay in, some of whom will occasionally get lucky ("suck out")
Pot Size:	5—Can build very large pots with 6 betting rounds and many players staying in
Average Winners:	Full House. If a pair appears on the board, the full house has to be that high.
Good Starting Cards:	Trips, high two pair, pair of aces

Iron Cross

Description:

As in "Cincinnati", each player receives five cards face down, and there are five community cards dealt as well. The community cards, however, are dealt in the shape of a cross, three cards long and three cards wide (the middle card is part of both the vertical column and the horizontal row of three). Each player will make his best poker hand out of any combination of his five hole cards and either the horizontal row or the vertical column of the community card "cross". There can be six betting intervals, one after the hole cards and one after each community card is exposed. In more conservative versions, the number of betting intervals can be five (turn a community card before betting), or four (turn two community cards each time, and then the middle card before the last bet).

Comments:

Hands are stronger than "Seven Card Stud" since there are eleven cards to choose among, and stronger still if the board contains pairs or flush or straight draws. This game builds a fairly large pot if five or six betting rounds are used.

Dealing Notes:

It is important to decide ahead of time and announce how many betting intervals there will be and how the community cards will be exposed.

Variations:	This game lends itself to high-low with different combinations of cards and/or different rows of community cards being allowed for players going both ways. This game is sometimes played with the middle card in the cross and others like it being wild (but if you play it this way, you should turn the middle card first so players can apply more skill throughout the game).
Time to Play:	4—Takes longer than the average game if six betting intervals are used
Complexity:	3—Fairly straightforward
Skill Factor:	3—Skill will be a significant factor in player outcomes
Pot Size:	4—Larger than average pot size due to 4+ betting rounds and more players in
Average Winners:	Flush. If there's a pair on board, a full house is likely
Good Starting Cards:	Two pair, four to flush, pair of Aces or Kings

Other Shapes

There are a large number of other simple Community Card games that differ from each other only in the number of hole cards received, the number of cards "on the board", the shape in which they are arranged and the rules for which can be used in a hand. Here are some of the ones you may run into:

Tic Tac Toe Poker / Hollywood Squares: Players receive five hole cards (or four, or three) and there are nine cards dealt on the board in a 3 x 3 grid. Players can use any horizontal, vertical, or diagonal row of three cards on the board to make their best hand. To avoid having ten betting rounds the board is usually exposed in this order: top row, betting interval, bottom row, betting interval, middle row but not the middle card, betting interval, the middle card (center square for you Paul Lynde fans)*. The middle card and all like it are sometimes played as wild.

---

* Paul Lynde was an actor who is most famous for filling the center square in the tic-tac-toe based TV Game Show, Hollywood Squares. Peter Marshall was the game show host. Lynde was famous for acerbic responses to the questions the contestants had to answer. Examples:

Peter Marshall: When you pat a dog on its head he will usually wag his tail. What will a goose do?

Paul Lynde: Make him bark.

Peter Marshall: Is it possible for the puppies in a litter to have more than one daddy?

Paul Lynde: Why, that bitch!

Peter Marshall: If the right part comes along, will George C. Scott do a nude scene?

Paul Lynde: You mean he doesn't have the right part?

Merry Go Round: Also called "**Wheel**", "**Circle**", "**Clock**", etc. Two, three, or four hole cards are given to each player and five, six, seven, or even eight community cards are dealt on the board in the shape of a circle. Players make hands by combining their hole cards with any three community cards that are adjacent in the circle. In some varieties, players must play a fixed number of their hole cards.

Otis Elevator: This game has the community cards dealt in two columns of three cards each, plus one card somewhere between the columns. This in-between card is the "Elevator" and the two columns of cards form the elevator shaft. The players can think of the "Elevator" card as moving to complete the top, middle or bottom row of three cards on the board. Players use their hole cards in combination with any of the three horizontal rows of cards (top floor, middle floor, bottom floor), to make their best hand. The Elevator card can be used in any row, but does not have to be used in the final hand. Variations include a four or five story elevator, different numbers of hole cards, and/or constraints on how many hole cards must be used. And, of course, some play that the Elevator card and all like it are wild.

Double Board: "Hold 'Em", "Cincinnati", and other community games may be dealt with two sets of community cards. The flops or card exposing is performed on both boards at the same time. Players use their hole cards to make their best hand from either of the two boards, following the rules and restrictions of the regular (non-double-board) variety of the game. Players may not use cards from both boards, unless they are going both ways in a high-low variation, in which case, they can use one board for high and one board for low.

Twin Beds: In "Twin Beds", which is often played high-low, the community cards are dealt in two columns of five cards. The players, who receive two, three, or four hole cards, make their best poker hands by combining one or two of their hole cards with the five cards in either of the two columns. The community cards are exposed two at a time (one from each column) with a betting round after each exposure. Players going both ways in a high-low version are allowed, but not required, to use different hole cards for high than they do for low, and to use different columns of community cards for high than they do for low. When played high-low, with six betting rounds, this game attracts a lot of "action" and can build a significant pot.

Draw Poker Games

Five Card Draw

Also Known As:	"Guts to Open", "Draw Poker" or, if played low-only, "Lowball"
Description:	Players are dealt five cards face down. There is a round of betting. Players, in turn, choose to discard up to three cards (four if they show an Ace) and receive the same number of cards from the deck. There is a final round of betting, followed by the showdown.
Comments:	One of the oldest forms of poker, and one with which almost every poker player will be familiar. With all the cards being concealed until the showdown, the players must ascertain what their opponents' hold by carefully watching the size of their bets, and the number of cards they discard during the draw. Exchanging one card may indicate a player trying to fill a straight or flush or trying to improve two pair. Exchanging two may indicate a player holding trips or maybe holding a low pair with a high kicker. Drawing what is called "an honest three" likely means the player is drawing to a pair.

This is the game that spawned the expression "never draw to an inside straight". It is also the game featured in the great poker scene in "The Sting".

Dealing Notes:	With more than six players, it may be necessary to shuffle discards in order to provide the last player their requested number of draw cards.
Variations:	"Jacks or Better" requires that the hand be re-dealt if no one holds at least a pair of Jacks at the start. "Progressive" requires Queens or better to open the betting on the second deal, and Kings or better after that.
Time to Play:	1—very quick relative to other varieties of poker.
Complexity:	1—very simple and straightforward
Skill Factor:	3—Skill will be a significant factor in player outcomes
Pot Size:	1—Small pot size due to only 2 betting rounds
Average Winners:	Two pair, Jacks over
Good Starting Cards:	Pair of 8's or higher

Five Card Draw—Jacks to Open, Trips to Win

Description:

Played the same as standard Five Card Draw, except that a player must have at least a pair of Jacks to open the betting and the winning hand must be at least three of a kind. A player holding Jacks or better is not required to open. The game is re-dealt if there are no openers or if no one qualifies to win. However, players who fold at any time are not eligible for new cards if the hand is re-dealt. There may be a subsequent ante among active players for each deal.

Comments:

This game can go on for several deals and can build a substantial pot if it does. Players holding poor cards may play anyway and even call the final bet hoping that the best hand will not meet the three-of-a-kind qualifier and that the hand will be re-dealt. This means that a player who eventually gets the qualifying high hand will often get a good return on his final bet.

Dealing Notes:

Hands where no one can open are fairly common, so the second deck should be shuffled and ready at all times to keep the game moving.

Time to Play:

4—Will often take a long time to achieve qualifiers, but sometimes end quickly.

Complexity:	2—Fairly straightforward
Skill Factor:	2—Skill will be a factor but qualifiers make the pot arbitrarily large
Pot Size:	4—Large pot size due to multiple deals and incentives to stay.
Average Winners:	High three-of-a-kind.
Good Starting Cards:	A Pair. Many players start with nothing, not wanting to fold and be out of a potentially big pot with multiple re-deals.

Jacks or Back

Description:	Played like classic "Five Card Draw— Jacks or Better to Open" but instead of re-dealing the hand if no one can open, the hand converts to Lowball (Five Card Draw, low-only). Note that a player holding a pair of Jacks or better is not required to open the betting. Sometimes there is a compulsory second ante as the game converts to Lowball. Once the game is declared converted to Lowball (and second antes are obtained from all players, if that option was in effect), the initial round of betting begins again with the player on the dealer's left.
Comments:	The presumption is that if no one has Jacks or better, the competition should be pretty good for the best low hand.
Dealing Notes:	It will be rare that you run out of draw cards, since many fewer cards will be drawn to low hands.
Time to Play:	1—very quick relative to other varieties of poker.
Complexity:	2—fairly straightforward
Skill Factor:	3—Skill will be a significant factor in player outcomes
Pot Size:	1—Small pot size due to only 2 betting rounds

Average Winners:	Two pair, Jacks over, if the game stays high. 9-6-x-x-x if played low.
Good Starting Cards:	High Pair if the game stays high, four unmatched cards below a 9 if played low

Five Card Draw—Draw Twice

Description: Played like "Five Card Draw" but with a
                     second round of discards and draws and
                     a corresponding third round of betting.

Comments: The hands will improve some and the
                     pots will be larger.

Dealing Notes: Even with only four or five players, it
                     may be necessary to shuffle the discards
                     (sometimes two different times) in order
                     to provide each player their requested
                     number of draw cards.

Variations: Jokers wild, or other wild cards which
                     increase the value of the average winning
                     hands and the starting cards one should
                     hold before betting and drawing.

Time to Play: 2—quicker than average relative to
                     other varieties of poker.

Complexity: 2—fairly straightforward

Skill Factor: 3—Skill will be a significant factor in
                     player outcomes

Pot Size: 2—Modest pot size due to only 3 betting
                     rounds

Average Winners: Two pair, Jacks over

Good Starting Cards: Pair of 8's or higher

Other "Choice Card" Games

Reject (aka "Push", "Take It or Leave It")

Description:

A bit like "Five Card Stud High-Low" but with choice cards. Players are dealt a single hole card. There are then four rounds of face up cards followed by betting intervals. In each round of up cards, the players have the choice of accepting the first up card offered to them or rejecting it and pushing it towards the player on their left (who then has the same choice). Once an offered choice card is accepted by a player, the dealer first "backfills" cards from the deck to any previous player(s) who rejected that card, before continuing the deal by offering a choice card to the next player who has yet to receive cards that round. If the last player to be offered a card on a round rejects his offered choice card, that card is discarded from the game.

The first round of up cards begins with the player on the dealer's left, but in subsequent rounds, to avoid a dealer advantage, the deal begins with the high hand showing.

The game is played high-low. After all players have their five cards, there is a twist round where (again beginning with the high hand showing) players can choose to exchange any of their cards for a new card from the deck (for a fee equal to the standard large bet). They do not get a choice on this replacement card and it is dealt up unless the hole card is exchanged in which case it is dealt face down.

Comments:

This is a terrific game, with a lot of available information, the opportunity for players to have some control over the cards they get, and sudden reversals of direction (a player who has been trying to build a low hand, pairs up his Ace, for example). It is also a reasonably straightforward game that can be used to gradually introduce new players to "Choice Card" games before hitting them with more complicated versions.

Dealing Notes:

This can be a tricky game to deal. The dealer must be careful not to follow in the habit of dealing the up cards too quickly. If a second up card is exposed before a player has decided on his choice card, it is a misdeal that is difficult to correct. In each round, the dealer be careful to note when a choice card is accepted and to go back and deal the mandatory replacement card to everyone who rejected that choice card on the round.

Dealing to the high hand first eliminates what could otherwise be a significant dealer advantage.

Variations:	There can be a modest fee installed for each time a player rejects a card ("pay to pass"), or, instead, there can be a fee for each time a player chooses to accept the first card offered ("pay to keep"). The fee can escalate through the rounds.
Time to Play:	4—Takes longer than the average game.
Complexity:	4—Fairly complex to teach, play and deal
Skill Factor:	5—Skill will be the determining factor in player outcomes
Pot Size:	4—Large or very large pot but split two ways
Average Winners:	Two Pair—9's over for high, and 9-6-x-x-x for low
Good Starting Cards:	Pair, 2 below a 9, suited connectors, two face cards

Indecision

Description:

A "Six Card Stud High-Low" game with choice cards and fees. Each player receives two hole cards. There are four rounds of face up cards, each followed by a betting interval. The players make their best high and/or low hand using any five of their six cards.

In each round of up cards, the players are offered a choice of accepting the first up card offered to them or rejecting it and pushing it towards the player on their left (who then has the same choice). Once an offered choice card is accepted by a player, the dealer first "backfills" cards from the deck to any previous player(s) who rejected that card, before continuing the deal by offering a choice card to the next player who has yet to receive cards that round. If the last player to be offered a card on a round rejects his offered choice card, that card is discarded from the game.

The fee for rejecting a card is equal to the minimum bet or ante on the first round and increases by that amount each round thereafter.

Players may play for high, low, or both ways. If going both ways, they may use a different combination of their cards for each half of the pot. But they must

279

win outright (not tie) both ways or their entire hand is void.

Comments:

This is a fascinating game, with a lot of available information and the opportunity for players to have some control over the cards they get. The name "Indecision" comes from the frequency with which the game forces difficult decisions on choice cards when their hand has different possibilities. The very act of being indecisive can communicate a lot about your hand to your opponents.

Dealing Notes:

This can be a tricky game to deal. The dealer must be careful not to follow in the habit of dealing the up cards too quickly. If a second up card is exposed before a player has decided on his choice card, it is a misdeal that is difficult to correct. In each round, the dealer must be careful to note when a choice card is accepted and to go back and deal the mandatory replacement card to everyone who rejected that choice card on the round.

Dealing to the high hand first eliminates what could otherwise be a significant dealer advantage.

Variations:

This game can be played with "qualifiers" so that if no one makes a decent low hand, the game converts to high-only with a single winner. (The debate rages over whether "qualifiers" adds skill by preventing someone from "falling into" a low hand, or whether it subtracts skill by not allowing smarter players to "sneak into" an uncontested low pot.)

Time to Play:	4—Takes longer than the average game.
Complexity:	4—Fairly complex to learn, play and deal
Skill Factor:	5—Skill will be the determining factor in player outcomes
Pot Size:	4—Large or very large pot but usually split two ways
Average Winners:	Straight for high, 8 high for low
Good Starting Cards:	Pair, 2 below a 9, suited connectors, or two face cards

Do Ya?

Description:

A "Six Card Stud High-Low" game with choice cards and fees. Each player receives two hole cards. On each of four up-card rounds, the players have three choices of cards. Starting with the player on the dealer's left (and with the high hand showing in subsequent rounds), an initial card is offered. The player can take that card for free or decline that card for .50 (a red chip). A second offered card is placed on top of the rejected first card. The player can take that second card for free or decline it for $1 (a blue chip). If he declines, he gets the third card from the top of the deck. After he takes a card by choice or force, the pile of any rejected cards moves to the next player. **There may be 0, 1, or 2 rejected cards in the reject pile when it passes to the next player.**

If there are **2 rejected cards in the pile**, the next player can take the bottom one from the reject pile for free, or decline it for .50 and take the second card from the pile for free, or decline the second card, too, for another $1 and take a new card from the top of the deck.

If there is only **one card in the reject pile**, the next player can take it for free, or decline it for .50 and have a new card offered. He can take that new card for free or decline it for $1 and take the card off the top of the deck.

The reject pile is saved at the end of each round of up-cards and is used to start the next round of up-cards. Note that if a rejected card on the **bottom** of the pile has made it all the way around the table to the first player who declined it, it is mucked, temporarily reducing the size of the pile, and the next previously rejected card (if there is one) falls to the bottom of the reject pile. Place a marker in front of the first person to reject a specific card when it was on the bottom of the reject pile (or was his first option with an empty pile). Move the marker when the bottom card is chosen by a player or when it makes it all the way around to the person who holds the marker from rejecting that card previously. [You can simplify the dealing, but lose some key game elements by just mucking the entire reject pile at the end of each round. The last player in any round no longer has to play "defense" by taking a card needed by another player if the pile is mucked rather than used in the next round].

There are four rounds of face up cards, each followed by a betting interval. The players make their best high and/or low hand using any five of their six cards.

Players may play for high, low, or both ways. If going both ways, they may use a different combination of their cards for each half of the pot. But they must win outright (not tie) both ways or their entire hand is void.

Comments:	This is an entertaining game, with a lot of available information and the opportunity for players to have some control over the cards they get. The game forces difficult decisions on choice cards when your hand has different possibilities. And you need to watch what everyone else is doing and play a bit of defense with your choices.
Dealing Notes:	This can be a tricky game to deal. The dealer must be careful to properly pass the reject pile, and to get a clear choice from each player before exposing any new cards. Keeping track of when the bottom (free) card has been rejected all the way around the table is almost impossible without the marker.
	Dealing to the high hand first eliminates what could otherwise be a dealer advantage (although this is mitigated by the reject pile being "carried over" from round to round).
Variations:	This game can be played as 5-Card high only, either with wild cards or without. Declare deuces wild and people will fish

a little more by rejecting cards to get the deuce they hope is on top of the deck. Or, declare that the first "forced" card taken by each player (and the others of the same rank) are wild for that player. (A "forced" card means the third option, taken sight unseen after paying the decline fee and declining the first two options in that round)

This game can be played with "qualifiers" so that if no one makes a decent low hand, the game converts to high-only with a single winner. (The debate rages over whether "qualifiers" adds skill by preventing someone from "falling into" a low hand, or whether it subtracts skill by not allowing smarter players to "sneak into" an uncontested low pot.)

Time to Play:	4—Takes longer than the average game.
Complexity:	5—Complex to learn, play and deal
Skill Factor:	4—Skill will be a very significant factor in player outcomes
Pot Size:	4—Large or very large pot but usually split two ways
Average Winners:	Flush for high, 8,5,x,x,x for low.
Good Starting Cards:	Pair, 2 below an 8, suited connectors, or two face cards

Anaconda

Description:

All players are dealt seven cards face down and will work towards making their best high or low poker hand. All players pass three cards to the player on their left. All players pick up the cards passed them and then pass two cards to the second player on their left. Finally, players pass one card to the third player on their left. (If playing with six players, the last pass can be called going "across", if playing with five or four players, the last pass goes to the *right*.) When all the passing is completed, players discard two cards and keep their final five. They arrange these cards in the order they would like them exposed and place them face down in front of them. Everyone then simultaneously turns their first card, followed by a betting round. The second, third and fourth cards are also turned simultaneously with betting rounds after each. Then there is a simultaneous declare for high or low, followed by the final bet and the showdown.

Comments:

This is an extremely popular game in friendly poker evenings. High-low games are always popular because they keep more players in the game and create more winners. This game also allows players to see their ultimate hand before deciding to invest any money in it. The technique of players rolling their hands out one card at a time while betting on each is known as a "roll-out" and is sometimes added to other games as well.

The roll-out is the main feature of Anaconda and adds strategy considerations not found in other games where players do not control the sequence in which their cards are exposed.

This game takes a long time to play due to all the passing rounds. Players who do not end up with a full house or a 6 low will often fold after the passing, leaving only half the table going through the roll-out and betting intervals.

Dealing Notes:

This game takes a while to deal initially and it is easy to misdeal as some players pick up their cards as they are dealt, causing the dealer to skip them with the next card. There also many misdeals caused by players picking up the wrong cards from a pass, picking up a pass before making their own pass, passing the wrong number of cards, or a host of other mistakes. Many dealers like dealing this game because they think that once the initial cards are dealt, their role of dealer is over. Somebody has to

	police the passing of the cards, however, to reduce the frequency of misdeals.
Variations:	This game has a very popular variation called "8 Card Anaconda" where all players receive eight cards, discard three (there is no passing) and then roll-out their five card hand. Because the hands are not as strong as in "7 Card Pass Anaconda", the eight card variation brings trips, straights, flushes, and low bluffs into play and makes for a more competitive game and interesting roll-outs. And it is significantly quicker.
	The game can also be played with only a single pass of three cards. This variety means that you know one of the cards in the final hand of the person on your left and the player on your right knows one of yours.
	Another variation has players keeping all seven cards in their final hand. Flip 2 up, bet, flip 2 more up, bet, flip 2 more up, bet and showdown.

"7 Card Pass Anaconda":

Time to Play:	4—Takes longer than the average game
Complexity:	3—Some complexity keeping the passing straight and arranging final hand

Skill Factor:	4—Skill will be a very significant factor in player outcomes over multiple hands
Pot Size:	3—Large pot with more players in, but split two ways
Average Winners:	Full House

"8 Card Anaconda":

Time to Play:	3—About average relative to other varieties of poker
Complexity:	2—Fairly straightforward
Skill Factor:	4—Skill will be a very significant factor in player outcomes over multiple hands
Pot Size:	3—Large pot with more players in, but split two ways
Average Winners:	Average is a high flush, but the range is wide. Full Houses are not uncommon and are therefore bluffed often. Straights and trips and even busted boats can win.

"Double-Handed Games"

The "Double-Handed" games are among the most enjoyable, highest skill, and best action games in existence. Although I have never seen these games listed anywhere before, I am certain that I was not the only guy to "invent" them. When we were stuck with only three or four players, and we still wanted to deal some cards, necessity became the mother of invention. "Double-Handed" games made it possible and even enjoyable to play Poker with only four players. They also improved the action and fun of a five player game.

The basic concept started by just dealing two separate hands to each player. The players played them separately and bet them separately. Everyone had twice the chances to get a decent starting hand, and the action on the table simulated the action from twice as many players. When we played high-low games, a player would often keep both hands in for a while, since one might be looking low and the other, high.

Unlike regular Stud Poker, each player knew the hole cards of two of the hands. This led to the frequent complaint that cards needed by one hand were among the player's other hand's hole cards. So, being creative little buggers, we began to allow players to mix and match their four total hole cards at the beginning of double handed stud games. And we instantly saw the wisdom of this in high-low. Now, we were dealing double handed games of "Six Card High Low" but players could divide their four hole cards into a hand to build low and a hand to build high before the up cards were dealt.

We enjoyed these games so much, that we wanted to deal them when we had a full table of six players. But, alas, there were not enough cards in the deck for double-handed stud with six players. Inspiration hit once again, however. We realized that if a player only received a single set of up cards and had to use them on two different sets of hole cards, we could simulate double-handed "Six Card High-Low", and have enough cards for six players. And so, we were able to play double-handed games, even with six (and, with another tweak, seven) players.

With all "Double-Handed" games, there needs to be a few basic conventions or rules that are followed, including the following:

- Players keeping two hands alive, must bet for each of them. They will contribute twice as much to the pot than players who have folded one hand, but they will also have twice the chance to win.

- If a game requires a fee for keeping or passing a card ("Reject" or "Indecision") it must be clear ahead of time whether the fee is doubled for players with two live hands. I have found that the games work better if the fee is not doubled, so there is a bit more incentive for players to keep both hands in the game, which increases the action. The counter-argument is that the player still has twice the chance to win, so he should pay twice the fee.

- If a player has two hands alive, it needs to be clear whether one hand can raise the other, or whether they have to bet or raise in unison. My recommendation is to have the hands bet separately, even raising each other if desired, as long as they are two completely distinct hands with separate up cards and hole cards. In the hybrid games with two sets of hole cards and one set of up cards, the two hands should be bet in unison.

- In a high-low game, if one of a player's two hands goes high, and the other of his hands goes low, this is not the same as "going pig" or declaring a hand is going both ways. Such a player does not have to win both or lose everything. Each hand is independent of the other. If, however, a player takes a single one of his hands "both ways", then he is going pig and must win both ways outright or lose everything.

- Before a double-handed game is dealt, there must be agreement on recycling discards and folded cards as needed to complete the dealing and/or dealing a last "community card" in lieu of a separate last card to each hand. For example, double-handed "Six Card Stud" can be played with five players (which theoretically could take sixty cards), if everyone acknowledges that before a 6th card is dealt to all live hands, if there are not enough cards to go around, the 6th card will, instead, be a community card for everyone to use in all hands.

Once again, the "Double-Handed" games listed in this section are among the most enjoyable, highest skill, and best action games in existence for friendly poker games. Some of them take a little time to learn and understand, but that time is well invested given the popularity of the games.

Double Handed Stud Poker

Description:
Exactly the same games as the regular stud poker varieties, (i.e. Five Card Stud, Six Card Stud, Seven Card Stud, High-Low Stud, Baseball, Chicago,) but with each player receiving two separate hands which he bets separately as if they were being played by two players.

Comments:
Any Stud game can be played double-handed, as long as there are sufficient cards. In general, the value in playing double-handed is when you have three, four or five players.

Dealing Notes:
Compute the number of cards it will take to deal a complete hand to each player (total number of cards in each hand) x (number of players) x (2). Announce whether you will recycle folded cards and how community cards will be used if there are not enough cards to complete the deal. Generally, seven-card games should not be played double-handed with more than four players, but six-card games can be played with up to five players.

Time to Play:
About as long as the single-handed counterpart but with twice the players

Complexity:
Same as the single-handed counterpart with a big more confusion caused by playing two hands at once.

Skill Factor:	A bit higher than single-handed, because a player can control two sequential betting decisions to soak raises or make larger than normal raises.
Pot Size:	Same as single-handed versions played with twice the players.
Average Winners:	Same as single-handed versions when there are twice the players at the table
Good Starting Cards:	Same as single-handed versions.

Double Handed Community Card Poker

Description:
Exactly the same games as the regular Community Card Poker varieties, (i.e. Hold 'Em, Omaha, Iron Cross, Twin Beds) but with each player receiving two separate hands which he bets separately as if they were being played by two players.

Comments:
Any Community Card game can be played double-handed, as long as there are sufficient cards. In general, the value in playing double-handed is when you have three, four or five players.

Dealing Notes:
Compute the number of cards it will take to deal a complete hand to each player: (total number of hole cards in each hand) x (number of players) x (2) + (number of cards dealt to the board)). Even some games requiring too many cards can be played double-handed if you recycle folded hole cards and/or withhold the last hole card to the end and only deal it if you have one for everyone. Just figure it out and announce it ahead of time.

Time to Play:
About as long as the single-handed counterpart but with twice the players

Complexity:
Same as the single-handed counterpart with a big more confusion caused by playing two hands at once.

Skill Factor: A bit higher than single-handed, because a player can control two sequential betting decisions to soak raises or make larger than normal raises.

Pot Size: Same as single-handed versions played with twice the players.

Average Winners: Same as single-handed versions when there are twice the players at the table

Good Starting Cards: Same as single-handed versions.

Double-Handed Reject

Description:

Played the same as regular "Reject" (aka "Push", "Take it or Leave It") but every player is dealt two separate hands. Each hand bets separately and one hand can raise the other. Thus each player can take two of the raises to build the pot or to soak up raises. Because the two hands interact with one another during the take it or leave it decisions, this is a very different game than regular "Reject"

Comments:

Because of the way a player's two separate hands collude with one another, this game is particularly fascinating. A lot of information is conveyed by players as they make their take it or leave it decisions. The players' right hand, since it almost always acts immediately before the left hand is often used to "protect" the left hand by taking bad cards and passing good ones. This is a game that requires a lot of skill, and unlike most double-handed games, the player who folds one of his hands is at a distinct disadvantage since his remaining hand has no one with whom he can collude.

Dealing Notes:

Dealing is already tricky in "Reject". In the double-handed version, the dealer also has to watch out for a player saying "pass" or "reject" but only referring to his right hand. Each player has to reject a card on each hand before that card is offered to the next player.

Variations:	After dealing the down card for all the hands, players are allowed to choose which of these hole cards will be played on his left hand, and which will be played on his right. Once placed, they cannot change for the rest of the game. (Players often want the better hand on the left so their right hand can help it become a winner.)
Time to Play:	5—Takes significantly longer than the average game
Complexity:	5—Significantly more complex than average
Skill Factor:	5—Skill will be the determining factor in player outcomes
Pot Size:	4—Large or very large pot but split two ways
Average Winners:	Trips for high, and 8-5-x-x-x for low
Good Starting Cards:	Pair, 2 below an 8, suited connectors, two face cards

Scaggsville—The Greatest Game Ever

Description:

"Scaggsville" is a double-handed six-card, high-low, game with each player receiving two sets of hole cards and then four choice cards dealt face up that each go with both sets of hole cards. The player's left hand is formed from the two hole cards on the left plus his four up cards. The player's right hand is formed from the hole cards on the right plus the same four up cards. The bets are per hand, with the two hands acting simultaneously and in unison. Thus, if a hand is not being folded, a player will put in twice the per-hand bet to call and twice the per-hand raise to raise. The left hand cannot raise the right. The player is free, however, to fold one or both of his hands at any time during the game.

To begin the game, the dealer gives each player four cards face down. The players divide these into two sets of two hole cards that will be played as separate hands. Once these hole cards are divided, the combinations cannot be changed.

In each of four rounds of up cards, the players are offered a choice of accepting the first up card offered to them (in which case it becomes the first up card for *both* of their hands) or rejecting it and pushing it towards the player on their left (who then has the same choice). Once an offered choice card is accepted by a player, the dealer first "backfills" cards from the deck to any previous player(s) who rejected that card, before continuing the deal by offering a choice card to the next player who has yet to receive cards that round. If the last player to be offered a card on a round rejects his offered choice card, that card is discarded from the game.

The first round of up cards begins with the player on the dealer's left, but in subsequent rounds, to avoid a dealer advantage, the deal begins with the high hand showing.

Players who reject a card on the first round of up cards must pay a fee equal to the ante or the minimum bet. That fee is doubled for the second round, doubled again for the third round and doubled yet again (to 8 x the ante) on the last round. If, however, a player rejects a card and pays the fee, and gets a replacement card that round of the same rank as the one he rejected, he gets his rejecting fee back from the pot.

When the fourth round of up cards is completed, and before the final bet, it is time for each player to declare his remaining hands high or low. There are qualifiers, however, that apply. A player cannot declare for low if his hand is not a 9-high or better. A player cannot declare for high if his hand is not two pair, Jacks over, or better. Any hand that cannot qualify for high or low must be folded before the declare.

Assuming they qualify, a player can declare each of his remaining live hands high, low, or both. As always, if a single hand is declared both ways, it must win (not tie) both ways or be nullified at the showdown. A player with two hands that qualify, typically declares one for high and one for low. This is not the same thing as a single hand going both ways, and the win-both-or-lose-everything rule does not apply.

Comments:

Scaggsville has been called "the greatest game ever invented". Of course, that was within the poker circle in Scaggsville, Maryland, where the game was first devised. But it may be accurate. This game takes a while to explain, but once you play it once or twice, you will get it pretty quickly. It generates a large pot due to the heavy action from everyone having two hands, and the extra boost of the reject fees. It also results in a single winner more often than most high-low games due to the required qualifiers (which sometimes prevent anyone from going for one half of the pot) and the opportunity for strong, player-selected up cards to support a straight or a flush as well as a great low (which can lead to successful attempts for a player to win both ways). With six players keeping at least one hand live to the end, the game requires exactly 52 cards. The game rewards those who keep track of cards and those who watch carefully as other players make the multitude of take-it-or-leave-it and keep-both-or-fold-one decisions. Because it is double-handed, everyone, in theory, is playing a high hand and a low hand. That means that there is no card that is really "safe" to pass.

Dealing Notes:	Six player maximum. Deal to the highest hand showing once everyone has their first up card. It is a tricky game to deal since you need to wait for a decision on each up card before exposing the next up card in the deal. Remember to announce just before the high-low declaration that non-qualifiers must fold.
Time to Play:	5—Takes significantly longer than the average game
Complexity:	5—Significantly more complex than average

Skill Factor:	5—Skill will be the determining factor in player outcomes
Pot Size:	5—Can build very large pots, usually, but not always, split
Average Winners:	High straight for high, 8 high for low
Good Starting Cards:	Pair, 2 below an 8, suited connectors, or two face cards

Scaggsville—Community Center

Description:

Very similar to "Scaggsville", but utilizing some community cards so that it can be dealt to seven players. It is a double-handed six-card, high-low, game with each player making their best poker hands from two hole cards, one of three sets of 2 community cards dealt to the board, and two choice cards dealt face up to each player. As in "Scaggsville", to begin the game, the dealer gives each player four cards face down and the players divide these into two sets of two hole cards that will be played as separate hands.

Next, three piles of two cards each are dealt face down in the middle of the table. The dealer flips over one of these piles and there is a betting round. The second and third piles are exposed with a betting round after each. The first round of betting starts with the player to the left of the dealer. The second and third rounds begin with the last raiser from the previous round.

After the third round of community card exposure and bets, there are two rounds of up cards dealt to each player where the players are offered a choice. They can accept the first up card offered to them (in which case it becomes the first up card for *both* of their hands) or they can reject it and push it towards the player on their left (who then has the same choice). If they reject the choice card, they will get another card from the deck instead.

Once an offered choice card is accepted by a player, the dealer first "backfills" cards from the deck to any previous player(s) who rejected that card, before continuing the deal by offering a choice card to the next player who has yet to receive cards that round. If the last player to be offered a card on a round rejects his offered choice card, that card is discarded from the game.

The dealing of the first round of upcards begins with the last raiser from the previous round of betting. The dealing of the second and last round of up cards begins with the high hand showing. (This is to avoid a dealer advantage to always starting with the player on the dealer's left).

Players who reject a card on the first round of up cards must pay a fee equal to the four times the ante or the minimum bet. That fee is doubled for the second round (to 8 x the ante). If, however, a player rejects a card and pays the fee, and gets a replacement card that round of the same rank as the one he rejected, he gets his rejecting fee back from the pot.

When the second and last round of up cards is completed, and before the final bet, it is time for each player to declare his remaining hands high or low. There are qualifiers, however, that apply. A player cannot declare for low if his hand is not a 9-high or better. A player cannot declare for high if his hand is not two pair, Jacks over, or better. Any hand that cannot qualify for high or low must be folded before the declare.

Assuming they qualify, a player can declare each of his remaining live hands high, low, or both. As always, if a single hand is declared both ways, it must win (not tie) both ways or be nullified at the showdown. A player with two hands that qualify, typically (but not always*) declares one for high and one for low. This is not the same thing as a single

---

* a player who has two hands that tie might keep them both in if he anticipates being tied by a third player, so that he gets a larger share of the split half-pot. Players may also wish to declare both hands (if they qualify) simply as part of the posturing during the simultaneous declare. Even though they will immediately fold the weaker of their two qualifying low hands or two qualifying high hands once the declare is finished, it might prove advantageous to have both closed fists out there as players get ready to declare, to worry an opponent trying to decide which way to declare a hand he holds that qualifies both ways.

hand going both ways, and the win-both-or-lose-everything rule does not apply.

Comments:

Because Scaggsville, "the greatest game ever invented", could not be played with seven players, its creators devised this community version one night when they had seven players at the table. The community card aspect of the game added layers of intrigue, and skill that were enjoyable and unique, so "Scaggsville Community Center" is now often played regardless of how many players are at the table. Classic "Scaggsville" also retains its popularity.

"Scaggsville Community Center" takes even longer to explain than regular "Scaggsville", but once you play it once or twice, you will get it pretty quickly. It generates a large pot due to the heavy action from everyone having two hands, the extra boost of the reject fees, and the fifth betting round. (Regular "Scaggsville" has only four). It also results in a single winner more often than most high-low games due to the required qualifiers, the need for players to have play at least one of the six community cards, and the opportunity for strong, hand-chosen up cards to support a straight or a flush as well as a great low.

The game rewards those who keep track of cards and those who watch carefully as other players make the multitude of take-it-or-leave-it and keep-both-or-fold-one decisions. Because it is double-handed, everyone, in theory, is playing a high hand and a low hand. That means that there is no card that is really "safe" to pass to your neighbor.

Dealing Notes:

Tricky to deal. Betting is led by the player on your left for the first bet, the last raiser on the 2nd and 3rd bets and the high card showing on the 4th and 5th bets. The two rounds of up cards are dealt beginning with the last raiser on the previous rounds. Wait for a decision on each up card before exposing the next up card in the deal. Remember to announce just before the high-low declaration that non-qualifiers must fold.

Variations:

In a version dubbed "Scaggsville Town Square", instead of placing 3 piles of two cards each in the middle of the table, the dealer lays out four cards in a square. The dealer turns two corners of the square, followed by a round of betting, then the other two corners, followed by another round of betting, and then proceeds to the two rounds where each player gets their own choice cards. To make their final hand, players can use any two adjacent (but not diagonal) cards from the "Town Square" to add to their hands. (This was said to be because the roads run between any two adjacent points of the town square, but not diagonally in the middle. I have been to Scaggsville and I can verify that there are no diagonal roads or paths in the town square. In point of fact, however, there is no town square there, either.) In this version of the card game, there are fewer cards in the middle, and one less round of betting so the game is slightly less liberal than Community Center.

Time to Play:	5—Takes significantly longer than the average game
Complexity:	5—Significantly more complex than average
Skill Factor:	5—Skill will be the determining factor in player outcomes
Pot Size:	5—Can build very large pots, usually, but not always, split
Average Winners:	Flush for high (but a full house if the board has a pair), 7 high for low unless none of the six community cards are below an 8.
Good Starting Cards:	Pair, 2 below an 8, suited connectors, or two face cards

"Miscellaneous Odd Games"

If you were to define "poker" as any game involving wagering and playing cards, then I suppose the games listed here would qualify. Whether you consider them "poker" games or not, however, these games are widely known, and have sufficient entertainment value to make their way into many friendly poker evenings.

Generally speaking, these "Odd" games do not reward skill or strategy as well as most poker games. This is likely due to the relative difficulty of inventing new games of strategy and skill and the relative ease of inventing new games of luck. More traditional poker game varieties feature a set of game design elements that work together to reward skillful play. Examples of these design elements include:

- A defined ranking of hands with values corresponding to probability of attainment
- Multiple rounds of betting
- Variable size bets and raises
- Playing against other players instead of against "the house" or "the pot"
- Moderate-sized betting amounts relative to the evening's buy-in totals.
- Opportunities for bluffing and slow-playing
- Requirement for at least five cards to form a winning hand.

If these elements are incorporated in a new variety of poker, they help to ensure that skill is rewarded in the new game. By omitting some or all of these design elements, the "Odd" games become more luck-driven. Most of the "Odd" games can generate large pots with potential to redistribute a lot of chips very quickly, meaning that, without caution, a few unlucky breaks can undo an entire evening of careful play.

Despite these drawbacks, the "Odd" games can be worthwhile and entertaining as a change of pace. The trick is to plan ahead and use variations of the "Odd" games that mitigate against total arbitrariness. In the descriptions below, I have tried to point out the rule variations that help keep the game as far in line as possible with the overall goal of rewarding skill.

Description:

Each player receives two cards face down and one card face up. Aces count as 1 or 11, face cards count as ½ and all other cards count as their numerical value. The pot is eventually split between the hand closest to 7 total points and the hand closest to 27 total points. (Going over 7 points or 27 points does not exclude a hand for competing for closest to 7 or to 27).

A round of betting follows the dealing of the first three cards. Betting begins with the high hand (most total points) showing. After the betting round, there are as many dealing rounds as needed. Dealing begins with the high hand showing. In each round of dealing, each player has the option to take a card or to pass on that round. There is a betting round after each round of dealing.

A player who passes on two dealing rounds becomes "frozen" and is not offered any more cards for the rest of the game. Players who are not "frozen" may take a card on as many rounds as they like, provided that their up cards (counting aces as 1 point) do not total more than 26 points.

When all players have passed twice, or, when all but one player is frozen and the last player taking cards reaches 26 points showing or passes, the dealing is finished. There is a declaration for high/low, one final bet and the showdown. Players may declare for both ways (with, for example a 5 and two aces), but they must win both ways outright (not tie) or they are out completely.

If there is a tie for closest to 7 or to 27, the "insides beat outsides", meaning that a 7 ½ would beat a 6 ½, while a 26 ½ would beat a 27 ½. If there is still an exact tie, then fewest cards in the hand wins. If there is an exact tie and with the same number of cards, then the tied hands split their half of the pot.

Comments:

This game can feature a player getting dealt a perfect 7 and getting to raise through 7 or 8 rounds of dealing and betting while the players trying for the high half take additional cards. This opportunity makes 727 a popular game to deal for players looking for a big score with no risk. Some players refuse to play anything but a pat hand, since trying to draw cards to a winner can be expensive. (If you have 20 points after the initial deal, you may be one more card from seeing your final hand, but you may need four or five cards if you keep getting faces, aces and twos).

Dealing Notes:	It is helpful for a player who has passed once to put a chip on top of his up cards to keep track. Dealing to the high hand removes the dealer advantage of acting last on the take-a-card-or-pass decision.
Variations:	The first three cards can be dealt face down with players choosing a card to become their first up card.

In another version, the players can choose to pass on their first up card, leaving them only two cards to start. (Betting does not begin, though, until after the first up card dealing round.)

In yet another very popular version, the game is played with only two cards dealt in the beginning. It is a significantly better game with three, however. With only two cards to start, it is impossible to have a pat hand going high, and it is much easier to get a pat hand going low. Since the game already favors the guys going low, this is not helpful. Furthermore, having two down cards adds to the bluffing possibilities and reduces the already plentiful betting rounds by one. And it increases the surprise at the declaration, since a 4, 5, 6, or 7 showing and frozen as the only up card can be a good high or low hand.

Time to Play:	4—Takes longer than the average game.
Complexity:	3—Some complexity with all the tiebreakers and ½ point counting
Skill Factor:	2—Skill will be a factor but luck is prevalent too.
Pot Size:	4—Large or very large pot but split two ways
Average Winners:	7 or 7 ½ for low. 26 ½ for high
Good Starting Cards:	Anything totaling 7 or under or 20 or more

Screw Your Neighbor

Description:

A great change of pace, since the game requires no heavy thinking, and moves pretty quickly. Each player puts three medium-to-large sized bets in front of him (maybe 3 blue chips, or 3 stacks of blue chips). In each round of deals, at least one player will lose and throw one of these three bets into the pot. The last player with any of his three bets in front of him wins the whole pot.

On each round of dealing, each player is dealt a single card face down. Players who receive a King immediately turn it face up. They cannot lose that round, nor can their King be passed or taken. The player to the left of the dealer is "under the gun" and must act first. (In subsequent rounds, this obligation rotates around the table). The first player can choose to hold their card or can exchange it with the player to their left (who cannot refuse). Once the first player has held or exchanged, the next player has the same choice—hold their current card or exchange it with the player on his left. The last player to act may hold his current card or discard it and take the top card off the deck. When all players have acted, all cards are flipped up. The player or players holding the lowest ranking cards (Aces are low in this game), throws one of their three bets into the pot.

The last player with bets remaining wins the pot. If only two players remain with only one bet left for each, and they tie on the last deal, they simply deal another hand.

Comments:	Although there is a lot of luck involved, there is some skill also, and it can be rather entertaining to watch folks react to their cards. The game takes no longer than some other poker games and is popular as a 'mental break' after a few tough complicated games have been played. If this game is dealt more than once or maybe twice a night, however, it loses all of its novelty and appeal.
Dealing Notes:	It adds to both the speed and the skill level of the game to deal from the same deck without shuffling between the deals until that deck is exhausted.
Time to Play:	4—Takes a bit longer than the average game.
Complexity:	1—Very simple and straightforward
Skill Factor:	2—Skill will be a factor but luck is prevalent
Pot Size:	4—Medium to Large pot with a single winner

Guts

Description:

All players add a medium sized bet to the dealer ante to make a decent starting pot. Three cards are dealt face down. The best hand is trips, followed by a pair, and then high card. To determine who is in and who is out, all players hold their cards a couple of inches above the table top. The dealer counts "1-2-3-drop." Players who drop their cards are out and have no further risk. Players who hold their cards are in. If nobody stays, the hand is re-dealt with the initial pot still on the table. If only one player stays, he gets the pot and the game ends. If more than one player stays, the showdown is immediate. Players take the pot if they win, but if they lose, they will ante the amount of this pot into the next hand (up to the house rules' maximum limit—the max-limit). If three or more players stay in, there will be multiple losers and the pot for the next hand can double or triple or more.

Comments:

Very popular game, particularly among the risk-takers at the table. Because the penalty for losing is pretty steep, a lot of money can change hands quickly

Dealing Notes:

Typically, if the very first hand has only a single winner, and the game would therefore be over, the players all kick in to form a second pot to give the game a second chance. Also, the dealer should announce how he will handle pots that grow to exceed the max-limit. He can split the larger amounts into separate pots that can be played once the first pot is taken by a single player. Or, he can leave the larger pot intact, meaning that players staying in on the next hand will be risking less than they stand to gain by winning. In general, it is best to split up pots that are more than twice the max-limit.

Variations:	Instead of the "1-2-3 drop" declaration of in or out, players, in turn, verbally declare in or out. If only the last person to act goes in, players around the table have one more chance to go in against him so he does not 'steal the pot'.
Time to Play:	3—About average, but can end very quickly or go on for many hands
Complexity:	1—Very simple and straightforward
Skill Factor:	2—Skill will be a factor, but luck is prevalent also
Pot Size:	5—Large pots with single winners and large money swings.
Average Winners:	Usually takes a pair. Trips are very rare. Ace High can sneak in.

Balls

Description:

Similar to **"Guts"** but with 2-card hands and a round of betting among those that stay. Two cards are dealt face down. The rank of hands is straight-flush, pair, straight, flush, high card. (A straight is less likely and more valuable than a flush in this game). To determine who is in and who is out, all players hold their cards a couple of inches above the table top. The dealer counts "1-2-3-drop." Players who drop their cards are out and have no further risk. Players who hold their cards are in, and they risk having to ante the amount of the pot into the next hand. If nobody stays, the hand is re-dealt with the initial pot still on the table. If only one player stays, he gets the pot and the game ends.

If there are two or more players staying in, there is a round of betting. *Any money put into the pot increases the pot size that a losing player has to ante to the next hand.* A player who was "in" may choose to fold at any time, without waiting for his 'turn' to bet, and his ante to the next hand will match the size of the pot at that point. After the showdown, the player who wins takes the pot, and the players who lose must ante the amount that was in that pot to the kitty for the next hand. If three or more players stayed in, there will be multiple losers and the pot for the next hand can double or triple or more. A new hand is dealt to all players.

Comments:	Because the penalty for losing is pretty steep, and made steeper by the round of betting, a lot of money can change hands quickly. A player can really hurt himself by calling or raising on the betting round and then losing. Not only does he lose the chips he just bet or raised, but he loses them a second time by having to match them in the ante for the next hand. Like other varieties of poker that were invented for "pot limit" games, "Balls" is not an easy game to squeeze into a Limit game. Since a player who stays in past the drop is already at risk of losing the max-limit just for staying in the game, the limits on the round of betting should be the standard-limits, not the max-limit. Otherwise a player could lose twice the max-limit on a single decision.
Dealing Notes:	Typically, if the very first hand has only a single winner, and the game would therefore be over, the players all kick in to form a second pot to give the game a second chance. Also, the dealer should announce how he will handle pots that grow to exceed the max-limit. He can split the larger amounts into separate

pots that can be played once the first pot is taken by a single player. Or, he can leave the larger pot intact, meaning that players staying in on the next hand will be risking less than they stand to gain by winning. In general, it is best to split up pots that are more than twice the max-limit.

Variations: Instead of the "1-2-3 drop" declaration of in or out, players, in turn, verbally declare in or out. If only the last person to act goes in, players around the table have one more chance to go in against him so he does not 'steal the pot'.

Time to Play: 4—Somewhat longer than average, can end quickly or go on for many hands

Complexity: 3—Some complexity in the betting round pot counting

Skill Factor: 3—Skill will be a significant factor in player outcomes

Pot Size: 5—Large pots with single winners and large money swings.

Average Winners: Medium Straight

APPENDIX 1

Quick Reference Chart
for the Games

Stud Poker Games:

Game	Overall Rating	Time to Play	Comp-lexity	Skill Factor	Avg Pot Size	Average Winners	Variation in Winners	Good Starting Cards	Page
5 Card Stud	3	1	1	4	3	Pair of Jacks	Low	A pair, one card higher than any showing	239
6 Card Stud	*5*	2	1	5	4	Medium Two Pair	High	A pair, 3 high cards, 3 to a Flush, 3 consecutive	241
7 Card Stud	3	3	1	3	4	Two Pair, Aces Over	Med	A high pair, 3 high cards, or 3 to a Flush	243
5 Card Stud Hi-Lo w/ Twists (One Buck Two)	*5*	4	3	4	4	Hi: Pair of Kings. Low: 9 high	High	Anything except an unpaired 10, J or K	245
6 Card High/Low	4	3	3	4	3	Hi: Two Pair. Lo: 9-6-x-x-x	High	High Pair, 3 high cards, 3 suited, 3 below a 9	247
7 Card High/Low	3	4	3	3	3	Hi: 2 Pair Aces up. Lo: 8-6-x-x-x	Med	High Pair, 3 high cards, 3 suited, 3 below a 9	247
Baseball - 7 Card	1	3	3	2	4	4 Aces or Low Straight Flush	Low	Trips, Wild Card+2 high or Straight Flush cards	249
- 6 Card	4	2	3	3	4	Full House	Med	Wild Card, high pair, or 3 Straight Flush cards	249
Follow the Queen - 7 Card	1	3	3	2	3	4 Aces or Low Straight Flush	Low	A Queen, high pair, 3 Straight Flush cards	251
- 6 Card	3	2	3	3	3	Full House	Med	A Queen, high pair, 3 Straight Flush cards	251
Low Hole Roll Your Own (Mexican Stud) - 5 Card	4	2	3	3	3	Trip Kings	Med	A pair or an Ace or King that is turned up	253
- 6 Card	4	3	3	4	3	High Flush	High	A pair or 3 to a Flush	253
- 7 Card	2	4	4	2	3	Four of a Kind	Low	A pair or 3 Straight Flush cards	253
Shifting Sands - 5 Card	3	3	3	3	2	Trip Jacks	Med	Pair of Wild Cards or 3 above a 10 or suited	255
- 6 Card	4	2	3	4	3	High Flush	High	Pair of Wild Cards, or 3 to Straight Flush	255
- 7 Card	3	4	3	2	3	Four of a Kind	Low	Pair of Wild Cards, 3 to a high Straight Flush	255
Woolworths	1	3	3	2	4	4 Aces or Low Straight Flush	Low	Trips, Wild Card+ 2 high or Straight Flush cards	255
Dr. Pepper	1	3	3	2	4	4 Aces or Low Straight Flush	Low	Trips, Wild Card+ 2 high or Straight Flush cards	255
Kankakee - 5 Card	3	1	2	3	2	Trips	Med	Pair, or two cards above a Jack	255
- 6 Card	4	2	2	4	3	High Flush or low boat	High	Pair or two hole cards above a Jack	255
- 7 Card	2	3	3	2	4	Four of a Kind	Low	Pair or two hole cards above a Jack	255
Chicago - 6 Card	3	3	2	3	3	Hi: Two Pair. Lo: 4 of spades	Med	Medium Pair or 4 of spades in hole	255
- 7 Card	2	4	2	2	4	Hi: Aces up. Lo: 3 of spades	Low	Medium Pair or 3 of spades in hole	255
Sequence - 5 Card	2	2	3	2	2	Trips	Med	2 or 3 in the hole	256
- 6 Card	2	3	4	3	3	Straight	Med	3 or 4 in the hole	256
- 7 Card			3		4	High Flush	Med	3, 4 or 5 in the hole AND pair or 2 high cards	256

Game									Page
Limit Texas Hold 'Em	2	2	3	3	1	2 Pair incl. highest board card	Med	Pair, Ace, face card suited, suited connectors	258
Omaha	3	3	4	4	3	Trips. Higher with pairs on board	Med	High Pair, two good sets of connecters	260
Cincinnati	2	4	2	2	5	Full House high as pair on board	Med	Trips, high Two Pair, pair of Aces	262
Cincinnati High-Low	2	4	3	2	5	Hi: Full House. Lo: 6 high	Med	Trips, high Two Pair, or four perfect low cards	262
Iron Cross	3	4	3	3	4	Flush. Full House if board paired	Med	Two Pair, four to Flush, pair of Kings	264
Iron Cross Hi-Low	3	4	3	3	4	Hi: High Flush. Lo: 7-4-x-x	Med	Two Pair, four to a Flush, 4 perfect low cards	264
Other Shapes						TicTacToe/Hollywood Squares, Merry Go Round, Otis Elevator, Twin Beds, Double Board			266
Community Games	2-3	3-4	2-3	3-4	3-4	Varies by number of cards dealt to each player and the number of community cards	Med		
"Draw" Poker Games									
5 Card Draw	2	1	3	1	1	Two Pair, Jacks Over	Low	Pair of 8's or higher	269
5 Card Draw Lowball	1	1	3	1	1	8-7-x-x-x	Low	4 strong low cards	269
5 Card Draw Hi-Lo	2	2	3	2	2	Hi: Jacks Over, Lo: 8-7-x-x-x	Low	Hi: Pair of 8's or higher, Lo: 4 strong low cards	269
Jacks to Open, Trips to Win	1	4	2	4	4	Trips	Low	Jacks or better	271
Jacks or Back	2	1	3	2	1	Same as 5 Card Draw High or Lowball	Depending on whether it was opened high or not	Jacks or better	273
5 Card Draw -Draw Twice	2	2	3	2	2	2 Pair - Kings Over	Med	Pair of 8's or higher	275
Other "Choice Card" Games									
Reject (Push)	*5*	4	5	4	4	Hi: 9's Over. Lo: 8-6-x-x-x	High	Pair, 2 under a 9, suited connectors, two faces	276
Indecision	*5*	4	5	4	4	Hi: Straight. Lo: 8-6-x-x-x	Med	Pair, 3 under a 9, 3 suited connectors, 3 faces	279
Do Ya	4	4	4	5	4	Hi: Flush. Lo: 8-5-x-x-x	Med	Pair, 2 < an 8, suited connectors, or 2 faces	282
Anaconda, 7 Card Pass	4	4	3	4	3	Hi: Full House. Lo: 6-5-3-2-A	Low	NA - You see your whole hand at the start	286
Anaconda, 8 Card No Pass	4	3	2	4	3	Hi: Full House. Lo: 6-5-3-2-A	Low	NA - You see your whole hand at the start	289
Double Handed Games									
Double Handed Reject	*5*	5	5	4	4	Hi: Trips. Lo: 8-5-x-x-x	Med	Pair, 2 < an 8, suited connectors, two faces	297
Scaggsville - the Greatest	*6*	5	5	5	5	Hi: High Straight. Lo: 8 high	High	Pair, 2 < an 8, suited connectors, two faces	299
Scaggsville Com. Center	*6*	5	5	5	5	Hi: Flush. Lo: 7 high.	High	Pair, 2 < an 8, suited connectors, two faces	304
Miscellaneous Odd Games									
Seven Twenty-Seven (7-27)	2	4	3	2	2	Lo: 7 or 7 ½. Hi: 26 ½ for high	Low	Under 7, or between 20 and 27.5	312
Screw Your Neighbor	2	4	1	2	2	NA	NA	NA - you stay to the end regardless	316
Guts	3	3	1	2	5	A pair, Ace high can sneak in	Med	Same as average winners	318
Balls	2	4	3	3	5	Medium "Straight"	Med	NA	320

APPENDIX 2

Great Poker Quotations

From Movies and Television

The Sting:

Henry Gondorff: Jesus. Does he do anything where he's not alone?
J.J. Singleton: Just poker. And he cheats. Pretty good at it, too.

Floyd: Doyle, I KNOW I gave him four THREES. He had to make a SWITCH. We can't let him get away with that.
Doyle Lonnegan: What was I supposed to do—call him for cheating better than me, in front of the others?

Henry Gondorff: Glad to meet you, kid, you're a real horse's ass. Is Lonnegan after you too?
Johnny Hooker: I dunno...I ain't seen anybody.
Henry Gondorff: You never do, kid.

------ ♦ ♣ ♥ ♠ ------

Johnny Hooker: Luther said I could learn some things from you . . . I already know how to drink.

------ ♦ ♣ ♥ ♠ ------

[*Gondorff enters the poker game pretending to be drunk*]
Henry Gondorff: Sorry I'm late. I was taking a crap.

------ ♦ ♣ ♥ ♠ ------

Henry Gondorff: You not gonna stick around for your share?
Johnny Hooker: Nah. I'd only blow it.

------ ♦ ♣ ♥ ♠ ------

Doyle Lonnegan: Mr. Shaw, we usually require a tie at this table... if you don't have one, we can get you one.
Henry Gondorff: That'd be real nice of you, Mr. Lonniman!
Doyle Lonnegan: Lonnegan.
[*Gondorff nods and burps in response*]

------ ♦ ♣ ♥ ♠ ------

Henry Gondorff: Tough luck, Lonnehan. But that's what you get for playing with your head up your ass!

------ ♦ ♣ ♥ ♠ ------

328

Doyle Lonnegan: Your boss is quite a card player, Mr. Kelly. How does he do it?

Johnny Hooker: He cheats.

------ ♦ ♣ ♥ ♠ ------

Henry Gondorff: Five Hundred.

Doyle Lonnegan: Your five hundred. And one thousand.

Henry Gondorff: Your one thousand and I'll raise you two thousand.

Doyle Lonnegan: Your two thousand . . . Mr. Clemens, give me ten thousand more. [*Lonnegan gets the chips from the banker and puts them into the pot*]

Henry Gondorff: [*pauses, then casually:*] I'll call.

Doyle Lonnegan: [*lays his cards on the table*]: Four nines.

Henry Gondorff: [*pauses, smiles, lays his cards on the table, leans forward*]: Four Jacks! . . . You owe me fifteen grand, pal!

Doyle Lonnegan: [*searches through his jacket pockets*]: I must have left my wallet in my room.

Henry Gondorff: [*rises and flashes his own wad of cash at Lonnegan*] Don't hand me any of that crap! When you come to a game like this, you bring your money! How do I know you won't take a powder?

[*Lonnegan rushes at Gondorff, but is restrained by the other players*]

Henry Gondorff: All right. I'll tell you what I'll do. I'll send a boy around to your room in five minutes. You better have the money or it's going to be all around Chicago that you welched. You won't be able to get a game of Jacks. . . . [*pushes his chips over to the banker*] Cash me in for the rest of these bums.

------ ♦ ♣ ♥ ♠ ------

Rounders:

Mike McDermott: I feel like Buckner walking back into Shea.

Mike McDermott: Listen, here's the thing. If you can't spot the sucker in the first half hour at the table, then you ARE the sucker.

Worm: You know what always cheers me up?
Mike McDermott: No, what's that?
Worm: Rolled up aces over kings. Check-raising stupid tourists and taking huge pots off of them. Playing all-night high-limit Hold'em at the Taj, "where the sand turns to gold." Stacks and towers of checks I can't even see over.
Mike McDermott: Fuck it, let's go.
Worm: Don't tease me.
Mike McDermott: Let's play some cards.
Worm: Yes!

Teddy KGB: That ace could not have helped you.
[*drops all of his chips onto the table*]
Teddy KGB: I bet it all.
Mike McDermott: [*laughs*] You're right Teddy, the ace didn't help.
[*pushes chips towards the center and flops down his cards*]
Mike McDermott: I flopped a nut straight.

Teddy KGB: Lays down a monster. The fuck did you lay that down?

Worm: [*Interrupting the other two players' conversation in Russian*] Hey! If you want to see this seventh card you're gonna stop speakin' fuckin' Sputnick. I'm sure you guys were talking about pierogis and snow but let's cut that out.

Worm: I guess the saying's true. In the poker game of life, women are the rake, man. They are the fuckin' rake.
Mike McDermott: What the fuck are you talkin' about? What saying?
Worm: I—I don't know. There ought to be one though.

Mike McDermott: I want him to think that I am pondering a call, but all I'm really thinkin' about is Vegas and the fuckin' Mirage.

Mike McDermott: It's immoral to let a sucker keep his money.

Mike McDermott: In "Confessions of a Winning Poker Player," Jack King said, "Few players recall big pots they have won, strange as it seems, but every player can remember with remarkable accuracy the outstanding tough beats of his career." It seems true to me, cause walking in here, I can hardly remember how I built my bankroll, but I can't stop thinking about the way I lost it.

Teddy KGB: Nyet! Nyet! No More! No! Not tonight! This son of bitch, all night he, "Check. Check. Check." He trap me!

Teddy KGB: Aces full, Mike.

Mike McDermott: You were lookin' for that third three, but you forgot that Professor Green folded on Fourth Street and now you're representing that you have it. The DA made his two pair, but he knows they're no good. Judge Kaplan was trying to squeeze out a diamond flush but he came up short and Mr. Eisen is futilely hoping that his queens are going to stand up. So like I said, the Dean's bet is $20.

Butch Cassidy and the Sundance Kid:

Card player #1: Well, looks like you just about cleaned everybody out, fella. You haven't lost a hand since you got to deal. What's the secret of your success?
Sundance Kid: [*pause*] Prayer.

Card Player: I didn't know you were the Sundance Kid when I said you were cheating. If I draw on you, you'll kill me.
Sundance Kid: There's that possibility.

------ ♦ ♣ ♥ ♠ ------

Butch Cassidy: My, we seem to be a little short on brotherly love 'round here.
Sundance Kid: I wasn't cheating.

------ ♦ ♣ ♥ ♠ ------

Butch Cassidy: Do you believe I'm broke already?
Etta Place: Why is there never any money, Butch?
Butch Cassidy: Well, I swear, Etta, I don't know. I've been working like a dog all my life and I can't get a penny ahead.
Etta Place: Sundance says it's because you're a soft touch, and always taking expensive vacations, and buying drinks for everyone, and you're a rotten gambler.
Butch Cassidy: Well that might have something to do with it.

------ ♦ ♣ ♥ ♠ ------

Honeymoon in Vegas:

Jack Singer: Do you know what a straight flush is? It's like... unbeatable.
Betsy: "Like unbeatable" is not unbeatable.
Jack Singer: Hey, I know that now, okay.

------ ♦ ♣ ♥ ♠ ------

Jack Singer: [*laying down his cards*] Straight flush to the jack!
Tommy Korman: Boy. It's one for the books. . . . [*lays down his cards*]. To the queen.

The Odd Couple:

Oscar Madison: I'm in for a quarter.
Murray: Aren't you going to look at your cards first?
Oscar Madison: What for? I'm gonna bluff anyway. Who gets a Pepsi?

Oscar Madison: I'm $800 behind in alimony. Let's raise the stakes.

Oscar Madison: If you're my accountant, how come I need money?
Roy: If you need money, how come you play poker?
Oscar Madison: 'Cause I need money.
Roy: But you always lose.
Oscar Madison: That's why I need the money.

Murray the Cop: What are you yelling about? We're playing a friendly game!
[*the bickering continues*]
Murray the Cop: All right, all right, ALL RIGHT! Calm down, calm down, take it easy. I'm a cop, you know—I can arrest the whole lousy game.

[*they all quiet down*]

Oscar Madison: My friend Murray the cop is right. Let's just play cards and please hold them up. I can't see where I marked them.

------ ♦ ♣ ♥ ♠ ------

Murray: How many cards you got, four?
Speed: Yes, Murray, we all have four cards. When you give us one more, we'll all have five. If you gave us two more, we'd all have six. Do you see how that works now?

------ ♦ ♣ ♥ ♠ ------

Felix Ungar: [*serving refreshments at the poker game*] Cold glass of beer for Roy...
Roy: Thank you.
Felix Ungar: Where's your coaster?
Roy: My what?
Felix Ungar: Your coaster. The little round thing that goes under the glass.
Roy: I think I bet it.

------ ♦ ♣ ♥ ♠ ------

Oscar Madison: [*tosses the coaster back to Roy*] Here, here, here. I knew I was winning too much! Here.
Oscar Madison: Listen, he was driving us all crazy with his napkins and his ashtrays and his bacon, lettuce and tomato sandwiches. All of you said so.
Roy: We didn't say kick him out, Oscar.
Oscar Madison: Well, who do you think I did it for? I did it for us!
Roy: Us?

Oscar Madison: Yes, that's right. Do you know what he was planning for next Friday night's poker game as a change of pace? Do you have any idea?

Vinnie: What?

Oscar Madison: A luau! A Hawaiian luau! Roast pork, fried rice, spareribs—they don't play poker like that in Honolulu!

Felix Ungar: Marriages may come and go, but the game must go on.

Maverick:

Maverick: Well, now, I bring all sorts of plusses to the table. I hardly ever bluff and I never ever cheat.

Maverick: My old pappy always used to say, "there is no more deeply satisfying religious experience... than cheatin' on a cheater."

Zane Cooper: I never said that once. You've been misquoting me all your life.

Maverick: What, we're going to quibble over fine points?

Zane Cooper: You never even get close. Give me some credit.

Annabelle: How'd you know I was bluffing? I didn't do any of my tells. I didn't shuffle my cards, I didn't pull my hair, I didn't even flick my teeth.

Maverick: You held your breath. If you'd been excited, you would have started breathing harder.

Annabelle: I did not.

[*Looks at the Commodore*]

Annabelle: Did I?

[*Commodore nods*]

Annabelle: [*Annabelle looks at Angel*] Did I?

[*Angel nods*]

Annabelle: [*Annabelle looks at the dealer*] Did I?

[*the dealer nods*]

Annabelle: Well, I'll just pretend I was playin' with someone else's money.

Maverick: That shouldn't be too hard.

[*Annabelle gets up. Cooper leans toward her*]

Zane Cooper: [*whispering*] You did hold your breath, ma'am.

The Cincinnati Kid:

Lancey Howard: Gets down to what it's all about, doesn't it? Making the wrong move at the right time.

Cincinnati Kid: Is that what it's all about?

Lancey Howard: Like life, I guess. You're good, kid, but as long as I'm around you're second best. You might as well learn to live with it.

Cincinnati Kid: Listen, Christian, after the game, I'll be The Man. I'll be the best there is. People will sit down at the table with you, just so they can say they played with The Man. And that's what I'm gonna be, Christian.

Christian: I know.

Cincinnati Kid: You call that an argument?

Slade: No, that's a fact. The argument's leaning over there against the door jamb.

[*Referring to his muscleman*]

Slade: How the hell did you know I didn't have the king or the ace?

Lancey Howard: I recollect a young man putting the same question to Eddie the Dude. "Son," Eddie told him, "all you paid was the looking price. Lessons are extra."

Slade: Six stacks, is that right, Shooter?

Shooter: Six.

Slade: Well, we've been playing 30 hours... uh, that rate, six thousand, that makes roughly, uh, $200 an hour. Thank you for the entertainment, gentlemen. I am particularly grateful to Lancey, here; it's been a rewarding experience to watch a great artist at work. Thank you for the privilege, sir.

Lancey Howard: Well, now, you're quite welcome, son. It's a pleasure to meet someone who understands that to the true gambler, money is never an end in itself. It's simply a tool, as a language is to thought. Good evening, uh... Mr. Slade.

Slade: Good evening, Mr. Howard.

Lady Fingers: How you holdin' up, Lancey?

Lancey Howard: Lady Fingers, that young man is a stud poker playing son of a...

Lady Fingers: He's gettin' to you, ain't he?

Lancey Howard: [*thinking on what he said to Lady Fingers*] No, Lady; he hasn't gotten to me. Not yet; but he might, he just might.

Lancey Howard: Women are a universal problem in our business. Of course, uh, it's purely an academic question with me now, but, looking back, I think it's best not to look for a fixed thing. Just tie into something nice when you're away from the action and let it wear itself out.

Cool Hand Luke:

Dragline: Nothin'. A handful of nothin'. You stupid mullet head. He beat you with nothin'. Just like today when he kept comin' back at me—with nothin'.

Luke: Yeah, well, sometimes nothin' can be a real cool hand.

Luke: Kick a buck.

The Gambler From Natchez:

"How did you know he was bluffing?"
"He kept looking back at his hole cards. If you got it, you don't
need to keep looking back to see what you got."

------ ♦ ♣ ♥ ♠ ------

My Little Chickadee:

Cuthbert J. Twillie: During one of my treks through
Afghanistan, we lost our corkscrew. Compelled to live on food
and water—
Gambler: Will you play cards!
Cuthbert J. Twillie:—for several days.

------ ♦ ♣ ♥ ♠ ------

Cousin Zeb: Uh, is this a game of chance?
Cuthbert J. Twillie: Not the way I play it, no.

------ ♦ ♣ ♥ ♠ ------

Cuthbert J. Twillie: If a thing is worth having, it's worth
cheating for.

------ ♦ ♣ ♥ ♠ ------

You Can't Cheat an Honest Man:

Larson E. Whipsnade: As my dear old grandfather Litvak said,
just before they swung the trap—He said "You can't cheat an
honest man. Never give a sucker an even break or smarten up
a chump."

------ ♦ ♣ ♥ ♠ ------

Canary Murder Case:

"A man's true nature comes through when playing cards."

Flame of the Barbary Coast:

"A deck of cards is like a woman—usually when you pick one up, you wish you hadn't."

Cheyenne Autumn:

Wyatt Earp: [*to Doc Holliday discussing what to do with a card cheat in their three-handed game*]: "If we shoot him, we won't have anyone to play with."

The Gunfighter:

[*Passerby upon being asked to sit in an ongoing poker game*] "I wouldn't sit in this game with cards I made myself."

A Big Hand for the Little Lady:

Dennis Wilcox: "Now look, mister, the first rule of the game of poker, whether you're playing Eastern or Western rules, or the kind they play at the North Pole, is put up or shut up!"

Mary Meredith: Gentlemen all. All such gallant gentlemen.

Henry Drummond: Well, we're gallant on Sunday, this is Friday and we're playing poker. Now, you wanna play with us, you ante up $500!

Sparrow the Stagedriver: I wouldn't play poker with Henry Drummond if his back was to a mirror! Even if I had the money!

Henry Drummond: My daughter, Celie, was getting married.

Jesse Buford: Celie?

Henry Drummond: That's right! When Tropp come for me, she was in the middle of getting married. And they're holding up the "love, honor and obey" part until I get back.

Dennis Wilcox: You mean you walked out in the middle of the wedding?

Henry Drummond: I did! I ain't been late for the game in sixteen years and I ain't about to start now... wedding or no wedding.

The Simpsons:

Homer: Your mother has this crazy idea that gambling is wrong. Even though they say it's okay in the Bible.

Lisa: Really? Where?

Homer: Eh, somewhere in the back.

Lenny: You want another card or not?

Homer: Huh? Oh, OK. I'll take three.

[Moe deals the three cards and Homer looks at them one at a time]

Homer: Doh!... Doh! . . . Doh! [*looks at the other players*]
Homer: I mean... Woo hoo!

House of Games:

Mike: You can't bluff someone who's not paying attention.

Mike: I think you're bluffin', pal. I think you're trying to BUY it!
George: Then you're gonna have to give me some respect, or give me some money.

Oceans 12:

Rusty: Barry, your turn.
Barry: Uh, four.
Rusty: You don't want four. You want to fold.
Barry: I do? Is that a good thing?

Risky Business:

Miles: All right. What's the game?
Barry: Five Card Draw with a spit Anaconda high low. Pass 2 to the right 1 to the left. Deuces, aces, one-eyed faces wild . . . Guts to open.

------ ♦ ♣ ♥ ♠ ------

Sports Night:

Jeremy: Natalie, do you even know how to play poker?

Natalie: The guys at Sigma Kappa Pi let me play in their poker game any time I wanted. Now, why do you suppose that was?

Jeremy: 'Cause you're a knockout and your parents are loaded?

Natalie: 'Cause I got game, baby.

Jeremy: Have you fallen on your head?

Natalie: I know why you're beating me so much.

Jeremy: It's 'cause you're not a very good poker player.

Natalie: That's not why.

Jeremy: It really is.

Natalie: Or, isn't it just possible, you're sitting in the good chair?

Jeremy: No. What is possible is that the boys from Sigma Kappa Pi are a big honkin' bunch of LOSERS!

Jeremy Goodwin: Natalie, listen to me. You've lost a lot of money to me tonight. You're basically gonna be living the rest of your life on a charitable grant from the Jeremy Goodwin Foundation. Take the hundred bucks back and fold.

Natalie Hurley: Scared?

Jeremy Goodwin: I've got a straight, you've got three sevens.

Natalie Hurley: You don't have a straight.

Jeremy Goodwin: Look at me. I'm not lying to you. I have a straight.

Natalie Hurley: How do you know I don't have a big house?

Jeremy Goodwin: A FULL house. Dan already folded the six you needed, and I have the other one. You don't have a house of any sort, you don't have a pup tent. You've got trip sevens, and I have a straight. I want you to trust me right now. I want you to say to yourself, yeah, I've dated a string of jerks in my life, they were stupid, they were mean to me, but maybe this one's different. Maybe I should take a chance and not adopt the break-up-with-him-before-he-breaks-my-heart strategy. I want you to remember that when I started liking you, I didn't stop liking tennis. And I want you to know that I don't think there's a woman in the world that you need to be threatened by, no matter how glamorous you think she is. But mostly, I want you to trust me, just once, when I tell you that you have three sevens, and I have a straight.

------ ♦ ♣ ♥ ♠ ------

M*A*S*H:

Klinger: Okay, okay. Here we go. Down and dirty. *[deals the cards]*
Sidney: *[looks at his cards]* Ay-yi.
Hawkeye: What's your problem, poker face?
Sidney: I'm committing suicide.
Henry: Go out in turn, Sidney.

------ ♦ ♣ ♥ ♠ ------

Frank: Well, I see the conference is in full swing.
Sidney: Hi Frank. What's new up on the Mount?
Pak: Read any good Commandments lately?

------ ♦ ♣ ♥ ♠ ------

PA System: Will doctors Pierce and McIntyre kindly return to the conference? They need your money.

------ ♦ ♣ ♥ ♠ ------

[*After Hawkeye and Trapper explain why they had to operate on the CID man without another one standing by*]

Capt. Halloran: [*to Frank*] I split a gut getting down here.

Trapper: Well, look, if it'll make you feel any better, the blues are five, the reds are a dollar, and the whites are fifty cents.

Capt. Halloran: Deal me in.

Frank: [*very angry Trapper and Hawkeye weren't arrested*] It's amazing! Anyone who comes in here is instantly corrupted!

Hawkeye: Hurry up Frank. The good ship *Lollypop* is leaving.

Sidney: [*to Klinger*] I'm gonna beat the pants off you, lady.

Hawkeye: Okay, moving right along now, dealer's choice, five card stud. Sidney, what's the psychiatric basis for gambling?

Sidney: Sex.

Hawkeye: Why?

Sidney: I don't know. They told me to say it. Sex is why we gamble, sex is why we drink, sex is why we give birth.

Hawkeye: Thank you, doctor.

Sidney: I'm taking a five-dollar chip. That was a house call.

Cap. Halloran: Just a minute. Colonel, can these men be trusted?

Henry: Well, certainly.

Cap. Halloran: [*looking at Klinger*] What about her?

Cap. Pak: She's my wife.

Sidney: That's a very interesting joke, Sam.

346

Cap. Pak: *[flipping Sidney a poker chip]* Thanks for seeing me, Sidney.
Halloran: Hey, up close you're a guy.
Klinger: Far away, too.

------ ♦ ♣ ♥ ♠ ------

Hawkeye: How much did you win?
Trapper: About fifty bucks. I'm sending it to my wife for her private-detective fund.
Hawkeye: She gonna have you followed out here?
Trapper: No, it's for when I get back home—starting the second night.

------ ♦ ♣ ♥ ♠ ------

From *The West Wing:*

Josh Lyman: Who else is playing this game?
Toby Ziegler: Anyone with currency.

------ ♦ ♣ ♥ ♠ ------

Deborah Fiderer: Let me in the game sir, I beg of you.
President Bartlett: Why are you so eager to get in this game?
Deborah Fiderer: I enjoy poker, Mr. President, and your card skills are well known around the building and frankly I wanted to learn.
President Bartlett: Seriously?
Deborah Fiderer: I enjoy poker.
President Bartlett: This is a cash game, Debbie. These are hard-working people blowing off some steam and taking each other off their coin. We don't play for matchsticks and we don't play for . . .

[*Debbie flashes a wad of $20 bills*]
Ok, can I ask you something? I forgot to have Charlie draw cash for me. Can you float me a little . . . ?
Deborah Fiderer: I can *play*?
[*Leo interrupts, needing the President's attention*]
Yeah, you can play.
Deborah Fiderer: Thank you, sir.

------ ♦ ♣ ♥ ♠ ------

CJ: Nine, no help. Jack, no help. Eight, possible flush. King possible flush. Ace, no help. Six, possible straight. Knave of love for the dealer. Ace bets.
Mandy: Check.
Sam: Check.
CJ: Check.
Leo: Check.
Josh: Check.
Toby: [*pause*] Check.
[*long pause*]
CJ: Mr. President?
President Bartlett: There is one fruit . . .
[*Group groans. Toby rubs his eyes. CJ takes a drink . . . *]
President Bartlett: There is one fruit . . .
Toby: Mr. President, check or bet, sir? Those are your choices.
President Bartlett: There is one fruit . . .
Josh: Or you should feel free to give us a quiz on inane trivia.
President Bartlett: There is one fruit, whose seeds are on the outside. Name it please.
CJ: Is it the Kumquat?
[*laughter*]
Toby: Check or bet, sir.
President Bartlett: I bet five.
Mandy: Call.

Sam: See it.

CJ: Fold.

Leo: See it.

Josh: Call.

Toby: I see it . . . And, I raise you five.

[*murmurs at the table. Another pause*]

CJ: Mr. President?

President Bartlett: It's the strawberry.

[*Group agrees "oh, right," "sure"*]

Toby: Well, thank you, sir. I just raised your bet.

President Bartlett: Yes, you did, Toby. And I thought it was a bold move, when you consider that Leo is holding the six you are looking for.

Toby: Do you call the raise, sir?

President Bartlett: It depends.

Josh: Depends on what?

President Bartlett: There are fourteen punctuation marks in standard English grammar. Can anyone name them, please?

CJ: Period.

Josh: Comma.

Mandy: Colon.

Sam: Semi-colon.

Josh: Dash.

Sam: Hyphen.

Leo: ahhh . . . apostrophe.

President Bartlett: That's only seven. There are seven more –

Toby: Question mark, quotation marks, exclamation point, parentheses, brackets, braces, and ellipses. [*group murmurs approvingly*]. Do you call the raise, sir?

President Bartlett: There are three words in the English language and three words only that begin with the letters "DW . . .

Josh: This is a pretty good demonstration of why we get nothing done.

President Bartlett: Can anyone name them for me please?

Sam: Three words that begin with the letters "DW"

President Bartlett: Yes.

Sam: Dwindle.

President Bartlett: Yes.

Toby: Dwarf.

President Bartlett: Yes.

Toby: Dwindle, . . . dwindle and dwarf . . . c'mon folks, we got dwindle and dwarf . . .

President Bartlett: Ah, I'll see your five and raise you five, by the way.

Toby: Dwarf . . . Dwindle . . .

Leo: Fold.

Josh: Fold.

CJ: Last card down. [*deals to Toby and Bartlett*]

President Bartlett: A witches' brew, a magic spell, an enchanted forest where . . .

Toby: Faeries dwell. Dwell. Dwell. Dwindle, dwarf and dwell.

President Bartlett: Well, the answer's correct, but let's check with our judges and see. Oh, Noooo. I'm sorry. Time expired.

Toby: What? What time?

President Bartlett: My time. [*throws in a final bet*]

Josh: You have your own time?

Toby: I call.

President Bartlett: Trip nines.

Toby: Take your money sir. . . .You'd d'well to report that to the IRS, because, God knows I will.

Other Great Poker Quotes

Your first duty is to the Game; then come Mother, God, and Country.

—*Anonymous, Motto at the National Press Club, Washington D.C.*

When a man with money meets a man with experience, the man with experience leaves with money and the man with money leaves with experience.

—*Anonymous*

Besides lovemaking and singing in the shower, there aren't many human activities where there is a greater difference between a person's self-delusional ability and actual ability than in poker.

—*Steve Badget*

Bad beats only happen to good players.

—*Joe Crow*

Show me a good loser and I'll show you a loser.

—*Stu Ungar*

Last night I stayed up late playing poker with Tarot cards. I got a full house and four people died.

—*Steven Wright*

It's unlucky to be superstitious.

—*Dave Enteles, Card Player*

Perception is reality.

—*Immanuel Kant*

Cards are war, in disguise of a sport.

—*Charles Lamb*

Poker is the game closest to the western conception of life,
where life and thought are recognized as intimately combined,
where free will prevails over philosophies of fate or of chance,
where men are considered moral agents and where—at least
in the short run—the important thing is not what happens but
what people think happens.

—*Johnny Luckacs*

The game exemplifies the worst aspects of capitalism that have
made our country so great.

—*Walter Matthau*

Poker is the only game for a grown man. Then, your hand is
against every man's, and every man's hand is against yours.
Teamwork? Who ever made a fortune by teamwork? There's
only one way to make a fortune, and that's to down the fellow
who's up against you.

—*Somerset Maugham*

If you know poker, you know people; and if you know people,
you got the whole dang world lined up in your sights.

—*Brett Maverick*

It's easy to be a tough competitor and still be the kind of person with whom people love to compete.

—*Chuck Thompson*

Man is a gaming animal. He must always be trying to get the better in something or other.

—*Charles Lamb*

There are few things that are so unpardonably neglected in our country as poker. The upper class knows very little about poker. Now and then you find ambassadors who have sort of a general knowledge of poker, but the ignorance of the people is fearful. Why, I have known clergymen, good men, kind-hearted, liberal, sincere, and all that, who did not know the meaning of a "flush." It is enough to make one ashamed of the species.

—*Mark Twain*

Learning to play two pairs is worth about as much as a college education, and about as costly.

—*Mark Twain*

A card player should learn that once the money is in the pot, it isn't his any longer.

—*Herbert Yardley*

I never go looking for a sucker. I look for a champion and make a sucker of him.

—*Amarillo Slim*

Never perform card tricks for the people you play poker with.

—unknown

Shallow men believe in luck. Strong men believe in cause and effect.

—Ralph Waldo Emerson

The next best thing to gambling and winning is gambling and losing.

—Nick 'The Greek' Dandalos

No wife can endure a gambling husband, unless he is a steady winner.

—Thomas Robert Dewar

Poker reveals to the frank observer something else of import— it will teach him about his own nature. Many bad players do not improve because they cannot bear self-knowledge.

—David Mamet

Poker is... a fascinating, wonderful, intricate adventure on the high seas of human nature.

—David A. Daniel

An aggressive poker player looks for a reason to stay in every hand. A passive player looks for a reason to get out of every hand.

—VP Pappy

He's a self-made poker player, which shows you what can happen when you don't read the instructions.

—*VP Pappy*

The gambling known as business looks with austere disfavor on the business known as gambling.

—*Ambrose Bierce*

I used to be a heavy gambler. But now I just make mental bets. That's how I lost my mind.

—*Steve Allen*

The point is that it looks like gambling because the language of the game is money.

—*Al Alverez*

Most of the money you'll win at poker comes not from the brilliance of your own play, but from the ineptitude of your opponents.

—*Lou Krieger*

Money won is twice as sweet as money earned.

—*Eddie Felson in "The Color of Money"*

The saddest words I ever spoke were "Deal around me boys, I'm broke."

—*unknown*

You can shear a sheep a hundred times, but you can skin it only once.

—*Amarillo Slim*

Poker is a microcosm of all we admire and disdain about capitalism and democracy. It can be rough-hewn or polished, warm or cold, charitable and caring, or hard and impersonal, fickle and elusive, but ultimately it is fair, and right, and just."

—*Lou Krieger*

Even Your Poker Face Is Ugly

—*Unknown*

[Poker is] as elaborate a waste of human intelligence as you could find outside an advertising agency.

—*Raymond Chandler*

Old card players never die, they just shuffle away.

—*Unknown*

I bluffed. You caught me. I outdrew you. Shut up.

—*Unknown*

The urge to gamble is so universal and its practice so pleasurable that I assume it must be evil.

—*Heywood Hale Broun*

Someone once asked me why women don't gamble as much as men do and I gave the commonsensical reply that we don't have as much money. That was a true but incomplete answer. In fact, women's total instinct for gambling is satisfied by marriage.

—*Gloria Steinem*

I don't gamble, because winning a hundred dollars doesn't give me great pleasure. But losing a hundred dollars pisses me off.

—Alex Trebek

Casinos and prostitutes have the same thing in common; they are both trying to screw you out of your money and send you home with a smile on your face.

—VP Pappy

I heard 007 doesn't play baccarat anymore; now it's Hold 'em. I keep waiting for Phil Hellmuth to talk smack at the table right up until Bond puts one right between his eyes.

—Matt Bramanti

Look at it this way: Think of how stupid the average poker player is, and then realize half of 'em are stupider than that.

—Adapted from a George Carlin quote about stupid people

We are put on this earth to fart around. Don't listen to anyone who tries to tell you otherwise.

—Kurt Vonnegut

Son, when a man bets you that the jack of spades will rise out of the deck and squirt water in your ear, son don't take that bet, for as sure as eggs is eggs, you'll end up with a wet ear.

—Damon Runyon

Don't look at when a player sucks out on you with a trash hand as a loss. Think of it as an investment that will be returned with interest.

—Unknown

They anticipate losing when they sit down and I try my darnedest not to disappoint one of them.

—*Amarillo Slim*

The only bad luck for a good gambler is bad health. Any other setbacks are temporary aggravation.

—*Benny Binion*

There is less luck involved than a bad player thinks there is, and there more luck involved than a good player will admit there is.

—*Unknown*

You gotta know, when to hold 'em; know when to fold 'em, know when to walk away, and know when to run.

—*Don Schlitz*

Now, every gambler knows that the secret to survival is knowing what to throw away and knowing what to keep. Cuz every hand's a winner and every hand's a loser And the best you can hope for is to die in your sleep.

—*Don Schlitz*

Who needs balls when you've got the "nuts"?

—*Unknown*

So again, do not raise in No Limit Hold'em—especially tournaments—if there is a reasonable chance that a reraise will make you throw up.

—*David Sklansky*

I have found that when my reasoning for making a call amounts to, "Aww, fuck it," it is usually the wrong move.

—*Unknown*

"So, what did you have?" "A pair... Of balls."

—*Unknown*

Whether he likes it or not, a man's character is stripped at the poker table; if the other players read him better than he does, he has only himself to blame. Unless he is both able and prepared to see himself as others do, flaws and all, he will be a loser in cards, as in life.

—*Anthony Holden*

The one who bets the most wins. Cards just break ties.

—*Sam Fahra*

Life is like a game of cards. The hand that is dealt you is determinism; the way you play it is free will.

—*Jawaharlal Nehru*

Marriage is like a deck of cards. . . . In the beginning, all you need are two hearts and a diamond. But years later, you'll be wishing for a club and a spade.

—*Unknown*

You can't lead a horse to water, but a donkey will follow you all the way to the river.

—*Unknown*

If you could lose all of your money again... what would you have done differently?

—*Unknown*

A great poker player knows when he is playing poorly.

—*Unknown*

The poker player learns that sometimes both science and common sense are wrong; that the bumblebee can fly; that, perhaps, one should never trust an expert; that there are more things in heaven and earth than are dreamt of by those with an academic bent.

—*David Mamet*

Playing poker for play money is like going to a strip club for the food.

—*Uncle Waldo*

Some days you're the pigeon, some days you're the statue.

—*J. Andrew Taylor*

I don't mind getting beaten by a good player, and I don't even mind getting beaten by a bad player, but I can't stand getting beaten by a bad player who thinks he is good.

—*H.L.B. Tunica*

To win a bit of money, make your opponent think your hand is stronger than it is. To win a lot of money, make him think your hand is weaker than it is.

—*Josh Avery*

Nobody would play the game if the best hand always won.

—*Will Schwarz*

The all-in play works every time but once.

—*Unknown*

The problem with slowplaying the nuts is that there might be somebody else slowplaying a hand they only think is the nuts.

—*Gary Carson*

Darwin takes a toll on the worst poker players because they lose money, Darwin takes a toll on average poker players because they don't make money and they will never be a great poker player. Darwin takes the greatest toll though, on the greatest poker players, because they could be doing something greater.

—*Unknown*

Overheard at Author's Poker Game

Rick: I knew I shoulda stayed in! That would have been my Ace!

Mark: You don't know that.

Rick: Of course I do! I just looked at it. That was the card on top of the deck, the one I woulda got! And it's the Ace of Clubs!

Mark: But it might not have been the Ace of Clubs when you made your decision. It did not become the Ace of Clubs until you saw it. It could have been anything when you made your decision.

Rick: What are you talking about? Are you saying the card can change by magic?

Mark: It doesn't have to change. It may not have yet become. All possible universes can exist simultaneously and things may only become constrained by our perception once we perceive them. There is no way to prove otherwise.

Rick: So are you saying that, in some other, unseen parallel universe that existed at the instant I made my decision, that card might not have been the Ace of Clubs?

Mark: Quite possibly.

Tim: Yeah, but in that universe, Spock would have had a beard. Let's deal.

Applied from "Dirty Harry" to a player who is trying to decide whether to purchase a choice card or stay in the pot to see a final bet:

Harry Callahan: You've gotta ask yourself one question: "Do I feel lucky?" Well, do ya, punk?

And when he folds but wants the dealer to show him what his card would have been or the winner to show the cards he did not pay to see, he pleads:

Bank Robber: Hey!... I gots to know!

------ ♦ ♣ ♥ ♠ ------

Applied from "Paradise by the Dashboard Light" to a player taking a long time to decide on whether to accept a choice card that has been offered to him:

Well? What's it gonna be, boy? ... Yes? ... Or No?

Index

Made in the USA
Middletown, DE
12 June 2021